Freedom of Expression in a Pluralistic World Order

AF757533

Freedom of Expression
in a Pluralistic World Order

Ambrogino G. Awesta

eleven
international publishing

Published, sold and distributed by Eleven International Publishing
P.O. Box 85576
2508 CG The Hague
The Netherlands
Tel.: +31 70 33 070 33
Fax: +31 70 33 070 30
e-mail: sales@budh.nl
www.elevenpub.com

Sold and distributed in USA and Canada
International Specialized Book Services
920 NE 58th Avenue, Suite 300
Portland, OR 97213-3786, USA
Tel: 1-800-944-6190 (toll-free)
Fax: +1-503-280-8832
orders@isbs.com
www.isbs.com

Eleven International Publishing is an imprint of Boom uitgevers Den Haag

ISBN 978-94-6236-532-2
ISBN 978-94-6274-234-5 (E-book)

Cover photo: *Cosmographia* by Nicolaus Germanus (1482)

© 2015 Ambrogino G. Awesta | Eleven International Publishing

This publication is protected by international copyright law.
All rights reserved. No part of this publication may be reproduced, stored in a retrieval system, or transmitted in any form or by any means, electronic, mechanical, photocopying, recording or otherwise, without the prior permission of the publisher.

Printed in The Netherlands

"***Whoever fights with monsters should see to it that he does not become one himself***"

Friedrich W. Nietzsche, *Beyond Good and Evil* (Aphorism 146)

Table of Contents

Introduction

We live in a world that is characterized by an intense plurality of worldviews. The growth in such a level of pluralism is being fostered by a process of globalization that continues unabated. In other words, we live in an era that is increasingly characterized by globalization, a process that has shrunk time and space and, as a consequence, intensified human interactions with their unavoidable tensions and clashes. This globalized era is, thus, a tumultuous epoch filled with uncertainties wherein the general will seems to have allowed 'security' to prevail over 'fundamental rights and freedoms'.[1] The quest for security is a result of contingencies and menaces that need to be confronted. This inconvenience whereby human rights and freedoms need to be confined and suspended in the name of security is often called 'the state of exception'[2], albeit not in the classical sense of the word.

The shrinking of space and time, which is among the most fundamental characteristics of globalization, has turned the world into a global village in which the interaction between diverse worldviews has vastly increased. Due to this plurality Samuel P. Huntington states that, in this era, politics is configured along views that are designated by the notions of 'culture' and 'civilization', which we have called 'the human dimension' of the process of globalization. Hence, it has become, in a way, the age of identity politics. This tense reciprocity among different if not competing worldviews is designated by the notion of *multicivilizationalism* at the international level and *multiculturalism* at the regional and national level – two notions that are used interchangeably in this study. However, the application of these concepts requires further clarification.

The prefix 'multi-' indicates plurality, i.e. multiplicity of the notions that follow this prefix. And regarding the notions of 'culture' and 'civilization', the following observations are timely. As Adda B. Bozeman observed in 1975 (whose description is adopted by Samuel P. Huntington), "The words 'culture' and 'civilization' carry different meanings for different scholars. [...] [Yet, as he deploys it] both stand for that which is most fundamental and enduring about the ways of a group persisting in time. That is to say, they cover those values, norms, institutions, and modes of thinking to which successive generations in a given society have attached primary importance".[3] Thus, as Huntington puts it, "Civilization and culture both refer to the overall way of life of a people, and a civilization is a culture writ large".[4] Elsewhere we see that he provides the same

---

[1] Report and Recommendations of the President's Review Group on Intelligence and Communications Technologies, '*Liberty and Security in a Changing World*' (12 December 2013)

[2] Giorgio Agamben, *State of Exception* (UCP, Chicago 2005)

[3] Adda B Bozeman, 'Civilizations Under Stress: Reflections on Cultural Borrowing and Survival' [1975] VQR 51

[4] Samuel P Huntington, *The Clash of Civilizations and the Remaking of World Order* (Simon & Schuster, London 2002) 41

description by defining culture "[...] in purely subjective terms as the values, attitudes, beliefs, orientations, and underlying assumptions prevalent among people in a society".[5] He describes the notion of civilization as the highest cultural grouping of people and the broadest level of cultural identity people have, short of that which distinguishes humans from other species. It is defined by common objective elements such as language, history, religion, customs, institutions, and by the subjective self-identification of a people. "[...] Civilizations are the biggest 'we' within which we feel culturally at home as distinguished from all the other 'thems' out there".[6] Hence, civilization is understood as the broadest cultural entity. It goes without saying that, in this context, religion is conceived as one of the crucial formative factors of civilization.[7] In other words, "Religion remains an important source of cultural rules, even in apparently secular societies; at the same time, religious rules are subject to a spontaneous evolution as they interact with a society's given historical environment".[8] Accordingly, usage of the notions of culture and civilization differ merely in their scope of application, but remain, for the rest, synonymous regarding their content which is also the line of thought that is followed in this research. This means thus that these two notions and their multiplicity are interchangeably employed in this survey. Yet, when the concept of civilization is taken as the overarching principle the notions of religion and culture are conceived as its formative components.

Furthermore, it has to be noted that the notions of culture and civilization have no universally accepted definitions and, as referred to above, carry different meanings for different scholars and disciplines. This is why also in this research no actual attempt has been made to define these notions. We have merely deployed the aforesaid descriptions of these notions which have also been used as a paradigm by Huntington for studying 'the intercivilizational clash of culture and religion'.[9] Thus, the concepts of multicivilizationalism and multiculturalism are taken at face value in this study for describing the multiplicity of worldviews among which clashes tend to occur within globalized societies. However, in reality the latter concept has been used as a political notion in the broadest sense of the word by policy makers and scholars in this field. Our research is not concerned with the political usage of the notion of multiculturalism, due to which also a discussion of multiculturalist theories does not fall within the scope of the present study. Nevertheless, for the sake of argument, it is important to provide a mere categorical understanding of this notion in view of its political deployment. The reason why a general survey suffices is because the old multiculturalism

[5] Lawrence E Harrison and Samuel P Huntington (eds), *Culture Matters: How Values Shape Human Progress* (Basic Books, New York 2000) xv

[6] Samuel P Huntington, *The Clash of Civilizations and the Remaking of World Order* (Simon & Schuster, London 2002) 43

[7] Ibid 47

[8] Lawrence E Harrison and Samuel P Huntington (eds), *Culture Matters: How Values Shape Human Progress* (Basic Books, New York 2000) 111

[9] Samuel P Huntington, *The Clash of Civilizations and the Remaking of World Order* (Simon & Schuster, London 2002) 54

paradigm has not been successful in integrating non-Western migrants into a rather liberal Western culture.[10] This explains, for instance, why the failure of this paradigm has been loudly voiced by policy makers.[11] Therefore, it is neither the functionality nor the desirability of this notion that is disquieting, but the perilous reality concerning the fundamental right to freedom of expression that is yet to be seriously investigated. It is thus the aim of this study to come to terms with this perilous reality. In other words, a thorough elucidation of the concept of multiculturalism has no added value to our inquiry. This is because we do not aim to conduct a normative evaluation of this concept, but rather to comprehend its effect on the fundamental right to freedom of expression. Hence, a diversity of worldviews, which is designated by the exchangeable notions of *multiculturalism* and *multicivilizationalism*, is used in this research as a mere paradigm shred of any political connotation. Therefore, for our stated purpose in this study, it suffices to provide an outline of the contexts in which this concept has been used. In so doing, three interrelated referents of 'multiculturalism' can be discerned.

Firstly, we have the demographic-descriptive usage of multiculturalism that refers to the existence of *ethnically* or *racially* diverse segments in the population of a society or state.[12] Secondly, multiculturalism is used as an ideological-normative approach to "[...] generate the greatest level of debate since it constitutes a slogan and model for political action based on sociological theorizing and ethical-philosophical consideration about the place of those with culturally distinct identities in contemporary society".[13] The third referent is the programmatic-political usage of 'multiculturalism'. This approach recognizes the existence of ethnic diversity and ensures the rights of individuals to keep their culture through specific types of programs and policy initiatives designed to accommodate such diversity. This is managed through assimilation, integration, inclusion, and social cohesion with the aim of creating a stable and harmonious social order, peace and security (passive social relationships).[14] Also, access to, participation in, and adherence to constitutional principles and commonly shared values prevailing in society are fostered with the aim of reducing social pressures based on disadvantage and inequality.[15] In other words, this approach aims to foster social justice, intercultural dialogue, as well as tolerance and respect for the diversity of cultures. This is done through, for instance, "cooperation and

---

[10] Francis Fukuyama, 'A question of identity' *The Australian* (Sydney 3 February 2007) <http://www.theaustralian.com.au/news/a-question-of-identity/story-e6frg6n6-1111112933880> accessed 3 January 2013

[11] Laura Kuenssberg, 'State multiculturalism has failed, says David Cameron' *BBC* (London 5 February 2011) <http://www.bbc.co.uk/news/uk-politics-12371994> accessed 7 January 2013. Kate Connolly, 'Angela Merkel declares death of German multiculturalism' *Guardian* (London 17 October 2010)

[12] Christine Inglis, 'Multiculturalism: New Policy Responses to Diversity', UNESCO Management of Social Transformation, *Policy Paper* (1997) No.4, 16-17

[13] Ibid

[14] Office of the Deputy Prime Minister, 'State of the English Cities' (2006) Vol 1, 109

[15] Christine Inglis, 'Multiculturalism: New Policy Responses to Diversity', UNESCO Management of Social Transformation, *Policy Paper* (1997) No.4

harmonious interaction among people and groups with plural, varied and dynamic cultural identities as well as their willingness to live together"[16] (active social relationships). Yet, we can discern that the usage of the notion of 'multiculturalism' has encompassed all the aforementioned interwoven approaches. This means that multiculturalism has been used for enacting – directly or indirectly – various multicultural policies and legal instruments in order to structure and accommodate a multicultural society. The purpose of doing this has been manifold. Firstly, the aim has been the enhancement of respect for cultural diversity, because cultural rights are considered to be 'an integral part of human rights'.[17] Subsequently, the defense of cultural diversity is conceived to be a commitment to human rights and fundamental freedoms, which is said to be an ethnical imperative inseparable from respect for human dignity.[18] It means that every individual[19] should have the right to participate in the cultural life and practices of his or her choice.[20] Therefore, the proponents of multiculturalism perceive this notion as enrichment to society as a whole. They consider "[...] cultural diversity as a source of exchange, innovation and creativity, [which] is [in their point of view] as necessary for humankind as biodiversity for nature. In this sense, as the common heritage of humanity, they claim that it should be recognized and affirmed for the benefit of present and future generations".[21] However, although cultural rights are said to be an integral part of human rights, it is acknowledged that "[...] cultural diversity can be protected and promoted only if human rights and fundamental freedoms, such as freedom of expression, as enshrined in the Universal Declaration of Human Rights"[22] (as well as other "[...] universally recognized legal instruments, such as the two International Conventions of 1966 relating, respectively, to civil and political rights and to economic, social and cultural rights"[23]) are guaranteed. This means that "[...] no one may invoke cultural diversity to infringe upon or to limit the scope of human rights and fundamental freedoms"[24] in general, and the right to freedom of expression[25] in particular.

Notwithstanding, the reciprocity among the worldviews, which we called the cultural dimension of globalization, has not garnered the attention it deserves,

---

[16] The Preamble and Article 2 of the 2001 UNESCO Universal Declaration on Cultural Diversity

[17] Article 5 of the 2001 UNESCO Universal Declaration on Cultural Diversity

[18] Article 4 (ibid)

[19] As Jurgen Habermas rightly argues, the right to practice and to participate in a cultural life is an 'individual right'; Amy Gutmann (ed), *Multiculturalism* (PUP, Princeton 1994) x

[20] The Preamble of the 2001 UNESCO Universal Declaration on Cultural Diversity

[21] Article 1 of the 2001 UNESCO Universal Declaration on Cultural Diversity

[22] Article 2 (1) of the 2005 UNESCO Convention on the Protection and Promotion of the Diversity of Cultural Expressions. Article 4 of the 2001 UNESCO Universal Declaration on Cultural Diversity

[23] The Preamble of the 2001 UNESCO Universal Declaration on Cultural Diversity

[24] Article 2 (1) of the 2005 UNESCO Convention on the Protection and Promotion of the Diversity of Cultural Expressions

[25] Article 19 of Universal Declaration of Human Rights. Article 19 of International Convention on Civil and Political Rights. Article 10 of European Convention on Human Rights

while the furtherance of interactions has had outrageous consequences. Especially when we bear in mind, in this context, that law and society are two interwoven concepts that reciprocally influence each other. Contemporarily, this reciprocity is made obvious from the impact of pluralistic society on the concept of law – about which we have narrowed the scope of this inquiry to the fundamental right to freedom of expression and the impact that this reciprocity has on this fundamental right, because "in a globalized world speech can be universally heard, as [for instance] the Mohammed cartoons that appeared 2005 in a local Danish newspaper illustrate. [The same sort of cartoons that were published by the satirical French magazine *Charlie Hebdo* resulted in a barbarous massacre in 2015]. Without the growing multiculturalism of European societies, these cartoons would not have garnered much attention. Without modern information technology, they would not have been universally noticed within days. In a globalized world [which is, thus, characterized by multicivilizationalism] speech can provoke universal reactions".[26] This is only one example among many assaults on this fundamental freedom that underpins this study. Thus, the form of pluralism fostered by the process of globalization, and yet downplayed in the discourse on it, tends to have an impact on the fundamental right to freedom of expression. Therefore, the aim of this study is to provide an understanding of the menace that this pluralism of worldviews and the clashes between them pose to the fundamental right to freedom of expression at the different strata of society. This aim leads us to the central question as to whether the reciprocal clashes among different worldviews in terms of civilizations and/or cultures have legally confined the fundamental right to freedom of expression. This question will thus guide this inquiry into whether multicivilizational (i.e. multicultural) clashes have posed *de jure* limitations on the fundamental right to freedom of expression, and if so, to what extent. This overriding research question consists of two main parts.

First, we have to determine whether the human dimension of the process of globalization, which has fostered pluralism, underpins the contemporary clash between worldviews, and if so, we need to grasp both the nature and the scope of this antagonism. Hence, the first part of this inquiry concerns pluralism which tends to have a limiting effect on the fundamental right to freedom of expression. As Samuel P. Huntington asserts, in this age of globalization, this pluralism and its perilous discontent have taken place along cultural lines.[27] Thus, in *Part I*, an attempt will be made to provide an understanding of the content and scope of the

---

[26] Ivan Hare and James Weinstein (eds), *Extreme Speech and Democracy* (OUP, Oxford 2009) 17

[27] Samuel P Huntington, *The Clash of Civilizations and the Remaking of World Order* (Simon & Schuster, London 2002) 19, 36. According to Huntington, "[…] the fundamental source of conflict in the new world will not be primarily ideological or primarily economic. The great divisions among humankind and the dominating source of conflict will be cultural. […] the principal conflicts of global politics will occur between nations and groups of different civilizations. […] Conflict between civilizations will be the last phase in the evolution of conflicts in the modern world". Samuel P Huntington, 'The Clash of Civilizations?' (1993) 72 (3) Foreign Aff 22, 22

contemporary tensions within the context of our globalized age. The process of globalization is used for apprehending the scope and effect of pluralism at the different levels – international, European, and national. The purpose of such attempt is thus to determine whether an actual clash between opposing worldviews has taken place which underpins current world affairs and by extension confines the fundamental right to freedom of expression. Therefore, we need to understand the process of globalization at face value. In so doing, the three waves of globalization – globalism, transformationalism, and skepticism – are surveyed in so far as they concern the human dimension wherein the current pluralistic antagonism is being vested. By taking this dimension into consideration, we will be able to comprehend the inherent rationale of the contemporary collisions and their disruptive, disintegrative, and marginalizing effects which we have tried to conceptualize. In other words, we will try to grasp the reciprocal antagonism that tends to limit the fundamental right to freedom of expression. To this end, a comparative approach is employed towards such antagonistic perspectives – whose roots can be retraced to the aforementioned waves – which are, at the same time, each other's dichotomies. Thus, our method concerns an interpretivist position and, in epistemological terms, a partially modern realist approach, since the antagonistic theories that we have comparatively elaborated in this study are discursive and provisional in nature.[28] Henceforth, understanding the effect of pluralism brought about by the reality of an increasingly globalized world is dependent on the interpretative theories that oftentimes reciprocally antagonize one another.

The purpose of conceptualizing this mutual antagonism, which is often designated by the notions of 'Orientalism' and 'Occidentalism', is to make evident its indisputable inherency which has led to perilous consequences. This is done by elaborating the essence of this antagonism which is drawn along civilizational lines, and hence defined in terms of 'Orientalism' and 'Occidentalism'. Such elaboration will render the inherent nature and underlying concept of this antagonism tenable. Based on this, we will then proceed with a substantiation of the underpinning concept of the aforementioned reciprocal antagonism in order to comprehend thoroughly the dichotomy between 'Orientalism' and 'Occidentalism'. The theoretical conceptualization of the essential contours and inherent features of this dichotomous antagonism makes it possible to understand the actual materialization of such animosity within the current process of globalization. Against this background, an attempt will be made to expound the continuation and vivacity of this antagonism. In so doing, we will try to explain how and through which concepts this continuation has taken place for antagonizing the West in this globalized era.

The discussion of the furtherance and continuation of such dichotomous antagonism in our globalized era will reveal that antagonism towards the West is not one-sided but rather reciprocal in nature; a reciprocity which is even fostered by globalism with its narrow comprehension of the human dimension. To make

[28] David Marsh and Gerry Stoker (eds), *Theory and Methods in Political Science* (2nd edn Palgrave Macmillan, Hampshire 2002)

this advancement tangible, the pivotal globalist theory of Francis Fukuyama, 'the-end-of-history' thesis, is taken as our point of departure. A discussion of this thesis will make its theoretical shortcoming evident, which is embedded in its negligence and misapprehension of the concept of civilization in the broadest sense of the word. Therefore, we will try to clarify that the notion of civilization – which concerns the human dimension within the process of globalization – is such a pivotal concept that cannot be ignored in terms of current world affairs. This notion cannot be ignored because it is, in fact, Oriental civilization that collides with its Occidental counterpart which is defined in terms of modernity for which the West is held liable. With regard to this latter, the historical and the psychological dimensions will be discussed. An elaboration of these two angles will make clear that the resurgence of civilization is unavoidably intertwined with modernity, because civilization is exactly invoked to palliate the effects of modernity. Thus, the inevitability of the concept of civilization – the palliating revival of which is fostered by its very negligence by globalism – will be made evident through a comprehensive look at the globalist thesis of Fukuyama. Accordingly, a discussion of the underlying mechanism of this globalist thesis will reveal its shortcoming(s). This will make clear why we need to go beyond this thesis if we are to grasp the reciprocity and continuation of the current antagonism which is underpinned by the neglected concept of civilization. Thus, both the importance of this concept and the danger of neglecting it should become obvious through a closer look at the antagonism towards the West. And yet, it remains crucial to understand that this perilous antagonism does not stop at a mere criticism of the West. This is because this criticism goes so far as to become apologetic about illegitimate discontent that, as we shall see in the second part, aims to undermine, among others, the fundamental right to freedom of expression.

Thus, after having determined that there is a pluralistic clash, we need to examine the ensuing question of whether this antagonism imperils the fundamental right to freedom of expression. In this sense, the survey of the second part of our research question will theoretically clarify why precisely the fundamental right to freedom of expression is prone to be legally confined by pluralistic tensions. Subsequently, the *de jure* limitation of pluralism, which tends to be imposed on this particular right, will be examined at different strata – international, European, and national level. In other words, *Part II* of this research is concerned with the danger posed to the fundamental right to freedom of expression which tends to be confined by the so-called reciprocal antagonism that characterizes our globalized world. Hence, our inquiry will reach beyond the normativity of the first part in order to assess the *de jure* effect of pluralism on the fundamental right to freedom of expression – after having philosophically conceptualized this right and its possible limitations within a pluralistic society. With this conceptualization, we will endeavor to apprehend why precisely this particular right is imperiled by civilizational clashes that are being fostered by an ever growing antagonism within pluralistic societies. This will be made evident through a discussion of the theory of Hannah Arendt which we have taken as our point of departure. In this discussion, it will be argued that pluralism is not only an undeniable fact, but is even the prerequisite for safeguarding fundamental rights and freedoms. And the denial of it would result in alienation and worldlessness and, thus, in the deprivation of rights and freedoms. This is because speech, as an authentic political action, cannot take place in isolation, but is ineluctably dependent on plurality and *vice versa*. As Arendt asserts, speech is the actualization of the human condition of plurality, that is, appearance as a distinct and unique being among equals. Thus, the loss of human rights amounts to being deprived of a place in the world that renders opinions significant and actions effective. In this sense, the significance of the fundamental right to freedom of expression becomes obvious when the state of absolute rightlessness is taken into consideration, which is a state of being deprived of the right to action, i.e. the right to form an opinion. This is why this fundamental freedom is, more than ever before, at stake in current pluralistic societies.

Notwithstanding, it has to be noted that although pluralism is the prerequisite for having rights and freedoms, simultaneously it tends to confine them for the sake of that same plurality. How this limitation that stems from pluralistic reciprocity can be approached is what will be discussed through the philosophy of John Stuart Mill. This discussion will reveal that, according to Mill and his harm principle, speech ought to be constrained when, as a consequence, it has mischievous acts that can harm others. However, he modifies this general principle by arguing that despite the difficulty of determining the bounds of offense, the freedom of expression in the public realm still has to meet the civilized conditions of interaction. He calls this 'the morality of public discussion', the violation of which should result in the limitation of speech in the same way as harmful action. This modification can become problematic when it is conceived against the background of Mill's utilitarianism whereby the interest of the majority is taken as the standard. Yet, this is not the menace of this multicivilizational epoch. It is rather another development whereby, for the sake of peaceful coexistence[29], the threshold of the morality of public discussion is reversed from the interests of the 'majority' to those of the 'minority'. It is also this reversal which can pose far-reaching limitations on the fundamental right to freedom of expression that are not only extrajudicial but also judicial in nature.

Henceforth, with the preceding discussion in mind, we will try to respond to the question: to what extent has the increase in antagonistic pluralism had a *de jure* impact on the fundamental right to freedom of expression? Thus, after having considered whether a civilizational antagonism has occurred at the international, European, and national level, we will examine the question: to what extent these civilizational clashes have *de jure* limited the fundamental right to freedom of expression? In assessing the limiting impact that pluralism tends to have on this fundamental right, the legal order is thus divided alongside the aforesaid layers of the pluralistic society into three different strata –

[29] Ivan Hare and James Weinstein (eds), *Extreme Speech and Democracy* (OUP, Oxford 2009) 119

international, European, and national legal orders. At each level, the scope and substance of the law in force is first explained and, subsequently, their limitations are discussed. Simultaneously, the impact of accelerating pluralism is expounded as it will underpin our response to the aforementioned question. With regard to the international level, our research is confined to the documents issued by the prominent organs of the United Nations which are concerned with this fundamental right. With respect to the European level, the scope of this research is confined to the European Court of Human Rights, since it is *this* Court that deals with the fundamental right to freedom of expression in a *legal* sense. The last stratum in which the interaction between civilizations is most vivid and has led to tensions and clashes is the national level. It is at this level that multiculturalism has made its mark in the reality of Western societies, the prime example of which is the Netherlands which we have studied in this research. In determining this, an attempt has been made to scrutinize the *de jure* impact of a plurality of civilizations on the fundamental right to freedom of expression. In so doing, the relevant national laws are first explained. Hereupon, the national jurisprudence is studied by taking the criminal law approach as our point of departure. This approach requires particular attention, because 'criminal law' is *the* instrument that – due to its coercive nature – has a sweeping impact on the fundamental rights and freedoms in general and on the fundamental right to freedom of expression in particular.

The methods and approaches adopted for this assessment are manifold in nature, depending on the aforementioned layers and sources that we use. As to the sources in each layer, it has to be noted that there are three different categories that we have used in this study. First, we have the primary sources which are the positive law tools – both hard and soft law – that are to be found in, among others, conventions, declarations, resolutions, and codes. To this category belong also the judicial judgments. The second category of sources concerns the preparatory works (*travaux préparatoires*) containing parliamentary acts and papers. The tertiary sources are the legal reports and literatures. In order to grasp the content and scope of the fundamental right to freedom of expression, a descriptive approach is adopted. Through this approach, we should be able to grasp the leitmotifs and significance of this right by expounding its underlying concepts and rationales. Furthermore, for analyzing these sources on the basis of their (legal) nature, the following methods are used. First, the grammatical interpretation, in other words, the black-letter method is used for studying the legal provisions at their face value. Second, the historical interpretation is employed for grasping the leitmotifs behind their codification as well as the stipulation of their reach. Furthermore, the fundamental right to freedom of expression is analytically studied with the aim of determining the extent to which this right is constrained by a plurality of worldviews.

Finally, we will conclude with a general assessment of our findings in this research, which should provide us with an answer to the central question of whether multicivilizationalism/multiculturalism has imposed a *de jure* limit on the fundamental right to freedom of expression in this age of globalization.

Part I
Pluralistic World Order

1. Pluralistic World Order: An Introduction

In this first part of our research, an attempt will be made to expound the scope and content of reciprocal antagonism which has reached its climax in the current process of globalization. For it is this process that has intensified the interaction among civilizations, i.e. cultures and, thereby, pluralized society in general. Thus, globalization has not only had a positive impact on human society but negative consequences as well. This is also why this reciprocity can be drawn along the three waves of globalization – globalism, transformationalism, and skepticism. Henceforth, we will try to expound the scope of the discontent (and its perilous consequences) between worldviews deemed to be fostered by the process of globalization. In other words, through the process of globalization with its enhancement of pluralism, an attempt will be made to grasp the scope and content of the current antagonism that, accordingly, imperils the fundamental right to freedom of expression.

After having explained that the process of globalization has engendered a reciprocal antagonism which is drawn along cultural lines, we will try to conceptualize this animosity which is often described in terms of 'Orientalism' versus 'Occidentalism'. Thus, in order to render the inherency and indisputability of contemporary dichotomous discontent and its perilous consequences obvious, the essence of this civilizational antagonism will be elucidated. This survey will make the inherent nature and the underlying concept of this reciprocal antagonism tangible. Based on this, we will proceed by substantiating this underlying concept in order to understand thoroughly both sides of the antagonistic clashes between 'Orientalism' and 'Occidentalism'.

Upon the theoretical conceptualization of the essential contours and inherent features of this dichotomous antagonism, it is exigent to grasp the actual materialization and continuation of this reciprocal animosity within the current process of globalization which we have pointed out. In this regard, we will make the continued exertion and vivacity of this antagonism tangible and will, subsequently, expound how and through which notions this continuity has taken place and is being upheld in the antagonizing of the West in our globalized era. In so doing, it will become plain that the increase in antagonism is not only fostered by Occidentalism as such, but is rather hastened by Orientalism in its own attitude towards the human dimension.

This comprehension requires, however, a further exposition of globalism, and its demeanor regarding the human dimension, which is conceived as Orientalism *par excellence* and, therefore, antagonized. In coming to such an understanding, 'the-end-of-history' thesis of Francis Fukuyama is taken as our point of departure. A thorough discussion of this will clarify the ineluctability of the human dimension in terms of civilization, as well as the continuity and acceleration of antagonism within the context of an increasingly globalized world. In other words, the unequivocality of this revived concept and its continuity will be enunciated through a comprehensive survey of the aforementioned globalist theory. In so doing, this study will reveal the shortcoming of this theory through a scrutiny of its underlying mechanism, namely, the concept of *thymos*. This will show the necessity for going beyond this theory if we are to grasp the underpinnings of current reciprocal antagonism. Accordingly, for clarifying both the importance and peril of this concept, we will elaborate further on the antagonism towards the West that is being fostered by globalism through its negligence of this very concept.

The menace to fundamental human rights and freedoms (that stems from globalism's disdain of the human dimension and which underpins the current reciprocal antagonism) will be made apparent in the succeeding part of this research. Yet, for the sake of argument, it is important first of all to give further thoughts to the rise in dichotomous antagonism that endangers these rights and freedoms in general and the fundamental right to freedom of expression in particular. Thus, we need to grasp thoroughly that this perilous antagonism does not stop at a mere criticism of the West. For it actually goes so far as to become apologetic about illegitimate discontent that imperils rights such as the fundamental right to freedom of expression.

1.1. Globalization and the Essence of Discontent

Our era is characterized by the disputatious phenomenon of 'globalization' which has challenged human life in all its facets. This means that while globalization has positive, innovative, and dynamic aspects, it also has negative, disruptive, and marginalizing consequences.[30] Despite diverging opinions about the definition, content, scope, and desirability of globalization – indicated as *globophilia* and *globophobia*[31] – this phenomenon remains a multidimensional process that has affected various realms of human society at the international, regional, and national level. To be more concrete, the process of globalization both informs and disrupts the concept of 'culture' in the broadest sense of the term. And it is also through this concept that globalization is experienced in a most direct way.[32] Thus, the relation between 'globalization' and 'culture' can be considered reciprocal. This means that it is not only 'globalization' that informs the notion of 'culture', but also the different cultures that inevitably shape the nature of their interaction with different aspects of globalization and thereby generate diverse responses.[33] It is also in this process of globalization where, as we will discuss later, "the infiltration of popular culture and the encroachment of the global marketplace pose an existential threat to some traditional societies as dire as conquering hordes".[34]

[30] UN Development Programme, 'Globalization with a Human Face' (1999)
[31] Michael McIvor, *Establishing a Heart Failure Program: The Essential Guide* (3rd edn Blackwell Publishing, Malden 2007) 16
[32] Paul Hopper, *Understanding Cultural Globalization* (Polity Press, Cambridge 2007) 2
[33] Ibid 3
[34] David P Goldman, *It's Not the End of the World, It's Just the End of You: The Great Extinction of the Nations* (RVP Publishers, New York 2011) 271

It has to be noted from the very outset that it is neither our aim to get involved in the unresolved theoretical discourse on the three waves of globalization, nor our goal to rehearse the normative arguments that stem from different disciplines. Instead, we merely adopt a constructive approach in studying the existing contributions to the process of globalization. The purpose of this is to comprehend this process in so far as it concerns its interconnectivity which has had an impact on the human dimension and has generated various responses. Thus, it suffices to grasp the concept of 'globalization' in the neutral sense of the word that would encompass the core characteristics of this phenomenon, and which can be deployed as the underlying framework for our comprehension of contemporary tensions. In doing so, various descriptive views stemming from the main actors and documents in the process of globalization will be considered.

One of the main actors that deals, to a certain extent, with globalization's human dimension is the World Trade Organization.[35] The Director-General of this organization, Pascal Lamy, has defined 'globalization' in his speech of 30 January 2006 as "a historical stage of accelerated expansion of market capitalism [...] [which] is a fundamental transformation in societies because of the recent technological revolution which has led to a recombining of the economic and social forces on a new territorial dimension. [...] Globalization has led to the opening, the vanishing of many barriers and walls, and has the potential for expanding freedom, democracy, innovation, social and cultural exchanges while offering outstanding opportunities for dialogue and understanding. [...] [However], globalization has reinforced the strong ones and weakened those that were already weak. It is this double face of globalization that [ought to be addressed in order] to 'humanize globalization' [which] is also in line with the millennium development goals [...]".[36] This description makes clear that the process of globalization is multidimensional and interconnected in all its facets with sweeping effect on human life. In other words, globalization is "a powerful, complex and essentially indeterminate and open-ended transformative force or process responsible for massive change within societies and world order".[37] A plain description of this effect on human life is provided by the 1999 UN Human Development Report which asserts that the distinctive features of 'globalization' in the modern era are the "shrinking space, shrinking time and disappearing borders [which] are linking people's lives more deeply, more intensely, more immediately than ever before".[38] This delineation contains two main features of the globalization process. The first feature is the shrinking of space and time,

---

[35] For further information concerning, among others, the role of this organization in this age of globalization, reference can be made to: UN Development Programme, 'Globalization with a Human Face' (1999)

[36] Pascal Lamy, 'Humanising Globalization' (Speech at the World Trade Organization in Santiago, 30 January 2006) <http://www.wto.org/english/news_e/sppl_e/sppl16_e.htm> accessed 1 March 2011

[37] Paul Hopper, *Understanding Cultural Globalization* (Polity Press, Cambridge 2007) 8-9

[38] UN Development Programme, 'Globalization with a Human Face' (1999)

which is often called the time-space convergence[39], time-space compression[40] or time-space distantiation.[41] The concept of time-space convergence implies the elimination of distance, that is, from a spatial perspective, a decrease in the distance between places[42] through the velocity of transportation technologies, whereas 'time-space compression' indicates[43] the annihilation of space by time "that lies at the core of the capitalist dynamic".[44] This implies that the compression of time and space is the result of the expansion of capitalism across the world. Anthony Giddens, however, goes beyond the technological velocities and the economic dimensions, and calls this feature of globalization the 'time-space distantiation'. By this he means "the processes whereby societies are 'stretched' over shorter or longer spans of time and space"[45], i.e. "the stretching of social systems across time-space, on the basis of mechanisms of social and system integration".[46] Despite the different contexts and disciplines wherein these phraseologies are applied, one notices that they all have one core aspect in common, namely, the shrinking of time and space. And this leads us to the second feature of the globalization process which is the disappearance of borders. This second trait is often called 'deterritorialization', which has connected people's lives more deeply, intensively, and immediately. In other words, the feature of 'deterritorialization' contains 'dislocation', that is, transcending territorial identities and boundaries and creating new links, i.e. fostering and intensifying 'interconnectedness'.

Despite the lack of universal consensus on the definition of 'globalization', I propose, for the purpose of this study and based on the aforementioned features, the following description. Globalization is a precipitating set of continuous processes involving miscellaneous flows that encompass ever-increasing numbers of the global spaces in a compressed time scale, which result in deterritorialization and lead to aggrandized integration, as well as an intensified and deepened interconnectedness. However, we can see that for a considerable period of time, the aforementioned features of the process of globalization have been applied merely to economic and technological flows across the globe. This means that the flow of human beings, in terms of 'global migration', has gained attention as one of the many flows while, at the same time, their modes of life, in

[39] Donald G Janelle, 'Central place development in a time-space framework' (1968) 20 The Professional Geographer

[40] David Harvey, *The Condition of Postmodernity* (Blackwell Publishing, Oxford 1989)

[41] Anthony Giddens, *The Consequences of Modernity* (Polity Press, Cambridge 1990)

[42] Ronald John Johnston and others (eds), *The Dictionary of Human Geography* (4th edn Blackwell Publishing, Malden 2000) 835

[43] David Harvey, *The Condition of Postmodernity* (Blackwell Publishing, Oxford 1989)

[44] Peter Droege (ed), *Urban Energy Transition: From Fossil Fuels to Renewable Power* (Elsevier, Oxford 2008) 61

[45] Anthony Giddens, *A Contemporary Critique of Historical Materialism: Power, Property and the State* (vol 1 UCP, Berkeley 1981) 90. See also Anthony Giddens, *The Consequences of Modernity* (Polity Press, Cambridge 1990) 28

[46] Anthony Giddens, *The Constitution of Society: Outline of the Theory of Structuration* (UCP, Berkeley 1984) 377

terms of 'culture', have been neglected. In other words, for a notable period of time, the cultural dimension of globalization has not gained the necessary attention from those involved in the globalization discourse.

In this discourse, globalism, as one of the three waves of the process of globalization, conceives this process merely in terms of 'modernization'. Hereby, the Western world in general and the United States in particular are considered to be the forerunners of 'modernization', i.e. exporters of a global techno-economic consumer culture. This view puts modernization on a par with the homogenization of cultures. However, as we will discuss later, such a narrow view is often conceived as Western capitalist expansionism and imperialism. Therefore, grasping 'globalization' merely in these terms entails a narrow understanding of our current globalized world, because the converging and homogenizing effect of techno-economic modernization, which we call the process of modernization, is rather *relative*. This means that the process of modernization does not imply an *absolute* homogenization, i.e. full convergence. What is more, the *relative* homogenizing effect of technological or economical modernity, as will become plain during our inquiry, does not mean that other traits of human life, such as '*politics*' or '*culture*', would necessarily homogenize, too. In other words, the globalization of modernity is considered to be the prerequisite for global connectivity, whereby "contacts between people and their cultures – their ideas, their values, their ways of life – have been growing and deepening in unprecedented ways [...]".[47] Yet, this interconnection does not entail the creation of a homogenized 'global consumer culture', viz. a *single* 'universal culture'.

The transformational challenges, that have ensued from the increased plurality and diversity of cultures, have raised the general level of awareness of the parties involved. This has resulted in the second wave of globalization called 'transformationalism'. The transformationalist wave contends that cultural products flowing around the globe are differently received and used.[48] This means that despite the intensified interactions, cultures do not homogenize but evolve, transform, and hybridize. However, we have to add that cultural interactions can also result in clashes. In the same vein, Menachem Mautner pointed to anthropologists who defined 'culture' "[...] as an entity clearly bounded in terms of its contents and internal processes of development, and as widely shared and even agreed to by members of a society. [However], in recent decades, these views of culture have been abandoned and superseded by a new understanding of culture that is to a great extent the reverse of the former one: the culture of every society is viewed as highly fragmented, i.e., as composed of a large number of subcultures whose contents are mastered to varying extents by different members of a society. [...] the contents of every culture are both produced internally and borrowed from other cultures through varying means of contact with them. What all of this means is that people internalize cultural contents whose origins lie in various cultural systems and give meaning to what

[47] UN Development Programme, 'Globalization with a Human Face' (1999)
[48] Ibid

transpires in their lives by means of mind categories whose origins lie in various cultural systems. Put differently, most people are multicultural beings".[49] Thus, according to transformationalism, a greater role is given not only to techno-economic modernization, but also to human agents in the way they perceive modernization within the process of globalization.[50] The determinative and decisive factor in this regard is the human trait 'culture' in the broadest sense of the term.

Roland Robertson might be considered one of the few scholars who have incorporated the concept of culture, as a global human condition, into the process of globalization. In this context, he has introduced the term 'glocalization' which entails that the *global* and *local* are interacting and interpenetrating spheres that inform each other. Thus, in his point of view, "globalization involves the creation and incorporation of locality, processes which themselves largely shape, in turn, the compression of the world as a whole".[51] However, the transformationalist explanation is *partial* in that it does not take the aforementioned discordant dimension of this process into account. Thus, according to the second wave of globalization, cultures have coalesced and fused together, but it should not be forgotten that they also clash with each other. In other words, transformationalism defines this interrelationship as 'glocalization', viz. "a hybrid of globalization and localization, [which empowers] local communities through strategic linking of global resources to address local issues for positive social change and to balance changing cultural interests and community needs".[52] Yet, others go beyond this partial understanding and conceive this interrelationship as a disruptive and disintegrative force, since the *local* also gives rise to various, often traditional, forms of discord and resistance.

This latter perspective is highlighted by the third wave of globalization called 'skepticism'. According to this wave, the *global* and *local* levels do not always form a syncretic whole or hybridize, but rather differentiate, polarize, fragmentize and collide. This is because modernity, which is normally associated with the Western world, is perceived as the imposition and implosion of Western values on a global scale.[53] And by being thus experienced as a new form of Western imperialism – for which various terminologies such as '*Westernization*', '*Americanization*', and '*McDonaldization*' have been deployed – it is often antagonized and resisted. Therefore, Mautner is right when he observes that despite the assumption that people are multicultural beings, "[...] anthropologists, linguists and cultural researchers are well aware of the difficulties involved in attempts to understand foreign cultures and to 'translate'

[49] Menachem Mautner, 'Religion in Politics: Rawls and Habermas on Deliberation and Justification' (2013) Tel Aviv University Law Faculty Papers. Working Paper No. 167

[50] Paul Hopper, *Understanding Cultural Globalization* (Polity Press, Cambridge 2007) 8-9

[51] Ibid 97

[52] Patrick Mendis, *Glocalization: The Human Side of Globalization as if the Washington Consensus Mattered* (Lulu Press, Morrisville 2007) 2

[53] E Osei Kwadwo Prempeh, Joseph Mensah, and Senyo B-S K Adjibolosoo (eds), *Globalization and the Human Factor: Critical Insights* (Ashgate Publishing, Hampshire 2004) 73

meaning that is prevalent in one culture into the meaning terms extant in another culture without suffering misunderstandings, distortions and losses, as well as the difficulties involved in maintaining intercultural communication. Indeed, there are too many instances in which Western liberals have failed to understand the meaning of cultural practices prevalent in non-liberal groups. It is often the case that liberals attach certain meanings to such practices, while in the groups themselves they bear wholly different meanings".[54] Thus, globalization does not only homogenize and hybridize cultures, but, as we can now observe, it has also disruptive, disintegrative, and marginalizing consequences that are held to be reconfigured along cultural lines.

Based on the foregoing, we can infer that the process of globalization has hastened, if not brought about, pluralism while, at the same time, the human dimension herein has been neglected to the point that it has fostered discontent. In order to understand the menace of this antagonism, it is ineluctable to elaborate on the scope and content of this reciprocal discord, which is often defined as a clash between 'Orientalism' and 'Occidentalism'. In so doing, we have chosen Edward Said's two landmark works, '*Orientalism*' and '*Culture & Imperialism*', as our point of departure. Subsequently, our study of these two works is supplemented by additional literature.[55]

1.2. The Reciprocity of Antagonism: Orientalism *v.* Occidentalism

The contemporary menace being aimed at eliminating dissenters as well as undermining and destabilizing the social order seems to be a discord between Orientalism and Occidentalism that is drawn along cultural lines, i.e. constituted on the basis of civilization. This illustrates that this clash is not a new juncture, but in fact an old phenomenon in a new guise. Accordingly, to determine whether the human dimension of the globalization process, i.e. the notion of culture, inevitably fosters the current antagonism, it is important to expound the scope and nature of this discontent in a broader context. In so doing, the aforementioned landmark works of Edward Said, '*Orientalism*' and its sequel '*Culture & Imperialism*', are taken as the point of departure of this inquiry into the inevitability of the notion of culture for contemporary antagonism. This implies that criticisms emanating from various disciplines will not be rehearsed, since the focus will only be on the political dimension of Said's overall thesis in so far as it is relevant for our inquiry. It suffices to note only that, as we will see below, the core of the critique regarding Said concerns his arbitrary selectiveness which has resulted, among others, in various factual aberrations in his thesis. As

[54] Menachem Mautner, 'Religion in Politics: Rawls and Habermas on Deliberation and Justification' (2013) Tel Aviv University Law Faculty Papers. Working Paper No. 167. Menachem Mautner, 'A Dialogue between a Liberal and an Ultra-Orthodox on the Exclusion of Women from Torah Study' (2013). Tel Aviv University Law Faculty Papers. Working Paper No. 180

[55] Aijaz Ahmad, *In Theory: Classes, Nations, Literatures* (Verso, London 2008) 14

to his supposed arbitrary selectiveness, the following main categories can be distinguished.

Firstly, Said restricts his argumentation to the Arab heartland without any (substantial) devotion to, for example, the Turkish, Persian or North African Orientalism.[56] In this context, reference can be made to the critique by Bernard Lewis of Said's treatment of Orientalism. Lewis contends that Said's thesis, and all its blind spots, "reveals a disquieting lack of knowledge of what scholars do and what scholarship is about".[57] Also, the British historian, Robert Irwin, contests Said's arbitrary selectiveness of the historical facts. He argues that "Orientalism is not a history of Oriental studies, but rather a highly selective polemic on certain aspects of the relationship of knowledge and power".[58] It is also this relationship that underpins our research, because, as James Clifford suggests, "If Said's primary aim were to write an intellectual history of Orientalism or a history of Western ideas of the Orient, his narrowing and rather obviously tendentious shaping of the field could [indeed] be taken as a fatal flaw. But his undertaking is conceived otherwise and is openly an oppositional genealogy".[59] This is why the aim of this inquiry is not to focus on or to rehearse the critique about the *historical* aspects of Said's work, but, as elaborated below, to take the *political* dimension of his overall thesis as our point of departure in studying the nature and inherency of contemporary antagonism.

The second remark regarding arbitrary selectiveness that needs to be borne in mind concerns the exclusion of the following groups and facts. As Ibn Warraq asserts, "In the view of Edward Said, the Arabs and "Orientals", by which he seems to mean only Muslims, were always the victims of European imperialism. His hugely influential *Orientalism* does not mention the inconvenient fact that Jews were a significant part of the population of Middle Eastern countries and made great contributions to them, but were chased out or persecuted, especially during moments of intensified Arab nationalism or Muslim fervor. [...] It makes no sense to talk of Israel as a European colony – not to reduce everything to an East-versus-West anti-imperialist struggle, as Said did. [...] Said claimed that the Islamologists were all colluding with imperialists. But he left out any reference to the German Islamologists, since that would have undermined his argument. [...] Said clearly preferred to forget that imperial Germany encouraged Muslims to revolt against the British and the Russians during World War I, and that Arab leaders allied themselves with the Nazis during World War II".[60] And not only

---

[56] Robert Irwin, *Dangerous Knowledge: Orientalism & Its Discontents* (Overlook Press, Woodstock 2006) 282

[57] Bernard Lewis, 'The Question of Orientalism' *The New York Review of Books* (New York 24 June 1982) 1, 10 <http://www.nybooks.com/articles/archives/1982/jun/24/the-question-of-orientalism/?pagination=false> accessed 18 July 2012

[58] Robert Irwin, *Dangerous Knowledge: Orientalism & Its Discontents* (Overlook Press, Woodstock 2006) 281-282

[59] James Clifford, *The Predicament of Culture: Twentieth-Century Ethnography, Literature, and Art* (HUP, Cambridge 1988) 267-268

[60] Ibn Warraq, *Why the West Is Best: A Muslim Apostate's Defense of Liberal Democracy* (Encounter Books, New York 2011) 143

are the German Orientalists excluded but also the Russian Orientalists are left out by Said since including them – as in the case of German Orientalism – would have undermined his thesis. This is why Irwin, by relying on Russian Orientalism, rightly rejects the presumption that Orientalism of the nineteenth century had been Eurocentric.[61]

Furthermore, as Ibn Warraq summarizes and as we will see in the course of our inquiry, "Said attacks not only the entire discipline of Orientalism, which is devoted to the academic study of the Orient and which Said accuses of perpetuating negative racial stereotypes, anti-Arab and anti-Islamic prejudice, and the myth of an unchanging, essential "Orient", but [as stated before] he also accuses Orientalists as being a group of complicit with imperial power and holds them responsible for creating the distinction between Western superiority and Oriental inferiority, which they achieve by suppressing the voice of the "Oriental" and by their antihuman tendency to make huge, but vague, generalizations about entire populations that in reality consist of millions of individuals".[62]

In this light, two additional comments are in order. Firstly, as regards the Orientalists, it is important to note that "a part of Said's tactic is to leave out Western writers and scholars who do not conform to his theoretical framework. Since, for Said, all Europeans are a priori racist, he obviously cannot allow himself to quote writers who are not".[63] And this is why "[...] the generalization which is intended here simply boggles the mind, for it is so obviously contrary to what one knows about numerous intellectuals of the colonial period who never thought of themselves as ever standing *inside* the 'Western cultural tradition' ".[64] Irwin goes a step further and clarifies that "there has [even] been a marked tendency for Orientalists to be anti-imperialists, as their enthusiasm for Arab, or Persian or Turkish culture often went hand in hand with a dislike of seeing those people defeated and dominated by the Italians, Russians, British or French".[65] Secondly, it has to be noted that Said eloquently deplores the fact that Orientals are never given a voice, "But what is remarkable is that with the exception of Said's own voice, the only voices we encounter in the book [*Orientalism*] are precisely those of the very Western canonicity which, Said complains, has always silenced the Orient".[66] Therefore, it is Said himself who denies the Orientals a voice and uses them merely as passive victims for his oppositional ideology.

Thenceforth, despite the factual and historical evasions in Said's thesis which have already gained enough attention from numerous commentators, the point of

[61] Robert Irwin, *Dangerous Knowledge: Orientalism & Its Discontents* (Overlook Press, Woodstock 2006) 158

[62] Ibn Warraq, *Defending the West: A Critique of Edward Said's Orientalism* (Prometheus Books, New York 2007) 19

[63] Ibid 33

[64] Aijaz Ahmad, *In Theory: Classes, Nations, Literatures* (Verso, London 2008) 206

[65] Robert Irwin, *Dangerous Knowledge: Orientalism & Its Discontents* (Overlook Press, Woodstock 2006) 204

[66] Aijaz Ahmad, *In Theory: Classes, Nations, Literatures* (Verso, London 2008) 172

concern in our inquiry is the *political* dimension of his thesis that has been neglected thus far. Therefore, the aim of our inquiry below is not to rehearse the existing canon written about Said's thesis from different approaches and disciplines. Instead, the focus will be on the mere political dimension of his thesis. This dimension will be studied only to the extent that it is relevant to our inquiry about the nature and scope of contemporary antagonism that tends to be based on pluralism. In other words, for grasping the danger of the current clashes, it is indispensable to contemplate further on current antagonism being drawn along civilizational lines and, hence, defined in terms of 'Orientalism' and 'Occidentalism'.

1.2.1. The Essence of Reciprocal Antagonism

In order to comprehend the essence and inhesion of reciprocal antagonism that is grounded in the notion of culture, it is important to elaborate on the political dimension of Said's thesis which underscores our inquiry below. For a better understanding of this political dimension, it is important to envisage the core notion that underpins his thesis, namely, the notion of 'Orientalism'. In so doing, we will start by expounding the course and nature of this notion according to Said. But before doing so, it is important to bear in mind that "Said never defines Orientalism but rather qualifies and designates it from a variety of distinct and not always compatible standpoints".[67]

The essence of his description is tantamount to the following. Said perceives the notion of Orientalism as a discursive mechanism that, as a malefactor, underlies the continuous attitude of the West towards 'the rest', that is, the dichotomy between the East and West. He traces the roots of this attitude back to the colonial and imperial times by arguing that while "[...] direct colonialism has largely ended; imperialism [nevertheless] lingers where it has always been, in a kind of general cultural sphere [in the form of dehumanizing attitudes of cultural hostility[68]] as well as in specific political, ideological, economic, and social practices [...]".[69] Subsequently, he is of the view that, after the Second World War, this attitude is inherited by the American Orientalists. This means that, as will be elaborated below, not the *character* of Orientalism but only the *source* of it has changed, and a mere shift in attitude, from *academic* to *instrumental* approach[70], has taken place. This is apparent in the development of the notion of '*modern* Orientalism' which, according to Said, is nothing but the modernization, secularization and laicization of eighteenth-century European culture for Christian supernaturalism.[71] As to the continuity of Orientalism in history, Said

---

[67] James Clifford, *The Predicament of Culture: Twentieth-Century Ethnography, Literature, and Art* (HUP, Cambridge 1988) 259
[68] Edward W Said, *Orientalism* (Penguin Books, London 2003) 290, 291
[69] Edward W Said, *Culture & Imperialism* (Vintage, London 1994) 8
[70] Edward W Said, *Orientalism* (Penguin Books, London 2003) 246
[71] Ibid 120, 122-123

notes that "the role of the early Orientalists [...] was to provide their work and the Orient together with *a mise en scene*; later Orientalists, scholarly or imaginative, took firm hold of the scene. Still later, as the scene required management, it became clear that institutions and governments were better at the game of management than individuals. This is the legacy of nineteenth-century Orientalism to which the twentieth century has [thus] become inheritor".[72] In this context, four secularizing elements of the eighteenth century – expansion, historical confrontation, sympathy, and classification[73] – have formed the basis of 'modern Orientalism'. As such, Orientalism in the twentieth century has been characterized by the following elements: the use of generalization, binomial opposition, synchronic essentialism, and generalizing narrative descriptions.[74] However, to grasp the notion of '*modern* Orientalism', we first need to understand the nature of the concept of 'Orientalism' itself as expounded by Said.

The essence of Orientalism is the interrelationship between '*knowledge*' and '*power*'. Knowledge means the "[...] rising above immediacy, beyond self, into the foreign and distant" and [...] "To have such knowledge of such thing is to dominate it, to have authority over it. And authority, that is, power means for 'us' to deny autonomy to 'it' – the Oriental country – since we know it and it exists, in a sense, *as* we know it".[75] As Ian Buruma and Avishai Margalit assert, this had made Europe – to which much of the rest of the world had been reduced – into the metropolitan center from where the periphery was dominated.[76] The effect of this view has thus been that the Orientals were perceived to be a subjected race dominated by a superior race that knows the Orientals better than themselves, and knows what is good for them. In other words, the Orientals "[...] are useful in the modern world only because the powerful and up-to-date empires have effectively brought them out of the wretchedness of their decline and turned them into rehabilitated residents of productive colonies".[77] Thus, in Said's view, this comprises the dichotomy that "there are Westerners, and there are Orientals. The former dominate; the latter must be dominated, which usually means having their lands occupied, their internal affairs rigidly controlled, their blood and treasure put at the disposal of one or another Western power".[78] According to him, the discourse on Orientalism insinuates that "[...] the Oriental is *contained* and *represented* by dominating frameworks', [that is to say] Orientalism was ultimately a political vision of reality whose structure promoted the difference between the familiar (Europe, the West, 'us') and the strange (the Orient, the East, 'them')".[79]

---

[72] Ibid 197
[73] Ibid 120
[74] Ibid 227-240
[75] Ibid 32
[76] Ian Buruma and Avishai Margalit, *Occidentalism: A Short History of Anti-Westernism* (Atlantic Books, London 2005) 22-23
[77] Edward W Said, *Orientalism* (Penguin Books, London 2003) 35
[78] Ibid 36
[79] Ibid 40, 43

This was inevitable for the colonizer in terms of establishing his identity against the 'otherness' of the colonized according to the *knowledge* of the former, based on which the colonized, consequently, began to define his own identity. In other words, "The creation of the Orient as the 'other' is necessary so that the Occident can define itself and strengthen its own identity by invoking such a juxtaposition".[80] Thus, Orientalism is about constructing 'the Orient' that goes beyond the Oriental reality itself and surpasses the Oriental experience. This is the worldliness inherent in 'Orientalism' that becomes the doctrine of power, for which, according to Said, Western cultural institutions are responsible. Orientalism is thus seen as the generic term for Western systematic, i.e. particularizing and dividing approach towards the Orient, which has transited from academia to administrative and executive institutionalization, with the aim of (re-)producing authority over it.[81] As James Clifford puts it, "For Said a discourse is [thus] the cultural-political configuration of "the textual attitude'. [...] In certain conditions this textual attitude hardens into a body of rigid cultural definitions that determine what any individual can express about certain reality. This 'reality' coalesces as a field of representations produced by the discourse. The conditions for discursive hardening are not clearly defined by Said, but they appear to be related to an ongoing imbalance of power that permits – perhaps obliges – a politically and technologically stringer culture or group to define weaker groups. Thus in Said's analysis occidental culture through the discourse of Orientalism "suffused" the activity of orientals with "meaning, intelligibility, and reality' ".[82]

Thus, according to Said, Orientalism is more than just an idea, for it has a reality and presence in and for the West through the configuration and institutionalization of power that ensure its durability. This means that Orientalism is not a mere *reflection* or *result* of the imperialist tradition, but that Orientalism is *the* tradition[83] which encompasses "[...] a *distribution* of geopolitical awareness into aesthetic, scholarly, economic, sociological, historical, and philological texts; it is an *elaboration* not only of a basic geographical distinction [...] but also of a whole series of 'interests' which, by such means as scholarly discovery, philological reconstruction, psychological analysis, landscape and sociological description, it not only reacts but also maintains; it *is*, rather than expresses, a certain *will* or *intention* to understand, in some cases to control, manipulate, even to incorporate, what is a manifestly different [...] world [...]".[84] In other words, Orientalism, as the dominating cultural enterprise of imperialism[85] or rather a political doctrine willed over the

---

80 Bill Ashcroft and Pal Ahluwalia, *Edward Said* (Routledge, London 2001) 64

81 Conor McCarthy, *The Cambridge Introduction to Edward Said* (CUP, Cambridge 2010) 84

82 James Clifford, *The Predicament of Culture: Twentieth-Century Ethnography, Literature, and Art* (HUP, Cambridge 1988) 264

83 Conor McCarthy, *The Cambridge Introduction to Edward Said* (CUP, Cambridge 2010) 73

84 Edward W Said, *Orientalism* (Penguin Books, London 2003) 12

85 Edward W Said, *Culture & Imperialism* (Vintage, London 1994) xxviii

Orient[86], is the discursive framework wherein – through the interplay between 'knowledge' and 'power' – the differences between the 'familiar' and the 'strange' are represented, so that the latter can be dominated. Based on this, knowledge is considered to be a matter of *representation*. And representation is grasped as a process of giving concrete form to ideological concepts and assumptions, that is, making certain signifiers signify signified.[87] More concrete, this suggests that the imperial culture is built on unchallenged assumptions, whereby the cultural production of it has a deep investment in the political character of its society that simultaneously drives and energizes it.[88] Thus, culture and its productions have a deep and complicated investment in as well as an invisible interwovenness with the political character and ideology of a society.[89] This implies that Orientalism is not only a *representation*, but rather a dimension of modern political-intellectual culture[90], i.e. Orientalism is both a political and cultural *fact*. The interest of imperialism has been *political*, yet it has been *culture* that created that interest in the Orient. Thence, Orientalism, as a political and cultural fact, exposes culture *as* imperialism.[91]

It is in this light that, in Said's opinion, "continued investment made Orientalism, as a system of knowledge about the Orient, an accepted grid for filtering through the Orient into Western consciousness, just as that same investment multiplied – indeed, made truly productive – the statements proliferating out from Orientalism into the general culture".[92] This interwovenness has to do with culture operating within civil society, which acknowledges a gradation of political importance in various fields of knowledge[93] that stem from sources of power in political society. Within civil society, some cultural forms gain hegemony which then gives Orientalism – encompassing Western superiority and non-Western inferiority – its strength and durability. And according to Said, we can better understand "[...] the persistence and the durability of suturing hegemonic systems like culture when we realize that their internal constraints upon writers and thinkers were productive, not unilaterally inhibiting".[94] Due to this durable productivity, Said contends that "[...] every European in what he could say about the Orient, was consequently a racist, and imperialist, and almost totally ethnocentric"[95], antihuman, hegemonic, and anthropocentric – the scope, the institutions and all-pervasive influences which have lasted up to the present.[96] With this in mind, Said considers the West itself to be culpable for the resistance and opposition

[86] Edward W Said, *Orientalism* (Penguin Books, London 2003) 204
[87] Bill Ashcroft and Pal Ahluwalia, *Edward Said* (Routledge, London 2001) 65
[88] Ibid 88
[89] Ibid
[90] Edward W Said, *Orientalism* (Penguin Books, London 2003) 12
[91] Bill Ashcroft and Pal Ahluwalia, *Edward Said* (Routledge, London 2001) 90
[92] Edward W Said, *Orientalism* (Penguin Books, London 2003) 6
[93] Ibid 10
[94] Ibid 14
[95] Ibid 204
[96] Ibid 44

that it faces. To this end, he insists that from the beginning, "[...] given the discrepancy between European colonial power and that of the colonized societies, there was a kind of historical necessity by which colonial pressure created anticolonial resistance".[97]

The preceding discussion on the notion of Orientalism shows, thus, the inevitability of the concept of culture (in the broadest sense of the word) within this discursive mechanism for which the West is held liable. Yet, this is only half of the story, for we need to inquire further if we are to gain a thorough understanding of both sides of the current dichotomous antagonism. That being said, it is indispensable to start with the two descriptions of 'culture' that Said provides. By reading these two descriptions together, it becomes clear that while culture entails "[...] all those practices, like the arts of description, communication, and representation, that have relative autonomy from the economic, social, and political realms and that often exist in aesthetic forms, one of whose principal aims is pleasure"[98], it is nevertheless a concept which as a source of identity includes "[...] a refining and elevating element, [that is] each society's reservoir of the best that has been known and thought"[99], in which various political and ideological causes engage one another.[100]

Based on the foregoing survey and Said's second description of culture, it would seem inconsistent to conceive this concept only as the (aesthetic) practices that are autonomous and independent of the other realms of life. This is because, as mentioned already, culture and its products have a deep and complicated investment in, and an invisible interwovenness with, other realms of life such as the political and ideological.[101] In confirming the inseparability of culture with other realms of life, and thus the necessity of reading conjunctively the aforementioned descriptions, Said relies on the notion of Orientalism which he conceives as a discourse, i.e. the political configuration of a 'structure of attitude and reference' that finds its existence in the cultural product of 'the novel'. To put it differently, in reinforcing the interwovenness of the European culture and imperialism, the phraseology of 'structure of attitude and reference' is invented. This expression encompasses "[...] the way in which structures of location and geographical reference appear in the cultural language of literature, history, or ethnography [...] across several individual works that are not otherwise connected to one another or to an official ideology of 'empire' ".[102] This phraseology is underpinned by his technique of 'contrapuntal reading' that encompasses a 'reading back' and 'rethinking geography'. In other words, "Contrapuntal reading is a technique of theme and variation by which a counterpoint is established between the imperial narrative and the post-colonial perspective, a 'counter-narrative' that keeps penetrating beneath the surface of

---

[97] Ibid 45

[98] Edward W Said, *Culture & Imperialism* (Vintage, London 1994) xii

[99] Ibid xiii

[100] Ibid vi

[101] Bill Ashcroft and Pal Ahluwalia, *Edward Said* (Routledge, London 2001) 88

[102] Edward W Said, *Culture & Imperialism* (Vintage, London 1994) 61

individual texts to elaborate the ubiquitous presence of imperialism in canonical culture".[103] This implies that while the interest of imperialism has been political, it has been the culture that created that interest. That is, even though this attitude is prevalent in many ways, forms and places, it has been principally the textual attitude – especially the 'novel' – which has broadened the domestic imperialist culture, without which territorial acquisition would not have been possible.[104]

Conversely, it has been the phenomenon of imperialism that has made it possible for the novel of the nineteenth century to develop. This is, however, not to say that "[...] the novel – or the culture in the broad sense – 'caused' imperialism, but that the novel, as a cultural artifact of bourgeois society, and imperialism are unthinkable without each other. Of all the major literary forms, the novel is the most recent, its emergence the most datable, its occurrence the most Western, its normative pattern of social authority the most structured; imperialism and the novel fortified each other to such a degree that it is impossible [...] to read one without in some way dealing with the other".[105] Thus, the 'novel' is seen as an important cultural institution "[...] with a particular capacity for representing society, reproducing its values and ideas, and displaying its forms of authority".[106] As regards the notion of 'authority', Conor McCarthy pointedly notes that "novelists locate their work in, and derive its authority from, the empirical reality of society [...]. Fictional authority is constructed, firstly, out of authorial authority – the author who gives narrative form to the processes of society; secondly, out of the authority of the narrator [...]; thirdly, out of the authority of the community [...]. But the power of the novel also comes from its appropriation of historical discourse: the novel historicizes the past, and narrativises the society. In so doing, it also differentiates and valorizes social space. Underlying this fictional space lies real political geography".[107]

Thus, the novel mirrors the discourse of Orientalism, as a political and cultural fact that is filtered into the Western consciousness. For that reason, Said contends that what every European could say about the Orient was racist, imperialist, ethnocentric, antihuman, hegemonic, and anthropocentric.[108] Buruma and Margalit share this view, but – unlike Said who argues that no corresponding equivalent of Orientalism is present in the Orient itself[109] – they go a step further by applying this view also to the notion of Occidentalism. In so doing, they argue that "the view of the West in Occidentalism is like the worst aspects of its counterpart, Orientalism, which strips its human targets of their humanity. Some Orientalist prejudices made non-Western people seem less than fully adult

---

[103] Bill Ashcroft and Pal Ahluwalia, *Edward Said* (Routledge, London 2001) 93
[104] Edward W Said, *Culture & Imperialism* (Vintage, London 1994) 114
[105] Ibid 84
[106] Conor McCarthy, *The Cambridge Introduction to Edward Said* (CUP, Cambridge 2010) 114
[107] Ibid 115
[108] Edward W Said, *Orientalism* (Penguin Books, London 2003) 44, 108, 204
[109] Ibid 204

human beings; [...]. Occidentalism is at least as reductive; its bigotry simple turns the Orientalist view upside down".[110]

The preceding elaboration leads us to the conclusion that the concept of culture is not independent and autonomous from other realms of life such as the political domain. To the contrary, this human dimension of globalization is the underlying fundament, which is inevitably interwoven with these realms. This underlines the inherency and inextricability of this concept from dichotomous antagonism, especially now that, as Said warns, "a growing, more and more dangerous rift separates Orient and Occident".[111] Thus, the importance of this concept for the current antagonism is also elucidated through Said's thesis about Orientalism or as discussed below, *mutatis mutandis*, applicable to the notion of Occidentalism. Although the roots of this dichotomy can be traced back to the imperial and colonial times, its presence is, more than ever before, tangible in our globalized world which has, coupled with the current pluralism, aggravated the clashes with far-reaching consequences. It is in this context that we need to grasp the manifestation of this reciprocal antagonism in our globalized era, the essence of which has been expounded in this part.

1.3. Dichotomous Antagonism within the Process of Globalization

After the theoretical conceptualization of the essential contours and inherent features of the dichotomous antagonism, it is important to examine the actual materialization of this reciprocal discord within the current process of globalization that we have touched on before. The preceding discussion has revealed that the underpinning fundament of the reciprocal clashes between Orientalism and Occidentalism is the unequivocal concept of culture, what we have called the human dimension of the process of globalization. The continuity of this reciprocal antagonism is best seen in Said's reasoning, whereby the West is held liable for the current state of affairs. For he argues that the discourse of Orientalism, being *the* imperial tradition, has laid the fundament for what is now a fully global world.[112] Thus, the notion of globalization has actually become the new word for imperialism[113], with which this epoch has been marked as 'the rise of the West'.[114] The distinct feature of this century is, hence, the process of globalization which, in Said's point of view, entails "[...] a world tied together as never before by the exigencies of electronic communication, trade, travel, environmental and regional conflicts that can expand with tremendous speed, [wherein] the assertion of identity is by no means a mere ceremonial matter'.

[110] Ian Buruma and Avishai Margalit, *Occidentalism: A Short History of Anti-Westernism* (Atlantic Books, London 2005) 10

[111] Edward W Said, *Orientalism* (Penguin Books, London 2003) 109

[112] Edward W Said, *Culture & Imperialism* (Vintage, London 1994) 4

[113] Ian Buruma and Avishai Margalit, *Occidentalism: A Short History of Anti-Westernism* (Atlantic Books, London 2005) 36

[114] Edward W Said, *Culture & Imperialism* (Vintage, London 1994) 6

[This contains the menace of mobilization of atavistic passions whereby people can be thrown back to] '[...] an earlier imperial time when the West and its opponents championed and even embodied virtues designed not as virtues so to speak but for war".[115]

What is remarkable about Said's view of the process of globalization is that it is a typical example of the skeptical wave of globalization. For according to this wave, as stated above, globalization is to be comprehended in terms of modernity, which is associated with the Western world and, accordingly, perceived as the perilous imposition and implosion of Western values on a global scale.[116] Consequently, this is experienced as Western imperialism which, therefore, is antagonized and resisted. However, it has to be borne in mind that Said does not provide a consistent description of the process of globalization, due to which he jumps from one wave of globalization to another. More concretely, depending on the topic at hand, Said switches back and forth from the skeptical paradigm to the transformationalist or globalist paradigm.

Nevertheless, Said's definition of 'globalization' brings the following essential aspects to the fore, all of which are underpinned by the fundamental concept of 'culture'. The first aspect is that globalization is a precipitating set of continuous processes, which involves miscellaneous flows across global spaces in a compressed timescale. Consequently, this development results in deterritorialization, and leads to aggrandized integration, as well as intensified and deepened interconnectedness. The second significant aspect that Said acknowledges is the inevitability of identity, and by that, the assertion of culture as its source. The third important aspect that ought to be addressed is the mere association of the menace that stems from the assertion of identity with the West and its imperial history.

With this narrow understanding, Said fails, wittingly or not, to face the danger ensuing from the assertion of identity by 'others', that is, the assertion of non-Western identities. In focusing on the West, he argues that there are two major Orientalist methods that have delivered the Orient to the West and accomplished the supremacy of Western culture in the twentieth century. First, the delivery took place through the diffusion of modern learning in the broadest sense of the word. Second, the delivery of the East to the West took place by means of the convergence between, what he calls, 'latent Orientalism' and 'manifest Orientalism'.[117] And against this background, two core *factors* have finally made the triumph of Orientalism in our modern world obvious. First, we have the tendencies of the contemporary culture in the Near East that are guided by American and European models. Hereby, the remainder of the Arab and Islamic world is seen as an inferior power in terms of the production of culture.[118] The

[115] Ibid 42

[116] E Osei Kwadwo Prempeh, Joseph Mensah, and Senyo B-S K Adjibolosoo (eds), *Globalization and the Human Factor: Critical Insights* (Ashgate Publishing, Hampshire 2004) 73

[117] Edward W Said, *Orientalism* (Penguin Books, London 2003) 221-223

[118] Ibid 323

second factor that confirms the triumph of Orientalism – and inextricable from the first – is Oriental consumption of Western ideological and material products.[119]

Two comments are here called for in order to better understand this consumption. Firstly, Said notes that a modern feature of the ideological component is its claim to being an educational movement that aims to modernize, develop, instruct, and civilize.[120] He is of the view that this is, however, nothing but an attitude of superiority of the West in general and the United States in particular. In this context, the United States is considered to be the symbolic representative of the West. Hereby, he asserts that the American attitude to American greatness, hierarchies of race, and to the perils of other revolutions have remained constant, and have obscured and dictated the realities of empirehood.[121] Said continues to contend that apologists for overseas American interests insist on American innocence, doing good, and fighting for freedom.[122] Meanwhile, the United States does not accept any infringements or sustained ideological challenges to what is conceived to be 'freedom'.[123] Due to this, he considers the West in general and the United States in particular to be imperialistic *par excellence*, by stating for example, as regards the United States, that the American experience "[...] was from the beginning founded upon the idea of 'an *imperium*- a dominion, state or sovereignty that would expand in population and territory, and increase in strength and power".[124] Secondly, concerning the material commodities, Said notes that "granted that American expansionism is principally economic, it is still highly dependent and moves together with, upon, cultural ideas and ideologies about America itself, ceaselessly reiterated in public"[125], which has "[...] the effect of depoliticizing, reducing, and sometimes even eliminating the integrity of overseas societies that seemed in need of modernization [...]".[126]

Thence, in this age of globalization, the assertion of identity is by no means a mere ceremonial matter, for it has marked the clashes between Orientalism and Occidentalism. What underpins this reciprocal antagonism is, as already said, the concept of culture, due to which freedom, peace, and security are put into perspective. It is also in this same context that antagonistic utterances such as 'the rise of the West', 'the triumph of Orientalism', and the linkage between imperialism and culture ought to be understood. Another example that illustrates the undeniability of the concept of culture for the current reciprocal clashes is the presence of Muslim populations in the West. Said acknowledges that there is a considerable and significant Muslim population in the Western countries because

[119] Ibid 324
[120] Ibid 269
[121] Edward W Said, *Culture & Imperialism* (Vintage, London 1994) 7
[122] Ibid
[123] Ibid 352
[124] Ibid 7
[125] Ibid 350
[126] Ibid 351

of which Islam is no longer on the fringes of the West but at the center of it. Yet, he denies that the notion of culture in general and the culture of this group in particular can be the underlying fundament of the current clashes. The paradox in this, however, is that Said denies the ineluctability of the notion of culture when he deals with 'others' and their opposition; while his own thesis is grounded on this notion based on which he antagonizes the West by, for example, arguing that the current threats do stem not from this particular group, but from the hostile memories buried in the collective culture of the West.[127]

Therefore, the ineluctability of the concept of culture in the broadest sense of the term makes Said's opposition to the notion of the 'clash of civilizations' spurious. This notion – coined by Bernard Lewis and later elaborated by Samuel P. Huntington – is severely criticized by Said in his critical article '*The Clash of Ignorance*', in which he argues that "[...] neither Huntington nor Lewis has much time to spare for the internal dynamics and plurality of every civilization, or for the fact that the major contest in most modern cultures concerns the definition or interpretation of each culture, or for the unattractive possibility that a great deal of demagogy and downright ignorance is involved in presuming to speak for a whole religion or civilization. No, the West is the West, and Islam Islam".[128] This betrays the ambiguity of Said's argument. And this equivocation is embedded in his thesis on Orientalism, based on the notion of culture and, in opposing the West, grounded on this civilizational clash that he, nonetheless, aims to repudiate when uttered by Huntington. Thus, based on the above survey, including Said's own thesis, it can be inferred that the dichotomous antagonism is, indeed, civilizational in nature. However, before continuing, it is important to devote some thoughts to this civilizational antagonism (viz. 'the clash of civilizations' thesis) which we have touched on above in order to explore its underlying cause.

Against all odds, what Said and Huntington have in common – despite differences in their views of the West – is that they are both skeptical about the homogenization and universalization of Western civilization. As Huntington puts it, the idea of a 'universal civilization' "[...] implies in general the cultural coming together of humanity and the increasing acceptance of common values, beliefs, orientations, practices, and institutions by peoples throughout the world".[129] However, he argues that "[...] the assumptions, values, and doctrines currently held by many people in Western civilization and by some people in other civilizations"[130], at least at the intellectual level, are far from a reflection of one 'universal culture'. Instead, "what is universalism to the West is imperialism to the rest".[131] Thus, Huntington is of the view that the concepts developed

[127] Edward W Said, 'The Clash of Ignorance' *The Nation* (New York 22 October 2001) <http://www.thenation.com/article/clash-ignorance?page=full> accessed 25 July 2012

[128] Ibid

[129] Samuel P Huntington, *The Clash of Civilizations and the Remaking of World Order* (Simon & Schuster, London 2002) 56

[130] Ibid 57

[131] Ibid 184

within Western civilization are not universal and will never take root beyond the boundaries of the Euro-Christian culture. This concurs thus with Said's view, according to which Western civilization's ambition, defined in terms of modernization, is nothing but the imposition of Western values on a global scale, which, as Western imperialism, is opposed. In the same vein, Huntington contests the utopian claims of globalists in general and the theory of Francis Fukuyama in particular. In so doing, he argues that the 'soft power'[132] of the West has faded, whereas the relative power of other civilizations has increased and has made them "increasingly immune to Western pressure concerning [among others] human rights and democracy".[133]

It is against the background of this antagonism that Huntington's 'civilizational approach'[134] has to be understood. According to this approach, "[...] the fundamental source of conflict in the new world will not be primarily ideological or primarily economic. The great divisions among humankind and the dominating source of conflict will be cultural. [...] the principal conflicts of global politics will occur between nations and groups of different civilizations. [...] Conflict between civilizations will be the last phase in the evolution of conflicts in the modern world".[135] This is attributed to the fact that "people use politics not just to advance their interests but also to define their identity [...]".[136] As Said also acknowledges, the assertion of identity is by no means a mere ceremonial matter anymore. Hence, Huntington defines world politics as a '*multipolar*' and '*multicivilizational*' system, meaning that a civilization-based world order has emerged.[137] Hereby, "[...] local politics [the so-called 'micro-level'] is the politics of ethnicity; [and] global politics [called the 'macro-level'] is the politics of civilizations. The rivalry of the superpowers is thus replaced by the clash of civilizations"[138] at the international level. As to the micro-level, Huntington argues that "[...] the most pervasive, important, and dangerous conflicts will not be between social classes, rich and poor, or other economically defined groups, but between peoples belonging to different cultural entities".[139]

While the most pervasive and devastating clashes take place at the micro-level, Huntington's thesis is, nonetheless, mainly if not only, concerned with the macro-level. This is why, unlike Huntington's sole focus on the macro-level,

---

[132] The idea of 'soft power' entails the ability to get the adherents of other cultures to want what you want through the appeal of your culture and ideology, and by means of the promotion of your political values and institutions that have resulted in material success and influence

[133] Samuel P Huntington, *The Clash of Civilizations and the Remaking of World Order* (Simon & Schuster, London 2002) 92, 195. It is important to bear in mind that Huntington considers individualism and the tradition of individual rights and liberties not as universal values, but as the distinct and essential features and qualities of Western civilization

[134] Ibid 36

[135] Samuel P Huntington, 'The Clash of Civilizations?' (1993) 72 (3) Foreign Aff 22, 22

[136] Samuel P Huntington, *The Clash of Civilizations and the Remaking of World Order* (Simon & Schuster, London 2002) 21

[137] Ibid 20

[138] Ibid 28

[139] Ibid

both realms will be comprehensively assayed in our research. It is worth noting that in his focus on the macro-level, Huntington observes that since "[...] international politics moves out of its Western phase, and its centerpiece becomes the interaction between the West and non-Western civilizations, and among non-Western civilizations"[140], in order to survive, the West should defend itself against the non-Western many[141] by reaffirming the uniqueness of Western civilization and identity.[142] And the prime candidate for doing this, according to him, is the United States.[143] It is precisely this behavior that Said defines as the imperialist superiority of the West in general and the United States in particular. Accordingly, he rejects this attitude and considers it to be highly dependent on consumerism and cultural ideas and ideologies of America and the West.[144] Thus, his antagonism is based on the idea that this attitude depoliticizes, reduces, and eliminates the integrity of overseas societies that seem to be in need of modernization.[145] Yet, as stated before and as will be further clarified in this survey, Said contradicts himself. This is because his own thesis is inextricably entrapped in this reciprocal antagonism, while he himself actually attempts to repudiate its existence. And as our discussion above shows, the vividness of this reciprocal antagonism that underpins globalized world affairs is beyond any reasonable doubt.

The foregoing discussion leads us to the conclusion that reciprocal antagonism, the essence of which is traced back to the colonial and imperial era, has continued to exert cultural influence even in this age of pluralism. The continuity of this dichotomous antagonism is, as already intimated, noticeable in Said's claim that the discourse on Orientalism (as *the* imperial tradition) has laid the groundwork for the current global world. But the question that might arise is *how* this continuity has come to antagonize the West as in the present. A thorough understanding of the continuity of this dichotomous antagonism will thus concern us in the following paragraph.

1.3.1. Continuation of Antagonism within a Globalized Era

As we have seen above, dichotomous antagonism, the roots of which are traced back to colonial and imperial times, has continued to exert civilizational influences in the present. The continuity of this antagonism is, as mentioned, clear from the discourse on Orientalism – which is understood as *the* imperial tradition that laid the groundwork for the current global world – against which Occidentalism aims to put up resistance. Thus, the vivacity of this continuity has

---

140 Samuel P Huntington, 'The Clash of Civilizations?' (1993) 72 (3) Foreign Aff 22, 23

141 Samuel P Huntington, *The Clash of Civilizations and the Remaking of World Order* (Simon & Schuster, London 2002) 36

142 Ibid 20-21

143 Ibid

144 Edward W Said, *Culture & Imperialism* (Vintage, London 1994) 350

145 Ibid 351

been made visible in our discussion above. Yet, the question of *how* this continuity has come to antagonize the West in this age of globalization remains.

As previously discussed, in antagonizing the West and holding it liable for the current clashes, appeal is made to the notion of 'modernization', which is considered to be the underlying core mission of Western imperialism in our globalized world. However, to grasp the continuity of antagonism in this age and reveal the ineluctable crux that underlies the current clashes, it is imperative to reflect on the assumed linkage between modernization and imperialism. In so doing, Said's overall thesis remains our point of departure despite his brief and obscure discussion of this issue and the chronological inconsistency about the aforementioned linkage.[146] However, it is worthwhile to note that on this latter linkage, Valerie Kennedy provides a plain summary that we may quote here at length: "Said compares modernism to the 'ironic disillusion' in the mainstream nineteenth-century novel and contrasts it with the 'infection of excitement' of the colonial experience via late nineteenth-century travel narratives and adventure novels. Specifically, he contrasts the latter with the modernist anxiety [...] and sees the anxiety as having an imperial source".[147]

Nonetheless, Kennedy refrains from elaborating on this connection by contending that, due to Said's brief discussion, any judgment must be suspended out of fear of speculation and the inability to provide a convincing demonstration of Said's ideas. Yet, a thorough reading of Said's works reveals sufficient continuity in his line of thought, despite the obscurities in his works in general and on this issue in particular. In this context, the prime issue that comes to the fore is the comparison between 'the interwovenness of modernization and imperialism' and 'the entwining of the novel and imperialism'. This comparison is possible because, as Said puts it, "A whole range of people [like Said himself] in the so-called Western or metropolitan world, as well as their counterparts in the Third or formerly colonized world, share a sense that the era of high or classical imperialism [...] has in one way or another continued to exert considerable cultural influence in the present".[148]

Thus, it is this continuity that makes, among others, the aforementioned comparison, and by that the comprehension of the interrelationship between modernization and imperialism, possible. The interrelationship between the 'novel' and 'imperialism', as discussed above, entails the 'novel' as a means of reflection by the high culture, thereby broadening the domestic imperialist culture[149] and *vice versa*. Nonetheless, this does not mean that the 'novel' – or rather 'culture' in the broad sense of the term – *caused* imperialism, but that high culture – by means of the 'novel' – and imperialism inevitably fortified each other.[150] Thus, the 'novel' is seen as an important cultural institution that has a

---

[146] Robert Irwin, *Dangerous Knowledge: Orientalism & Its Discontents* (Overlook Press, Woodstock 2006) 285

[147] Valerie Kennedy, *Edward Said: A Critical Introduction* (Polity Press, Cambridge 2000) 85

[148] Edward W Said, *Culture & Imperialism* (Vintage, London 1994) 6

[149] Ibid 114

[150] Ibid 84

particular ability for representing society, reproducing its values and ideas, and displaying its forms of authority.[151] That is why it is perceived to be an institution that perfectly mirrors the discourse of Orientalism as it is filtered into the Western consciousness.

When we analogously draw the same line of thought with the interrelationship between modernization and imperialism, the result will be that, through the 'media' (conceived as a crucial institution), modernization (in terms of global consumerism of Western culture) and imperialism (termed *expansionism* in the current context) have reciprocally fortified each other – which is, however, not to say that by means of the media, modernization has *ipso facto* caused expansionism. Thence, the 'media', as a modernist cultural institution, mirrors the discourse of modern Orientalism as imbedded in the contemporary Western consciousness. In other words, while the novel mirrored the discourse of classical Orientalism in the nineteenth century – which was filtered into the Western consciousness for manufacturing consent – it is the Western media that currently fulfills this task.[152] And while according to Said's understanding of Orientalism, 'others' previously seemed to be in need of culture to become civilized, currently they seem to be in need of modernization in order to become civilized. Thus, modernization, in terms of missionary tendencies to *modernize* 'others', is the same core feature of modern Orientalism just as civilization had previously been the core mission of classical Orientalism that aimed to *civilize* others.

Therefore, it is not surprising that the concepts of modern Orientalism and modernization are considered to be dovetailed.[153] Put differently, modernization is considered to be the core feature of modern Orientalism that has delivered the East to the West, and hence the Western expansionism in the contemporary world. For that reason, Said sees Orientalism as a racist, imperialist, ethnocentric, and antihuman approach the influences of which are still visible[154] in modern Orientalism. In other words, the contention here is that the era of high or classical imperialism, aimed at civilizing others, has continued to exert considerable cultural influence in the current era, which is being designated as the age of neo-imperialism. The reason for this lies in the assumption that 'modernization', as the core feature of 'modern Orientalism', is perceived to be the new trait of Western global domination that aims to impose internationally the Western civilizational values.[155] This is, for instance, apparent from Rasheed El-Enany's exposition of Ahmad Amin's reasoning. According to this reasoning, antipathy among the Orientals, which has led them to become suspicious of representatives

[151] Conor McCarthy, *The Cambridge Introduction to Edward Said* (CUP, Cambridge 2010) 114
[152] Edward W Said, *Culture & Imperialism* (Vintage, London 1994) 391-392
[153] Bill Ashcroft and Pal Ahluwalia, *Edward Said* (Routledge, London 2001) 126
[154] Edward W Said, *Orientalism* (Penguin Books, London 2003) 44
[155] E Osei Kwadwo Prempeh, Joseph Mensah, and Senyo B-S K Adjibolosoo (eds), *Globalization and the Human Factor: Critical Insights* (Ashgate Publishing, Hampshire 2004) 73

of modern civilization, is, in essence, engendered by the violence of colonial and imperial times.[156]

Thus, the discussion above has brought to light the importance of the notion of 'modernization', which is held to be the inextricable crux of the Western civilization that now underlines the clashes of our globalized era. This is because this notion, perceived to be the underlying core mission of Western civilization, is seen as a new form of imperialism. For that reason, the West is antagonized and held liable for the current clashes. In other words, it is believed that through the notion of 'modernization' – conceived as the civilizational mission of modern Orientalism – the dichotomous antagonism between Orientalism and Occidentalism has found its way into this age of globalization. Yet, for the sake of argument, it is important to bestow some thought on the nature and extent of this rudiment.

Some scholars have contested the aforementioned *ex parte* view on Western liability by contending that in this way, the notion of 'the West' is (ab-)used as a scapegoat for one's own interests. Yet, the aim of our survey is not to engage in this reciprocal blame-rhetoric and recrimination, since both views contain some nucleus of the truth. However, what is indisputable is that the resistance towards the West stems not only from the demeanor of the antagonists but, as it will become obvious in this research, also from the shortsighted bearing of the Western protagonists. What is more, these proponents are considered to be Orientalists *par excellence* who have paved the way for the antagonists to oppose and resist the Occident. This shortsightedness lies, as discussed before, in globalism's comprehension of the notion of modernization in terms of ideological, economic and technological advances, without taking the human dimension of the globalization process into consideration. Thus, in this process, the concept of culture in the broadest sense of the term, i.e. civilization[157], is not, if at all, taken into account. Consequently, this results in the failure to grasp the scope and significance of the perilous antagonism towards the West. As elaborated hereafter, this is made manifest in the reaction of antagonism to the partial bearing of globalism. Therefore, to grasp globalism's flaw, the antagonist approach will be taken as our point of departure with Said's antagonism as its pivotal basis.

The bearing of antagonists in general and Said in particular towards (modern) Orientalism might be said to be grounded in globalism's neglect of the human dimension, i.e. the notion of civilization. For this antagonism encompasses not just the opposition to economic and technological advances, but also to modernization in terms of 'global consumerism of the Western ideological and material products'. This is evident from Said's argument, who contends that

---

[156] Rasheed El-Enany, *Arab Representations of the Occident: East-West Encounters in Arabic Fiction. Culture and Civilization in the Middle East* (Routledge, Oxon 2006) 63

[157] It is important to observe that the terms 'culture' and 'civilization', as explained in this research, are interchangeably used, since in all fairness to the consulted theories in which scholars use these notions according to their own subjective preferences, it is impossible to provide a harmonized and/or universalized definition of either term

"what is crucial about the cultural productions of the West is the subtle way in which the political realities of imperialism are present in them".[158] In the same vein, opposition towards the West is considered to be the result of Orientalism itself because, as he asserts, "Those people [who are] compelled by the system to play subordinate or imprisoning roles within it emerge as conscious antagonists, disrupting it, proposing claims, advancing arguments that dispute the totalitarian compulsions of the world market".[159] In other words, a sense of inferiority and humiliation – held to be caused by Western domination and superiority – is considered to be the inevitable reason for the resistance to Western civilization.[160] Thence, the breeding ground for the contemporary antagonism towards the West, which is defined in terms of global expansionism of civilizational commodities, is to be sought within globalism. In this regard, the major globalist device, which is here opposed from the very outset, is 'the-end-of-history' thesis of Francis Fukuyama which, as elaborated below, heralds the triumph of 'liberal democracy'. Said considers such globalist theories as fallacious Western imagination that entails the completion of the imperialist project, whereby "[...] Westerners have assumed the integrity and the inviolability of their cultural masterpieces [...]. Yet [as regards this imagination, Said is of the view that] [...] it is a radical falsification of culture to strip it of its affiliations with its setting, or to pry it away from the terrain it contested or – more to the point of an oppositional strand within Western culture – to deny its real influence".[161]

Against the background of this globalist shortsightedness, Said contends that "we are nowhere near 'the end of history', but we are still far from free from monopolizing attitudes toward it".[162] In brief, this globalist theory contends that liberal democracy has a universal significance for all mankind[163] due to which, at the end of this evolutionary process, there will be more democracy than at the beginning.[164] Thus, Fukuyama claimed that "[...] liberal democracy may constitute the 'end point of mankind's ideological evolution' and the 'final form of human government', and as such constituted the 'end of history' ".[165] In other words, as Huntington has meticulously summarized it, according to Fukuyama, "we may be witnessing [...] the end of history as such: that is, the end point of mankind's ideological evolution and the universalization of Western liberal democracy as the final form of human government. [...] The war of ideas is at an end. [...] Overall liberal democracy has triumphed. The future will be devoted not to great exhilarating struggles over ideas but rather to resolving mundane

[158] Bill Ashcroft and Pal Ahluwalia, *Edward Said* (Routledge, London 2001) 8
[159] Edward W Said, *Culture & Imperialism* (Vintage, London 1994) 406
[160] Ibid 45
[161] Ibid 313
[162] Ibid 401
[163] Francis Fukuyama, *The End of History and the Last Man* (Free Press, New York 2006) 343
[164] Ibid
[165] Ibid xi

economic and technical problems".[166] Yet, "exactly thirty years after the fall of communism, though, America has lost its self-confidence, the European Community is at risk of disintegration [...]".[167] Neglecting the concept of civilization within this theory shows the shortcoming of globalism, especially since Fukuyama claims that "the realm of politics remains autonomous from that of culture".[168] Nevertheless, it is worth noting that the ineluctability of this concept, as we will see later, has, *inter alia*, forced Fukuyama to relativize his thesis. However, Fukuyama's failure to acknowledge the indispensability of the concept of culture, i.e. civilization in general and the inherency of this concept within the realm of politics in particular, has paved the way for Said to refute this thesis by arguing that it is a radical falsification of culture that strips it of its affiliations, pries it away from the terrain it contests, and denies it real influence.

In the same vein, Alastair Bonnett considers the contemporary portrayal of the West to be a self-confident attitude, whereby the Western 'liberal democratic' blueprint is held to represent the only viable choice for humanity.[169] In Bonnett's view, this is actually a moderate form of utopianism[170] that contains a hubristic rationalist and universalist vision of the perfect society. Thus, theories that claim the triumph of Western commodities are negligent of the fact that they foster antagonism towards the West, since they are considered to be, *de facto*, a new form of Western imperialism.

This is apparent, for instance, in Said's argument that this Western demeanor stems from the "twinning of power and legitimacy, one force obtaining in the world of direct domination, the other in the cultural sphere, [which] is a characteristic of classical imperial hegemony. [And he adds that] where it [only] differs in the American century is the quantum leap in the reach of cultural authority".[171] By applying this more concretely, Said asserts that "[...] modern Orientalism already carried within itself the imprint of the great European fear of Islam [...]".[172] And since the United States is considered to be the inheritor of Orientalism in this century, Said contends that "for decades in America there has been a cultural war against the Arabs and Islam. [...] The very notion that there might be a history, a culture, a society [...] has not held the stage for more than a moment or two, not even during the chorus of voices proclaiming the virtues of 'multiculturalism' ".[173] However, unlike Said's understanding of modern Orientalism as an anti-Arab field that is occupied by Westerners, Irwin points out that one of the salient features of modern Orientalism has been the number of

---

[166] Samuel P Huntington, *The Clash of Civilizations and the Remaking of World Order* (Simon & Schuster, London 2002) 31

[167] David P Goldman, *It's Not the End of the World, It's Just the End of You: The Great Extinction of the Nations* (RVP Publishers, New York 2011) 1

[168] Francis Fukuyama, *The End of History and the Last Man* (Free Press, New York 2006) 220

[169] Alastair Bonnett, *The Idea of the West: Culture, Politics and History* (Palgrave Macmillan: New York 2004) 123

[170] Ibid 140

[171] Edward W Said, *Culture & Imperialism* (Vintage, London 1994) 352

[172] Edward W Said, *Orientalism* (Penguin Books, London 2003) 253-254

[173] Edward W Said, *Culture & Imperialism* (Vintage, London 1994) 364

prominent Arabs in it.[174] Thus, what comes to the fore in our elaboration above is that globalism's neglect of the concept of civilization and the failure to acknowledge its indispensability have paved the way for antagonists to oppose the Western world. This antagonism is also evident from Said's demarcation of his oppositional approach, whereby he focuses on the United States as the symbol of the West. According to this delineated antagonism, apologists for overseas American interests insist on its innocence and defense of freedom[175], while at the same time the United States does not accept infringements or ideological challenges.[176] In other words, he argues that as in the past but now in a different guise, responsibility towards the world is claimed. As regards 'world responsibility' – which is currently perceived as 'humanitarian imperialism' – Said reckons that this phenomenon "[...] corresponds to the growth in the United States' global interest after World War Two and to the conception of its enormous power as formulated by the foreign policy and intellectual élite".[177] This shows that the contemporary forms of Occidentalism, as with Buruma and Margalit, are focused on America and specific American globalization policies that are perceived as U.S. imperialism.[178] Thus, it is evident that what underscores such forms of antagonism is the ineluctable concept of culture in the broadest sense of the word, which is wrongly neglected by globalism.

The foregoing discussion leads to the conclusion that antagonism, the essence and scope of which we have previously explained, has found its way into our age of globalization, and is even fostered by it due to the accelerated pluralism. Currently, this continuance of the dichotomous antagonism between Orientalism and Occidentalism is grounded in the notion of modernization, which is – as the core feature of modern Orientalism – considered to be the civilizational ambition of Western expansionism. This animosity is further hastened by its reciprocity as well as globalism and its perception of the human dimension, which is conceived as Orientalism *par excellence*. Thence, to explain the current acceleration of antagonism, it is necessary to elaborate on the demeanor of globalism towards the human dimension, upon which the globalist thesis of Fukuyama is based.

1.4. Globalism and the Continuation of Dichotomous Antagonism

As previously observed, reciprocal antagonism has found its continuance in our globalized era. This antagonism is considered to be reciprocal for it is not only fueled by Occidentalism as such, but it is rather hastened by Orientalism with its approach towards the human dimension in the process of globalization.

[174] Robert Irwin, *Dangerous Knowledge: Orientalism & Its Discontents* (Overlook Press, Woodstock 2006) 245

[175] Edward W Said, *Culture & Imperialism* (Vintage, London 1994) 7

[176] Ibid 352

[177] Ibid 345

[178] Ian Buruma and Avishai Margalit, *Occidentalism: A Short History of Anti-Westernism* (Atlantic Books, London 2005) 8

We have seen that the human dimension is the underpinning foundation of the reciprocity between Orientalism and Occidentalism which characterizes the contemporary clashes. This further implies that antagonism is not only unilateral but also reciprocal, i.e. it is fostered by the demeanor of the protagonists of the West as it is mirrored in one of the three waves of globalization called globalism. And so, through a discernment of globalism and its perception of the human dimension, we will try to come to terms with the question as to why, contemporarily, perilous antagonism is not only unilaterally but also reciprocally accelerated. Hence, the survey conducted hereafter will expound the acceleration and continuation of antagonism in this globalized world as well as the ineluctability of the human dimension, i.e. civilization, within the current clashes. In so doing, the prime example of globalism (the meteoric thesis of Fukuyama that heralds the triumph of liberal democracy) serves as our point of departure to be elucidated from a civilizational angle. In other words, in determining that the concept of civilization is the ineluctable core notion that fuels the contemporary antagonism, we need to scrutinize Fukuyama's globalist thesis from a civilizational angle.

For this scrutiny, the main critic of Fukuyama's thesis, the theory of Kenneth Jowitt, provides us with an apt starting point. As to his thesis, Jowitt rejects that the "liberal capitalist civilization is the absolute end of history, the definitively final civilizatiom"[179]; to the contrary, "liberal capitalist democracy will always generate opposing challengers".[180] According to Jowitt, "in coming to grips with the Leninist extinction's global impact we must be ready for chaos in some places, opportunities in others, and for the slim but persistent possibility that new civilizations might emerge".[181] He clarifies this by stating that "[...] in a turbulent, dislocating, traumatic Genesis environment the dissolution of existing boundaries and identities can generate a corresponding potential for the appearance of genuinely *new ways of life*".[182]

Thus, liberal capitalist democracy "[...] will regularly witness the rise ofboth internal and external movements dedicated to destroying or reforming it – movements that in one form or another will stress ideals of group membership, expressive behavior, collective solidarity, and heroic action".[183] This leads then to the emergence of a "[...] worldwide conflict between liberally oriented 'civics' and insular 'ethnics', a conflict that directly calls into question the value and status of liberal democratic individualism even in the West".[184]

While being aware of the emergence of various disruptive movements and acknowledging that "Islam has indeed defeated liberal democracy in many parts of the Islamic world [and still forms] a grave threat to liberal practices even in

---

[179] Kenneth Jowitt, 'After Leninism: The New World Disorder' (1991) 2 (1) JoD 11, 12

[180] Kenneth Jowitt, *New World Disorder: The Leninist Extinction* (UCP, Berkeley 1992) 263

[181] Kenneth Jowitt, 'After Leninism: The New World Disorder' (1991) 2 (1) JoD 11, 14-15

[182] Ibid 15

[183] Ibid 17

[184] Ibid 20

countries where it has not achieved political power directly"[185], Fukuyama still believes that, in general, there will not again arise a *major* ideology with universalist aspirations that might fundamentally challenge or replace liberal democracy. Even political Islam, perceived as a disruptive universalist ideology, is assumed to not form a challenge or alternative to democracy in any sense since it does, among others, not attract "many adherents outside the Islamic world".[186] This means that it has, on the level of ideas, "virtually no appeal outside those areas that were culturally Islamic"[187], and "[...] outside the Islamic world, [in Fukuyama's point of view] there appears to be a general consensus that accepts liberal democracy's claims to be the most rational form of government [...]".[188]

Unlike Fukuyama, Walid Phares tries to come to terms with the reality of this menace by observing that "Islamism [...] is not one ideology clashing with the West, in parallel to other anti-Western ideologies, but in reality is an ideology clashing with all other ideologies, Western, non-Western, and anti-Western alike".[189] According to him, this is exactly the analytical mistake that is made by the West since "Jihadism is not another ideology competing for the existing world order [...]. Rather, it is an ideology trying to destroy the current order and replace it with another world order altogether".[190] In the same vein, other commentators argue that "[...] cultural differences in themselves are not bound to produce conflicts; it is the approaches to cultural questions, which are largely determined by ideology and power relations, that matter".[191] Yet, it remains questionable whether we are still living in this age of ideology wherein Phares tries to fit the Islamic menace since, as Huntington clearly asserts, "September 11 dramatically symbolized the end of the twentieth century of ideology and ideological conflict, and the beginning of a new era in which people define themselves primarily in terms of cultures and religion. The real and potential enemies of the United States now are religiously driven militant Islam [...]".[192] To put it more broadly, not ideology or economics but 'culture' in the broadest sense of the term – including politicized religion, that is, not being privatized within the cocoon of the individual or family, but being set against a liberal and

---

[185] Francis Fukuyama, *The End of History and the Last Man* (Free Press, New York 2006) 45
[186] Marc F Plattner, *Democracy without Borders? Global Challenges to Liberal Democracy* (Rowman & Littlefield Publishers, Maryland 2008) 31
[187] Francis Fukuyama, *The End of History and the Last Man* (Free Press, New York 2006) 46
[188] Ibid 211
[189] Walid Phares, *The War of Ideas: Jihadism against Democracy* (Palgrave Macmillan, New York 2008) 71
[190] Ibid 15
[191] Jenia Iontcheva, 'Power Clashes in a Multicultural World' [1998] Theory & Event <http://muse.jhu.edu/login?auth=0&type=summary&url=/journals/theory_and_event/v002/2.1r_iontcheva.html> accessed 10 January 2013
[192] Samuel P Huntington, *Who Are We? The Challenge to America's National Identity* (Simon & Schuster, New York 2004) 340

capitalistic society[193] with the aim of refashioning secular politics and culture[194] – is considered to be the fundamental source of conflict in our modern world.

In addition, Phares reminds us of the fact that political Islam's "[...] outreach is vertical across classes and horizontal across nations".[195] This entails thus that it is in essence a universalist aspiration, "[...] opposed to political pluralism and freedom of religion, the two pillars of democratic culture".[196] Thus, Islamism is against all other viewpoints worldwide[197], since "under the Islamist paradigm, there is simply no such thing as pluralism, neither political nor ideological. [...] In a manner analogous to Bolshevism, Jihadism rejects the plurality of political parties and doctrines on an existential level, because this concept is in absolute conflict with the doctrinal beliefs of Islamic fundamentalism".[198]Nonetheless, Fukuyama contends that it is not Islam as a *religion* but, like any other religion, the *political interpretation* of religion that is at the heart of the problem. However, this is a fictitious confinement of religion to the private sphere since, as Bernard Lewis contends, "From the lifetime of its Founder, and therefore in its sacred scriptures, Islam is associated in the minds and memories of Muslims with the exercise of political and military power".[199] This line of thought is also discernible from the reasoning of the European Court of Human Rights in, e.g., the *Refah Party* case whereby, as regards Islamic law, the Court asserts that "[...] Sharia, which faithfully reflects the dogmas and divine rules laid down by religion, is stable and invariable. Principles such as pluralism in the political sphere or the constant evolution of public freedoms have no place in it. [...] [Henceforth] the Court notes that [any attempt towards] the introduction of Sharia [is] difficult to reconcile with the fundamental principles of democracy [...]. [Since] it is difficult to declare one's respect for democracy and human rights while at the same time supporting a regime on Sharia, which clearly

---

193 Hans Jansen and Bert Snel (eds), *Eindstrijd: De finale Clash tussen het Liberale Westen en een Traditionele Islam* (Uitgeverij Van Praag, Amsterdam 2009) 180-192

194 Daniel Philpott, 'The Challenge of September 11 to Secularism in International Relations' [2002] World Politics: A Quarterly Journal of International Relations 66, 67

195 Walid Phares, *The War of Ideas: Jihadism against Democracy* (Palgrave Macmillan, New York 2008) 16

196 Ibid 67. The same line of thought comes to the fore in the reasoning of the European Court of Human Rights as is apparent in the case of *Refah Partisi and Others v Turkey* (App nos 41340/98, 41342/98, 41343/98, 41344/98) ECHR 13 February 2003

197 Walid Phares, *The War of Ideas: Jihadism against Democracy* (Palgrave Macmillan, New York 2008) 70

198 Ibid 68. Similar observations concerning the totalitarian nature of Islamism have been made by other experts in the field. In this regard, particular reference can be made to Afshin Ellian, 'The Legal Order of Political Religion: A Comparative Study of Political Islam and Political Christendom' in Gelijn Molier, Afshin Ellian and David Suurland (eds), *Terrorism: Ideology, Law and Policy* (Republic of Letters Publishing, Dordrecht 2011) 208-209. For further documented reading, reference can also be made to the following study: Emerson Vermaat, *Nazi's, Communisten En Islamisten: Opmerkelijke Allianties Tussen Extremisten* (Uitgeverij Aspekt, Soesterberg 2008)

199 Bernard Lewis, *The Crisis of Islam: Holy War and Unholy Terror* (Phoenix, London 2004) 17

diverges from [European Human Rights] Convention values, particularly with regard to its criminal law and criminal procedure, its rules on the legal status of women and the way it intervenes in all spheres of private and public life in accordance with religious precepts. [...]".[200]

The irreconcilability of Islam with the principles of non-discrimination and equality is also apparent from other cases of the Court. For instance, in the *Leyla Sahin*[201] judgment, the Court notes that wearing of a headscarf is not reconcilable with gender equality[202], and that it undermines the rights acquired by women. As regards the notion of gender equality, it is imperative to note that the Court recognizes this notion as one of the underlying and tacit principles of the Human Rights Convention.[203] In addition, the Court asserts in the *Dahlab v Switzerland* case that "[...] wearing of a headscarf might have some kind of proselytizing effect, seeing that it appears to be imposed on women by a precept which is laid down in the Koran and which [...] is hard to square with the principle of gender equality. It, therefore, appears difficult to reconcile the wearing of an Islamic headscarf with the message of tolerance, respect for others and, above all, equality and non-discrimination [...]".[204] Hence, the aforementioned fictitious confinement of Islam to the mere private sphere and, by that, the disdain for its incompatibility with fundamental rights and democratic principles is not widely shared.

Still, some countries have allowed or even accommodated religion in the name of multiculturalism, notwithstanding that it might imperil the fundamental rights and freedoms, especially of vulnerable groups such as women. A compelling example of this is the United Kingdom where Sharia courts have been set up that apply the Islamic law within the sphere of, among others, family wherein women's rights and freedoms are at risk.[205] A prime example wherein

---

[200] *Refah Partisi and Others v Turkey* (App nos 41340/98, 41342/98, 41343/98, 41344/98) ECHR 31 July 2001

[201] *Leyla Sahin v Turkey* (App no 44774/98) ECHR 2005-XI

[202] Ibid

[203] *Schuler-Zgraggen v Switzerland* (App no 14518/89) (1993) Series A no 263, *Burghartz v Switzerland* (App no 16213/90) Series A no 280-B, *Van Raalte v Netherlands* (App no 20060/92) ECHR 1997-I, *Petrovic v Austria* (App no 20458/92) ECHR 1998-II

[204] *Dahlab v Switzerland* (App no 42393/98) ECHR 2001-V. The same reasoning is present in other cases like in the *Leyla Sahin v Turkey* (App no 44774/98) ECHR 2005-XI

[205] These worries have become apparent from developments in the United Kingdom. For instance, it has been voiced in *The Telegraph* that "calls for a parliamentary inquiry into the scale of Islamic law in the UK are mounting after the body representing solicitors in England and Wales issued formal guidance on making 'Sharia compliant' wills. The Law Society was accused of giving its stamp of approval to discriminatory practices after it published advice on writing wills which deny women an equal share and exclude 'illegitimate' children or unbelievers" John Bingham, 'Sharia law in UK: Calls for Parliamentary inquiry' *The Telegraph* (London 23 March 2014) <http://www.telegraph.co.uk/news/religion/10717575/Sharia-law-in-UK-calls-for-Parliamentary-inquiry.html> accessed 25 March 2014. With this guidance, "Islamic law is to be effectively enshrined in the British legal system for the first time under guidelines for solicitors on drawing up 'Sharia compliant' wills". John Bingham, 'Islamic law is adopted by

women's (human) dignity [206] and physical and mental integrity [207] might be imperiled is the case of marital rape.[208] And that in spite of many attempts to justify the establishment of such courts. For instance, the Lord Chief Justice of England and Wales, Lord Phillips, argues that "[...] there is widespread misunderstanding in this country as to the nature of the Sharia law. Sharia consists of a set of principles governing the way that one should live one's life in accordance with the will of God. These principles are based on the Qu'ran, as revealed to the Prophet Muhammad and interpreted by Islamic scholars. [...] They do not include forced marriage or the repression of women'. [...] [He, however, notes that] '[...] what would be in conflict with the law would be to impose certain sanctions for failure to comply with Sharia principles. Part of the misconception about Sharia law is the belief that Sharia is only about mandating sanctions such as flogging, stoning, the cutting off of hands, or death for those

---

British legal chiefs' *The Telegraph* (London 22 March 2014) <http://www.telegraph.co.uk/news/religion/10716844/Islamic-law-is-adopted-by-British-legal-chiefs.html> accessed 25 March 2014

[206] *C.R. v the United Kingdom* (App no 20190/92) (1995) Series A no 335-C

[207] Parliamentary Assembly of the Council of Europe Res 1691 'Rape of women, including marital rape' (2 October 2009) CoE Report Doc 12013

[208] Section 1 of the Sexual Offences Act 1956 defines rape as penetration of the vagina or the anus by the penis without the woman's consent. The definition of rape was, however, further broadened by the Criminal Justice and Public Order Act of 1994 in order to let it encompass male, spouses, and anal intercourse. This is further extended by a sequent Act in 2003. Imperative for this crime is not the manner of penetration, but the lack of consent due to which the victim's personhood, integrity and autonomy is undermined (*C.R. v the United Kingdom* (App no 20190/92) (1995) Series A no 335-C). A similar extension of the scope of this crime can be found in the Dutch legal system whereby penetration by means of a kiss is qualified as rape (HR 21 April 1998, *NJ* 1998, 781; HR 25 September 2007, *LJN* BA7257); yet, not the manner of penetration (HR 22 February 1994, *NJ* 1994, 379, HR 27 January 2004, *NJ* 2004, 121) but the intention of the perpetrator, the psychological threat (HR 22 March 1988, *NJ* 1988, 785; HR 28 March 1995, *NJ* 1995, 454) and independency (HR 16 November 1999, *NJ* 2000, 125) of the victim are decisive for the absence of consent (HR 16 November 2004, *LJN* AR3040). However, "The wording used for the definition of rape in national jurisdictions may either be specific (describing body parts as in *Persecutor v Furundzija* (Case No. IT-95-17/1-T and IT-95-17/1-A)) or unspecific in nature (without specifying body parts as in *Persecutor v Akayesu* (Case No. ICTR-95-4). [...] The focus now tends to be on the sexual autonomy of the individual [...]'" in Anne-Marie LM de Brouwer, *Supranational Criminal Prosecution of Sexual Violence: The ICC and the Practice of the ICTY and the ICTR* (Intersentia, Belgium 2005) 110. As regards 'marital rape', reference can be made to the case *SW v United Kingdom* (App no 20166/92) (1995) Series A no 335-B [which was decided together with *C.R. v the United Kingdom* (App no 20190/92) (1995) Series A no 335-C] whereby the applicant had been convicted of marital rape "[...] following the House of Lords' decision in *R v R* [1992] AC 599 (HL) to the effect that the marital exemption for rape should be abolished", see Mike Molan, *Cases & Materials on Criminal Law* (3rd edn Cavendish Publishing, Oregon 2005) 37. As Lord Chief Justice Lane has formulated in *R v R* [1992] AC 599 (HL), "This [marital rape] is not the creation of a new offence. It is the removal of a [common] law fiction which has become anachronistic and offensive". In other words, this is not a retrospective criminalization, for it is consistent with the *essence of the offence* and could *reasonably be foreseen*' see, e.g., Jaap de Hullu, *Materieel Strafrecht: Over algemene leerstukken van strafrechtelijke aansprakelijkheid naar Nederlands recht* (3rd edn Kluwer, Deventer 2006) 98

who fail to comply with the law'. [Lord Phillips continues that] 'it was not very radical to advocate embracing Sharia law in the context of family disputes [...]. There is no reason why principles of Sharia law [...] should not be the basis for mediation or other forms of alternative dispute resolution. It must be recognized, however, that any sanctions for a failure to comply with the agreed terms of the mediation would be drawn from the laws of England and Wales".[209] This reasoning conveys the impression that verdicts based on Sharia law may not contradict the laws of the state and basic human rights. Yet despite this benighted reasoning, no inquiry has been conducted so far concerning the *empirical* consequences of such Sharia rules and rulings and their impact, e.g. on the legal status of women.[210]

This becomes perilous when we bear in mind that the rulings of these courts are, according to the 1996 Arbitration Act, binding and enforceable. Thence, in the United Kingdom, the misrepresentation of *cultural* pluralism as *legal* pluralism[211], whereby Islamic law is formally institutionalized by means of courts that are allowed to coexist simultaneously with the official legal system of the state[212], puts fundamental human rights and freedoms in peril.[213] Especially

---

[209] Speech by Lord Phillips, Lord Chief Justice, *Equality before the Law*, East London Muslim Centre (3rd July 2008) "The speech was organized by Pro Bono in the LMC and the London Muslim Centre"

[210] It is worthwhile to note that "[...] the consequences of violence directed against women are difficult to ascertain because the crimes are often invisible and there is very little data on the subject. However, it is very clear that fear is perhaps the greatest consequence. Fear of violence prevents many women from living independent lives. Fear curtails their movement, so that women in many parts of the world do not venture out alone. Fear requires that they dress in a manner that is "un-provocative" so that no-one can say that "they asked for it" if they are violently assaulted. Fear of violence requires that they seek out male protection to prevent violence being directed at them. This protection can result in a situation of vulnerability and dependence which is not conducive to women's empowerment" in UN Economic and Social Council, Preliminary Report, para 73 <http://www.unhchr.ch/Huridocda/Huridoca.nsf/0/75ccfd797b0712d08025670b005c9a7d?Opendocument> accessed 10 December 2012

[211] Kirsten Hastrup (ed), *Human Rights on Common Grounds: The Quest for Universality* (Kluwer Law International, The Hague 2001) 139

[212] Steve Doughty, 'Britain has 85 sharia courts: The astonishing spread of the Islamic justice behind closed doors' *Mail Online* (London 29 June 2009) <http://www.dailymail.co.uk/news/article-1196165/Britain-85-sharia-courts-The-astonishing-spread-Islamic-justice-closed-doors.html> accessed 10 December 2012

[213] This has even forced Francis Fukuyama to falter relatively his universalistic thesis in the face of these developments and to acknowledge that the "contemporary Muslim communities are [indeed] making demands for group rights [exemptions] that simply cannot be squared with liberal principles of individual equality' [...] 'These demands include special exemptions from the family law that applies to everyone else in the society, the right to exclude non-Muslims from certain types of public events, or the right to challenge free speech in the name of religious offence (as with the Danish cartoons incident), [...] 'In some more extreme cases, Muslim communities have even expressed ambitions to challenge the secular character of the political order as a whole. These types of group rights clearly intrude on the rights of other individuals in the society and push cultural autonomy well beyond the private sphere". Francis Fukuyama, 'A question of identity' *The Australian* (Sydney 3 February 2007)

when we take note of the reasoning by the Muslim Arbitration Tribunal – in contrast to the assumption of Lord Phillips according to which only the official legal system of England possesses a monopoly of (legitimate) coercion, and that Sharia rules have to comply with fundamental human rights and the English law – highlighting the fact that although this organization has to operate within the legal framework of England and Wales, it does not prevent or impede the same tribunal from ensuring that all determinations reached by it are in accordance with one of the recognized schools of Islamic Sacred Law.[214] This becomes precarious when we take into account that Islamic law is considered to be "[...] superior and dominant over English law in the Muslim mind and in the eyes of the Muslim community".[215] This fact is independent of the question whether the official legal system recognizes this reality[216], let alone the inability[217] of this system to prevent Islamic practices that are inconsistent with both the English law[218] and fundamental human rights and freedoms. Especially when we take note of the fact that unlike Christianity[219], the Western distinction between church and state (that is, secularism) is alien to Islam.[220] This is apparent, for instance, from the reasoning of the reviver of the Islamic theocracy in the modern times, Ruhollah Khomeyni, who, by rehearsing the Islamic history, asserts that "in his days, the prophet, [...], was not content with explaining and conveying the laws. He also implemented them. God's prophet, [...], was the executor of the law. He punished, cut off the thief's hand, lashed and stoned and ruled justly. A successor is needed for such acts. A successor is not the conveyor of laws and not a legislator. A successor is [thus] needed for implementation"[221] of a static, immutable and infallible body of (divinely inspired) law.[222] In other words, "The idea that any group of persons, any kind of activities, any part of human life is in any sense outside the scope of religious law and jurisdiction is alien to Muslim thought. There is, for instance, no distinction between canon law and civil law,

---

<http://www.theaustralian.com.au/news/a-question-of-identity/story-e6frg6n6-1111112933880> accessed 3 January 2013

[214] Muslim Arbitration Tribunal <http://www.matribunal.com/> accessed 10 December 2012

[215] Brian Z Tamanaha, 'Understanding Legal Pluralism: Past to Present, Local to Global' [2007] Syd LR 375

[216] Ihsan Yalmiz, 'The Challenge of Post-Modern Legality and Muslim Legal Pluralism in England' [2002] Journal of Ethics and Migration Studies 343

[217] Brian Z.Tamanaha, 'Understading Legal Pluralism: Past to Present, Local to Global' [2007] Syd LR 375, 44

[218] Ibid 23

[219] Jacob Neusner (ed), *Religious Foundations of Western Civilization: Judaism, Christianity, and Islam* (Abingdon Press, Nashville 2006)

[220] Mark Juergensmeyer, *Global Rebellion: Religious Challenges to the Secular State, from Christian Militias to al Qaeda* (UCP, Berkeley 2008) 47

[221] Ayatollah Ruhollah Khomeyni, *Islamic Government: Governance of Jurisprudence* (UPPH, Hawaii 2005) 7

[222] It might be contested that the interpretation of this body of law is fallible and changeable – based on which Islam deems to be erroneously bifurcated into distinct realms – but it is imperative to bear in mind that this does, nevertheless, not diminish the sanctity and stability of the legal content of Sharia due to which any artificial bifurcation is and remains a fallacy

between the law of the church and the law of the state, crucial in Christian history. There is only a single law, the shari'a, accepted by Muslims as of divine origin and regulating all aspects of human life: civil, commercial, criminal, constitutional, as well as manners more specifically concerned with religion in the limited, Christian sense of that word".[223]

It is thus an analytical error to downplay or neglect the role and challenge of religion in general and Islam in particular within the contemporary civilizational collisions, especially when religion is institutionalized and accommodated by the state. The inseparability of the public and private realm within Islam is discernible from the reasoning of Khomeyni who asserts that it is the task of his followers to "familiarize the people with the truth of Islam so that the young generation may not think that the men of religion in mosques of Qum and al-Najaf believe in the separation of church from state [...]. The colonialists have spread [...] the need to separate church from the state and have deluded people into believing that the ulema of Islam are not qualified to interfere in the political and social affairs. [...] In the prophet's time, was the church separated from the state? Were there at the time theologians and politicians? At the time of the caliphs and the time of 'Ali, [...], was the state separated from the church? Was there an agency for the church and another for the state? The colonialists and their lackeys have made these statements to isolate religion from the affairs of life and society and to tacitly keep the ulema of Islam away from the people and drive people away from the ulema because the ulema struggle for the liberation and independence of the Moslems".[224] And thus, in the point of view of Islamists like Khomeyni, "The solution is [and has always been] the same for all these – to remove the alien and pagan laws and customs imposed by foreign imperialists and native reformers, and restore the only true law, the all-embracing law of God".[225]

The foregoing inquiry leads us to the inevitable conclusion that the aforementioned fictitious confinement of religion in general and Islam in particular to the private sphere is a contemptuous comprehension of the importance of the human dimension in terms of civilization, thus blurring the perilous reality of contemporary antagonism which has unprecedented and unforeseeable consequences for, among others, the dignity and integrity of the human person. The discussion above shows the unilateral and independent nature of antagonism towards the West. Yet, this antagonism is considered to be reciprocal for it is not only embedded in Occidentalism, but is rather fostered by Orientalism. In other words, some commentators are of the view that the current antagonism is not only unilateral but also reciprocal in nature. Therefore, they seek the source of the current clashes not only within the Oriental civilization,

[223] Bernard Lewis, *What Went Wrong? The Clash Between Islam and Modernity in the Middle East* (Harper Perennial, New York 2003) 100

[224] Ayatollah Ruhollah Khomeyni, *Islamic Government: Governance of Jurisprudence* (UPPH, Hawaii 2005) 8

[225] Bernard Lewis, *What Went Wrong? The Clash Between Islam and Modernity in the Middle East* (Harper Perennial, New York 2003) 105

which is often traditional in nature, but also within the sphere of modernity which, as explained above, is conceived as *the* mission of the Occidental civilization. Thence, while some scholars, like Fukuyama, contend that "[…] the contemporary challenge that the world faces in the form of radical Islamism or Jihadism is much more political than religious, cultural, or civilizational […]"[226], that is, it neither stems from Islam as a religion[227] nor is it "[…] the reassertion of some traditional Islamic cultural practice, [they, nevertheless, acknowledge that it takes place within] the context of modern identity politics"[228], meaning that our time is characterized by a global identity crisis.[229]

Thus, irrespective of whether one calls this challenge a *Muslim* resistance to democratization, *or*, as Fukuyama asserts, resistance stemming from the *Arab political culture*, it, nonetheless, "[…] emerges [as he also acknowledges] precisely when traditional cultural identities are disrupted by modernization and a pluralistic democratic order that creates a disjuncture between one's inner self and external social practice".[230] It is in this same context wherein Huntington asserts that due to globalized modernization, "Subnational cultural and regional identities are taking precedence over broader national identities. People identify with those who are most like themselves and with whom they share a perceived common ethnicity, religion, traditions, and myth of common descent and common history. In the United States [as in Europe] this fragmentation of identity manifested itself in the rise of multiculturalism and racial, ethnic, and gender consciousness".[231] It is worth noting that "this narrowing of identities, however, has been paralleled by a broadening of identity as people [due to globalization as we have elaborated above] increasingly interact with other people of very different cultures and civilizations and at the same time are able through modern means of communication to identify with people geographically distant but with similar language, religion, or culture. The emergence of a broader supranational identity has been most obvious in Europe [among the Muslim population], and its emergence there reinforced the simultaneous narrowing of identities".[232]

Although one may argue that the source of the current antagonism is political rather than religious or cultural in nature, it is, nonetheless, unassailable that it is not only unilateral but also reciprocal in essence. For it is the result of an interaction between two phenomena – tradition (of the Oriental culture) and modernity (of the Occidental culture) – within the context of civilization. This means that Muslims are actually entrapped between two worlds. On the one hand, the Western civilization characterized by the notion of modernity, and on

[226] Francis Fukuyama, *The End of History and the Last Man* (Free Press, New York 2006) 348
[227] Ibid 347
[228] Ibid 348
[229] Samuel P Huntington, *Who Are We? The Challenge to America's National Identity* (Simon & Schuster, New York 2004) 12
[230] Francis Fukuyama, *The End of History and the Last Man* (Free Press, New York 2006) 348
[231] Samuel P Huntington, *Who Are We? The Challenge to America's National Identity* (Simon & Schuster, New York 2004) 13
[232] Ibid 14

the other, the Islamic civilization characterized by ideology and tradition.[233] As we have previously inferred, this latter signals that it is an analytical error to bifurcate and classify religion into realms or to depoliticize and passivize it, for religion can be conceived as 'ideology', i.e. a perception of how the world should be, and 'culture', which entails an attempt to understand the world and oneself inside it. And, as we have said before, together they compose the formative components of 'civilization'. Thus, "If we think of culture as having cognitive, moral, and emotive components [...], religion is clearly implicated in all those dimensions, both as a force for change as well as for stasis".[234] However, it is worth remarking that, as Corwin Smidt puts it, unfortunately, in the process of globalization, "Little attention, as yet, has been devoted to the unique role that religion may play in building social capital.[235] [...] Different religious doctrines may affect the ways in which people may view human nature generally, the extent to which such believers choose to relate to those outside their religious community, and the priorities given to political life generally and personal political agendas specifically".[236] It is in this light that we need to be attentive to the fact that "over the past decades, there has been increased discussion within religious communities that they may be engaged in a cultural war".[237] Huntington is then right when he asserts that "the twenty-first century [...] is dawning as a century of religion. Virtually everywhere, apart from Western Europe, people are turning to religion for comfort, guidance, solace, and identity".[238] Therefore, religion has to be understood in this broad and comprehensive sense that represents an alternative means for reintegration with the capacity to challenge the modern culture, which tends to divide the objective material and subjective aesthetic harmony of the human wholeness.[239] The term 'culture' encompasses "[...] a heritage from which a society draws its strength. [It] is a resource which enables any given individual, community or society to survive and cope with the demands of social life. [...] For any given society, culture, through its shared and distinctive values, beliefs, forms of knowledge, symbols and language,

---

[233] Tony Blankley, *The West's Last Chance: Will We Win the Clash of Civilizations?* (Regnery Publishing, Washington 2005) 183

[234] Rhys H Williams, 'The Language of God in the City of Man: Religious Discourse and Public Politics in America' in Corwin Smidt (ed), *Religion as Social Capital: Producing the Common Good* (Baylor University Press, Waco 2003) 182

[235] The notion of 'social capital' is taken at face value and entails, for the sake of this inquiry, merely "[...] the set of norms, networks, and organizations through which people gain access to power and resources, and through which decision making and policy formulations occur", and which makes them able to cooperate at both the horizontal and vertical level, see Christiaan Grootaert, 'Social capital: The missing link?' in Paul Dekker and Eric M Uslaner, *Social Capital and Participation in Everyday Life* (Routledge, Oxon 2001) 10-11

[236] Corwin Smidt (ed), *Religion as Social Capital: Producing the Common Good* (Baylor University Press, Waco 2003) 2

[237] Ibid 12-13

[238] Samuel P Huntington, *Who Are We? The Challenge to America's National Identity* (Simon & Schuster, New York 2004) 15

[239] Amr G E Sabet, *Islam and the Politics: Theory, Governance and International Relations* (Pluto Press, London 2008) 34

expressiveness, and customs, charts life courses for its members. [...] Culture encompasses the symbolic, the non-material aspects as well as the material objects that society produces in order to guarantee individual and group survival".[240] Thus, the concepts of religion and culture – the two indispensable components for the formation of 'civilization' – are interwoven in such a way that they influence each other reciprocally at various levels, since "[...] culture is concerned with the meaning and significance of human activities and relations[241], [which] is also a matter of central concern to religion[242], [due to which] the two tend to be closely connected"[243] and can be defined within the broader notion of civilization. Against this background, we can infer that religious culture fulfills a vital role for the construction of a subjective, objective, and institutional worldview that underpins the social experience of the collectivity about, for instance, norms, beliefs, traditions, and charismatic leaders.[244] This is why religion is an unequivocal phenomenon that has underpinned the destinies of civilizations.[245] And in the case of Islam, "In the Muslims' own perception, Islam itself was indeed conterminous with civilization, and beyond its borders there was only barbarians and infidels".[246] Consequently, Islam is not only concerned

---

[240] E Osei Kwadwo Prempeh, Joseph Mensah, and Senyo B-S K Adjibolosoo (eds), *Globalization and the Human Factor: Critical Insights* (Ashgate Publishing, Hampshire 2004) 67

[241] "For its part, culture influences how a religion is interpreted, its rituals conducted, the place assigned to it in the life of society, and so forth [...]" in Bhikhu Parekh, *Rethinking Multiculturalism: Cultural Diversity and Political Theory* (Palgrave Macmillan, Hampshire 2006) 147

[242] "Religion shapes a culture's system of beliefs and practices [...]" in Bhikhu Parekh, *Rethinking Multiculturalism: Cultural Diversity and Political Theory* (Palgrave Macmillan, Hampshire 2006) 147. But it also provides culture with fundamental and existential worldviews. For an elaborated discussion on this latter from a sociological angle, see Matthias Koenig and Paul de Guchteneire (eds), *Democracy and Human Rights in Multicultural Societies* (Ashgate Publishing, Hampshire 2007) 255

[243] Bhikhu Parekh, *Rethinking Multiculturalism: Cultural Diversity and Political Theory* (Palgrave Macmillan, Hampshire 2006) 146

[244] Amr G E Sabet, *Islam and the Politics: Theory, Governance and International Relations* (Pluto Press, London 2008) 41

[245] Walid Phares, *The War of Ideas: Jihadism against Democracy* (Palgrave Macmillan, New York 2008) xiii

[246] Bernard Lewis, *What Went Wrong? The Clash Between Islam and Modernity in the Middle East* (Harper Perennial, New York 2003) 3. For further information, see the distinction between *'Dar al-Islam'* and *'Dar al-Harb'* in Stephen C Neff, *War and the Law of Nations: A General History* (CUP, Cambridge 2005) 39-46. However, it is worthwhile to observe that some commentators, like Bassam Tibi, contest this dichotomous worldview by arguing that "today, the Islamic civilizational model of an *umma*-based community of *dar al-Islam* vs the rest of the world no longer reflects any reality in the contemporary world. It can be safely stated that this model of *umma*-unity never reflected any unity in classical Islamic history, as well. Nonetheless, the scriptural doctrine has never engaged in any revising of this binary worldview". Despite this hypothetical contention, Tibi is forced to accept the current reality by asserting that "twisted in this inherited tradition contemporary Islamic worldview continues its own constructed dichotomy. Even though it is not in line with reality [as Tibi keeps denying, he nevertheless is forced to acknowledge that], the binary worldview remains dominant. [...]

with religious matters that are confined to the private realm, but it is an identity and loyalty that tends to transcend all others.[247]

Thence, as discussed above, the reciprocity of current antagonism lies in the fact that the notion of modernity is conflated and equated with Western civilization, against which the Islamic civilizational discourse[248] is on a collision course. This means the West is antagonized and resisted through an appeal to the process of modernization. In this regard, in exploring and explaining the crux of this civilizational clash, the following two dimensions of the process need to be elaborated: the *historical* and *psychological* angle. As regards the first dimension, the historical angle[249], attention is primarily drawn to the fact that "[...] Islamic culture has not collapsed in the face of modernity, as other cultures have. Instead, it has gotten stronger and reacted powerfully to the intruding world, and revolutionary leaders like bin Laden have infected this vigorous and angry culture with dangerous pathologies, including Islamist terror and jihad"[250], because "Muslim peoples, like everyone else in the world, are shaped by their history, but unlike some others, they are keenly aware of it".[251] Bernard Lewis, as the forerunner of this historical school, asserts that "[...] much of the anger in the Islamic world is directed against the Westerner, seen as the ancient and immemorial enemy of Islam since the first clashes between the Muslim caliphs and the Christian emperors, and against the Westernizer, seen as a tool or accomplice of the West and as a traitor to his own faith and people".[252]

With this historical animosity in mind, Lewis moves to the nineteenth century as the starting point of modernity and contends that "the cumulative effect of reform and modernization [in the Middle East was], paradoxically, not to increase freedom but to reinforce autocracy".[253] And above all, "[...] during the past three centuries, the Islamic world has lost its dominance and its leadership, and has fallen behind both the modern West and the rapidly modernizing Orient. This widening gap [subsequently] poses increasingly acute problems, both practical and emotional, for which the rulers, thinkers [like Edward Said], and

---

The Islamic Weltanschauung represent the cultural commitment of many religio-political groups in this period of re-politicization of Islam" in Bassam Tibi, *Islam in Global Politics: Conflicts and Cross-Civilizational Bridging* (Routledge, Oxon 2012) 40-41

[247] Bernard Lewis, *The Crisis of Islam: Holy War and Unholy Terror* (Phoenix, London 2004) 15

[248] For the historiography of civilizational discourse and Islam, see Peter J Katzenstein (ed), *Civilizations in World Politics: Plural and pluralist perspectives* (Routledge, Oxon 2009) 160

[249] It is worth noting that this reasoning is also applied within the international politics as we see, for instance, in the speech of Benjamin Netanyahu on 27 September 2012 at the UN. <http://www.algemeiner.com/2012/09/27/full-transcript-prime-minister-netanyahu-speech-to-united-nations-general-assembly-2012-video/> accessed 4 January 2013

[250] Tony Blankley, *The West's Last Chance: Will We Win the Clash of Civilizations?* (Regnery Publishing, Washington 2005) 183

[251] Bernard Lewis, *The Crisis of Islam: Holy War and Unholy Terror* (Phoenix, London 2004) xviii

[252] Ibid 113

[253] Bernard Lewis, *What Went Wrong? The Clash Between Islam and Modernity in the Middle East* (Harper Perennial, New York 2003) 53-54

rebels of Islam have not yet found effective answers"[254], and thus use the West as a scapegoat for their misfortune. More concrete, "For those nowadays known as Islamists or fundamentalists, the failures and shortcomings of the modern Islamic lands afflicted them because they adopted alien notions and practices. They fell away from authentic Islam, and thus lost their former greatness".[255] As regards the adoption of alien notions and practices, reference can be made, for instance, to "[...] the emancipation of women by modernizing rulers [which] was one of the main grievances of the radical fundamentalists, and the reversal of this trend is [thus] in the forefront of their agenda"[256], something they attempt to realize through, among others, the application and enforcement of Islamic law, as we have seen in our example above.

Hence, reciprocal antagonism is considered to have started and grown since the decolonization process whereby, in abandoning traditional beliefs, the now independent countries recognized the inherent relativism that underpinned all societies, systems of belief, and cultural practices.[257] Against this background, in our modern world, as Said rightly contends, "between the extremes of discontented, challenging urban mobs and the floods of semi-forgotten, uncared-for people, the world's secular and religious authorities have sought new, or renewed, modes of governance. None has seemed so easily available, so conveniently attractive as appeals to tradition, national or religious identity, patriotism. And because these appeals are amplified and disseminated by a perfected media system addressing mass cultures, they have been strikingly, not to say frighteningly effective".[258] It is in this context then that the concept of culture ought to be comprehended as a means that can palliate the ravages of a modern, aggressive, mercantile, culturally impoverished, and brutalizing (urban) existence.[259] The drawback of this is that, as Said emphasizes, "in time, culture comes to be associated, often aggressively, with the nation or the state; this differentiates 'us' from 'them' [...]. Culture in this sense is a source of identity, and a rather combative one at that, as we see in recent 'returns' to culture and tradition".[260] However, he employs this only when criticizing Orientalism, while currently this menace is more discernible from Occidentalism. For the invocation of tradition for palliating the ravages of modernity is the main cause of the current clashes, especially when it is accommodated and fostered by the states themselves through the enactment of multicultural measures, for example.

The second dimension of modernity from which the reciprocity of current antagonism towards the West ought to be approached is the psychological angle. As mentioned, the antagonizing reactions emanating from the Islamic

---

[254] Bernard Lewis, *The Crisis of Islam: Holy War and Unholy Terror* (Phoenix, London 2004) 4

[255] Bernard Lewis, *What Went Wrong? The Clash Between Islam and Modernity in the Middle East* (Harper Perennial, New York 2003) 156-157

[256] Ibid 73

[257] Edward W Said, *Culture & Imperialism* (Vintage, London 1994) 394-395

[258] Ibid 396

[259] Ibid xiii

[260] Ibid xiii-xiv

civilizational discourse is, by some commentators, considered to have been caused by the disruptive nature of modernity that currently underlies both pluralistic Western democracies and a rapidly transforming world. It is also in this context that modernization is conceived as the imposition of Western values on 'others', thereby undermining traditional values and ways of life and hence the resistance to such imposition.[261] And this is considered to be the challenge that also Islam in the broadest sense of the term has been facing with regard "[...] to its identity structure from a rapidly transforming world and a concomitantly changing order of values. The resulting imbalances and confusion that have afflicted Muslims in effectively all their social, political, economic, strategic, and religious domains, have imposed on them soul-searching question of existential significance".[262] To put it differently, it is believed that "modernity [...] has failed to achieve the multi-dimensional fulfillment required by human society. Its alluring promise of a better life has masked a dwindling concern with human self-realization through spiritual as well as material development. The internal dimension of the human essence has been externalized, and this has induced an unprecedented chaotic and conflicting relationship between body and spirit".[263] This tends to be caused by the process of modernity, which entails that one can become modern only when the substantive traditional values and manners are cast away.[264] Thus, the current clashes inevitably occur when the two constitutive human dimensions (the 'mental structures', that is, identity, and 'objective material conditions', that is, structural reality) dialectically collide. Due to this, "[...] a sense of crisis develops which is detrimental to [all social, political, economic, strategic, and religious realms of] a culture or a civilization's strength of character, equanimity, and consistency".[265] It is in this light that current world affairs can be defined as "[...] a universal conflict between two camps: the forces accepting and promoting a future with multiple types of democracies, and those heading back toward the past, armed with extreme religious injunctions. [...] The energies of the two outlooks have been unleashed against each other [...] culturally, politically, and increasingly militarily"[266], since "modernity exchanged the calm tyranny of traditional society for the anomie of the atomized individual, who was free, that is, free to wander alone in the universe and ask for an indication of his signification from an unhearing and indifferent cosmos".[267] Especially when it is borne in mind that in an epoch which is characterized by secularism and the decline of ideologies and loyalties, worldviews that are traditional in nature provide a solid basis for the palliation of

---

[261] Amr G E Sabet, *Islam and the Politics: Theory, Governance and International Relations* (Pluto Press, London 2008) 29
[262] Ibid 3
[263] Ibid 31
[264] Ibid 29
[265] Ibid 3
[266] Walid Phares, *The War of Ideas: Jihadism against Democracy* (Palgrave Macmillan, New York 2008) xviii
[267] David P Goldman, *It's Not the End of the World, It's Just the End of You: The Great Extinction of the Nations* (RVP Publishers, New York 2011) 4

psychological emptiness. This is because they offer, among others, "an emotionally familiar basis of group identity, solidarity, and exclusion; an acceptable basis of legitimacy and authority; an immediately intelligible formulation of principles for both a critique of the present and a program for the future".[268]

Thus, the process of modernization seems to have paved the way for antagonists who, in order to oppose this process, make an appeal to tradition, i.e. culture in the broadest sense of the term. Accordingly, Martin Albrow and Elizabeth King are right in asserting that the "[...] 'indigenization perspective' falls into the very trap of cultural globalization against which it wants to stand up: the claim of cultural and scientific authenticity in local traditions is in itself a production of modernity. To reject modernity and to search for alternatives in tradition already presupposes participation in a knowledge of modern culture".[269] However, others, like Mona Abaza and Georg Stauth, extensively argue that opposition in general and fundamentalism in particular do "[...] not appear as a reaction against too much modernization and secularization [...]'. 'Rather it is a reaction against an incomplete and false transposition of religious language into the language of 'modernity' ".[270] In the same vein, Alastair Bonnett argues that Oriental spirituality, i.e. indigenization perspective, is, due to its participation in the knowledge of modern culture, a form of reflexive modernization in that it entails a freedom of mind and not a slavery to materialism. The reflexivity of it entails a self-examining approach to the problem of modernity which is associated with the West. In addition, he asserts that Occidentalists' "[...] attitude towards the West represents an 'othering' of internal problems. It is a process of purification of the nation that sanctions and demands strict protection and self-discipline as well as the perpetuation of an image of the West as a spatially displaced 'folk-devil' ".[271]

It is worth noting that this antagonizing discourse is more vivid at the national level within pluralistic Western societies, where violent resentments are deemed to have occurred more tensely because of the breakdown of singular cultures. This breakdown entails, among others, the loss of old certainties of village life, the tightly knit clan relations, and the subservience to feudal or religious traditions.[272] It is in this context that, as noted before, the concept of culture is considered to be a crucial means of palliating the ravages of a modern, aggressive, mercantile, culturally impoverished, and brutalizing Western (urbanized) existence. This is why "commitment to traditional values [...] reflects a defensive posture which aims at rejuvenating the spirit of internal

---

[268] Bernard Lewis, *The Crisis of Islam: Holy War and Unholy Terror* (Phoenix, London 2004) 19

[269] Martin Albrow and Elizabeth King (eds), *Globalization, Knowledge and Society* (SAGE Publications, London 1990) 219

[270] Ibid 216

[271] Alastair Bonnett, *The Idea of the West: Culture, Politics and History* (Palgrave Macmillan: New York 2004) 116

[272] Ian Buruma and Avishai Margalit, *Occidentalism: A Short History of Anti-Westernism* (Atlantic Books, London 2005) 26, 31

cohesion and self-identification against the disintegrative effects brought in by patterns of modern life".[273] This rejuvenation is achieved by 'othering' the West in order to give shape and force to cultural revival. This 'othering' encompasses a negative image of the West for which various terms have been employed. Examples of these terminologies, as we also saw in the course of our inquiry, are spatially displaced folk-devil, aggressive, mercantile, culturally impoverished, imperialistic, racist, ethnocentric, undemocratic, and antihuman. All these notions have the core aspect of the 'soullessness' of Western civilization (that is, the vacuum of modernization) in common. This antagonistic 'othering' of the West is clearly spelled out in Said's line of thought in which he merely associates the menace of identifying with the West and its colonial and imperial times. While, at the same time, he fails to come to terms with the reciprocal nature of this antagonism, viz. the peril emanating from the assertion of identity by 'others' and their perception of the West, as we have previously observed.

Hence, the resisting indigenization is aimed at facing the fundamental dilemma of the process of modernity by means of and through a reliance on the concept of culture in the broadest sense of the word, i.e. civilization. More concrete, the dilemma of modernization in this age of globalization concerns, as elaborated hitherto, the mental vacuum created by the neglect of the internal dimension of the human essence, that is, the spiritual constituent. Consequently, to palliate this vacuum, modernization is resisted through an appeal to and by means of civilization. In other words, "Traditional peoples fight to the death, even in the knowledge that one day they must lose their existential fight for existence'. [...] 'The explanation for self-destructive behavior on a grand scale is that the spiritual death ensuing from the dissolution of traditional society provokes greater fear than does the fear of physical death".[274] And since modernization is conflated with the West, "any fundamental proposed resolution to problems of modernity [...] can only be violently anti-modern, anti-secular, anti-democratic, and therefore anti-Western. [...] This is expected to provoke a violent discourse [which we, however, are already witnessing in the Western world] between modernists and their opponents regarding the morally and ethically determinate and causal foundations of human, social and political organization".[275]

The inquiry above leads us thus to the inevitable conclusion that the current devastating antagonism is based on more than just an ideology or a mere political interpretation of religion[276] that aims to destroy or replace the contemporary order.[277] Religion is not merely 'ideology' but also 'culture'[278] which, as a social

[273] Amr G E Sabet, *Islam and the Politics: Theory, Governance and International Relations* (Pluto Press, London 2008) 157

[274] David P Goldman, *It's Not the End of the World, It's Just the End of You: The Great Extinction of the Nations* (RVP Publishers, New York 2011) 272

[275] Amr G E Sabet, *Islam and the Politics: Theory, Governance and International Relations* (Pluto Press, London 2008) 32

[276] Francis Fukuyama, *The End of History and the Last Man* (Free Press, New York 2006) 348

[277] Walid Phares, *The War of Ideas: Jihadism against Democracy* (Palgrave Macmillan, New York 2008) 15

capital[279], underlies the civilization of society.[280] This also means that the confinement of it to the private realm is a minimization and neglect of its relevance to the destinies of civilizations as well as contemporary antagonism and its perilous clashes. What is more, this civilizational antagonism is, as we have noted above, not only unilateral in nature but also, and for the most part, reciprocal in character. In other words, a negation of the importance of the concept of religion within the dichotomous antagonism or a bifurcation of it into artificial realms is a fallacy. For this concept is the underlying fundament of the notion of civilization, especially in the formation and mediation of identity in the process of modernization which has undermined traditional dogmas and, by that fact, created a psychological vacuum. As a result, we witness resistance emanating from this resurging concept which Jowitt describes as 'the appearance of new civilizations'.[281] Also, this latter remains dubious for it raises the question of whether we are witnessing the *appearance* of *new* civilizations or are we merely dealing with the *resurgence* of *traditional* civilizations along which Huntington draws the lines of his 'clash-of-civilizations' thesis. Either way, it is beyond doubt that – in contrast to Fukuyama's claim that "[...] the future will be devoted not to great exhilarating struggles over ideas but rather to resolving mundane economic and technical problems"[282] – the challenge that the world is now facing can only be apprehended from a civilizational prism, i.e. if we do not overlook let alone ignore the concept of civilization.

Especially when we bear in mind that the contemporary animosity towards the West "[...] goes beyond the level of hostility to specific interests or actions or policies or even countries, and becomes a rejection of Western civilization as such, not so much for what it does as for what it is, and for the principles and values that it practices and professes. These are indeed seen as innately evil, and those who promote or accept them are seen as the 'enemies of God' ".[283] This is why even the United States is not opposed as being a country, but as the exemplification and embodiment of Western civilization. Thus, it is undeniable that the Western identity in general and the "American identity [in particular has begun] a new phase with the new century. [Their] salience and substance in this phase are being shaped by [the West's and particularly] America's new vulnerability to external attack and by a new turn to religion, a Great Awakening

---

278 Rhys H Williams, 'The Language of God in the City of Man: Religious Discourse and Public Politics in America' in Corwin Smidt (ed), *Religion as Social Capital: Producing the Common Good* (Baylor University Press, Waco 2003) 182

279 Christiaan Grootaert, 'Social capital: The missing link?' in Paul Dekker and Eric M Uslaner, *Social Capital and Participation in Everyday Life* (Routledge, Oxon 2001) 10-11

280 Corwin Smidt (ed), *Religion as Social Capital: Producing the Common Good* (Baylor University Press, Waco 2003) 2

281 Kenneth Jowitt, 'After Leninism: The New World Disorder' (1991) 2 (1) JoD 11, 14-15

282 Samuel P Huntington, *The Clash of Civilizations and the Remaking of World Order* (Simon & Schuster, London 2002) 31

283 Bernard Lewis, *The Crisis of Islam: Holy War and Unholy Terror* (Phoenix, London 2004) 22

[especially] in America that parallels the resurgence of religion in most of the world".[284]

The indispensability of the notion of civilization for apprehending the acceleration and continuity of the dichotomous antagonism in this age of globalization also becomes evident once we elucidate the mechanism that underlies Fukuyama's globalist thesis. However, it is important to bear in mind that while Fukuyama is aware of the grave menace being posed to liberal democracy[285], yet he fails to explain why liberal democracy has no appeal within the Islamic world.[286] Similarly, Jowitt does not explain why the dissolution of existing boundaries and identities can generate a corresponding potential for the appearance of genuinely new ways of life[287] that would pave the way for internal and external movements that stress the ideals of group membership, expressive behavior, collective solidarity, and heroic action[288] in order to destroy or reform liberal capitalist democracy. The following inquiry into the underlying mechanism of Fukuyama's theory will provide us with answers to these questions. Hence, the following survey will explain the resurgence of antagonizing movements and alternative ways of life that imperil liberal democracy and, with that, the fundamental rights and freedoms within the Western world. Thus, this scrutiny should reveal the deficit of Fukuyama's globalist thesis and, by that, the necessity to go beyond it if we are to comprehend reciprocal antagonism and the discontent that we are confronted with in our globalized era. To put it simply, as elaborated hitherto, globalism neglects the notion of civilization in order to foster and universalize its relative political theory that consequently gives rise to alternative ways of life with perilous consequences. Therefore, the following inquiry into the underlying mechanism of Fukuyama's globalist thesis will shed further light on the indispensable role of the notion of civilization in the understanding of dichotomous antagonism in this age of globalization wherein pluralism is, more than ever before, being accelerated.

1.4.1. The Globalist Mechanism and Dichotomous Antagonism

As previously noted, globalism's neglect of the human dimension of the process of globalization, that is, the concept of civilization, bypasses the current global antagonism and the perilous clashes thereof. This has, as discussed before, provided the second wave of globalization – skepticism – with the necessary breeding ground to oppose this deficit which has fostered the current global clashes. However, this failure requires a thorough analysis before the roots of the

[284] Samuel P Huntington, *Who Are We? The Challenge to America's National Identity* (Simon & Schuster, New York 2004) 336

[285] Francis Fukuyama, *The End of History and the Last Man* (Free Press, New York 2006) 45

[286] Ibid 211

[287] Kenneth Jowitt, 'After Leninism: The New World Disorder' (1991) 2 (1) JoD 11, 15

[288] Ibid 17

existential threats and clashes emanating from dichotomous antagonism become apparent. In so doing, the underlying mechanism of Fukuyama's thesis is scrutinized, which will shed light on the indispensability of the human dimension of the globalization process – the notion of civilization – for comprehending the current reciprocal antagonism. Therefore, Fukuyama's book, '*The End of History and the Last Man*', is taken as our point of departure and, for a better understanding, supplemented with other relevant literature.

The fundamental mechanism that underpins his triumphalist thesis is the Platonic notion of *thymos*. By adopting a Hegelian approach, Fukuyama defines this concept as '*the desire for recognition*' which is the seat of 'values'[289] consisting of two constituents: *isothymia* and *megalothymia*. *Thymos* entails, according to him, "[...] the side of man that deliberately seeks out struggle and sacrifice, which tries to prove that the self is something better and higher than a fearful, needy, instinctual, physically determined animal [...]".[290] This is why Fukuyama, by criticizing the Hobbes-Locke tradition for banishing and constraining the desire for recognition from politics for the sake of physical security and material accumulation[291], conceives *thymos* to be "[...] an innately political virtue necessary for the survival of any political community, because it is the basis on which private man is drawn out from the selfish life of desire and made to look toward the common good'. [...] 'Construction of a just political order therefore requires both the cultivation and the taming of a *thymos*".[292]

The concept of *isothymia* entails the desire to be recognized as equal to others, whereas the concept of *megalothymia* contains the desire to be recognized as superior.[293] This latter concept is conceived to be the benign and dark side of *thymos*, i.e. highly problematic for political life, since it entails the desire to dominate as we could see with imperialism. This is why Fukuyama is of the view that *thymos*, even in its most humble manifestation, is just the starting point for human conflicts and, thus, capable of fanaticism, obsession, and animosity. For there is no guarantee that self-esteem would be confined to the bounds of 'moral self' which is, above all, not developed to the same level in all human beings. Therefore, there is no reason to contend that all human beings would evaluate themselves as each other's equals.[294] In this regard, *thymos* ought to be tamed by using *megalothymia* to counteract ambition[295] so as to prevent the emergence of tyranny. This can only take place in the democratic constitutional process, that is, a stage for the expression of *thymos* where men can seek recognition for their own views. Accordingly, he observes that the dialectical contradiction between these two concepts – *megalothymia* and *isothymia* – is best resolved and balanced out in the '*universal and homogenous state*', i.e. liberal democracy that

[289] Francis Fukuyama, *The End of History and the Last Man* (Free Press, New York 2006) 213
[290] Ibid 304
[291] Ibid 188-189
[292] Ibid 183
[293] Ibid 182
[294] Ibid 182, 214
[295] Ibid 187-188

rests on the twin pillars of economics and recognition.[296] This form of political organization is considered to be *universal* for it grants recognition to its citizens, not because they are members of certain ethnic, racial, or national groups but because they are human beings.[297] This recognition is also *rational* in as far as the state's authority does not stem from an ancient tradition or religious faith, but from the citizens' explicit consent to the conditions by which they cohabit. And it is also *homogeneous* due to its creation of a classless society in which the distinction between master and slave is erased.[298]

However, despite his eulogy of this utopian form of political organization and the alleged general consensus about its superiority, he admits that liberal democracy is yet to be globally accepted, as is the case in the Islamic world. This is also apparent from the reasoning of those who follow Fukuyama's line of thought. For instance, Amartya Sen defends the universality of liberal democracy by arguing that "[...] while democracy is not yet universally practiced, nor indeed uniformly accepted, in the general climate of world opinion, democratic governance has now achieved the status of being taken to be generally right".[299] In other words, Sen contends that the "[...] recognition of democracy as a universally relevant system, which moves in the direction of its acceptance as a universal value[300], is a major revolution in thinking, and one of the main contributions of the twentieth century".[301] Michael Goodhart also adheres to this understanding of the universality of the concept of democracy, and observes that "[...] calling democracy a universal value, then, does not imply that it is actually accepted by all, nor does it imply that people 'must' find it acceptable, reasonable, nonrejectable, the subject of an overlapping consensus, or otherwise 'valid' in any sense. The universality of democracy as a value does not concern its grounding".[302]

Despite a lack of empirical grounding, these commentators believe in the universality of liberal democracy, for it is considered to be, albeit in theory, the only mode of governance that, as Fukuyama puts it, is 'completely satisfying to man'.[303] This conviction is based on the conciliatory nature of liberal democracy between the *satisfaction of desire*[304] and "[...] the pursuit of *rational recognition*, i.e., recognition on a universal basis in which the dignity of each person as a free and autonomous human being is recognized by all".[305] The former component is

---

[296] Ibid 204

[297] M C Lemon, *Philosophy of History: A Guide for Students* (Routledge, Oxon 2003) 404

[298] Ibid 404

[299] Amartya Sen, 'Democracy as a Universal Value' (1999) 10 (3) JoD 3, 5

[300] According to Amartya Sen, the universality of any value is not dependent on the consent of all, but on the general view whereby this form of governance is generally conceived as a valuable concept, Amartya Sen, 'Democracy as a Universal Value' (1999) 10 (3) JoD 12

[301] Ibid

[302] Michael Goodhart, *Democracy as Human Rights: Freedom and Equality in the Age of Globalization* (Routledge, New York 2005) 138

[303] Francis Fukuyama, *The End of History and the Last Man* (Free Press, New York 2006) 206

[304] Ibid 301

[305] Ibid 200

designated through economics, which is considered to be vital in the formation of prerequisites that make autonomous choice probable. But if this economic homogenization would be undermined, the future of the process of democratization would become uncertain. It is also noteworthy that Fukuyama holds the view that, at the end, there is no economic rationale for democracy, which means that the choice for this mode of governance is autonomous and based on recognition instead of desire. While Fukuyama rejects "any *necessary* connection between capitalist economics and liberal-democratic politics"[306] he, nonetheless, considers economics to be a distinct, yet interwoven, feature that makes an autonomous choice for liberal democracy possible. He continues to argue that what has replaced *megalothymia* in our contemporary world is, firstly, a desiring part of the soul which manifests itself as an *economization* of life, and, secondly, an all-pervasive *isothymia*.[307] In other words, while modern liberalism has sought to banish *thymos* from the political life, we, nevertheless, witness the continued existence of *megalothymia* which is divulged in the *economization* of life and the transmutation of the desire for recognition in the form of *isothymia*[308] which, as the rational form of recognition, has to overcome the irrational desire for recognition.

Fukuyama is also cognizant of the fact that *megalothymia* has not completely disappeared from human life, and that the satisfaction of desire through material abundance and mere rational recognition is not sufficient for the survival of liberal democracy. For he argues that if 'man' is merely defined in terms of desire for recognition and material abundance, at the end of history, when these goals are achieved, he will cease to exist. This is because there will be no significant causes anymore to struggle and fight for.[309] This way of life, denoted by Fukuyama as 'the life of rational consumption', which we have designated as 'the mass consumerist culture', will become boring because human beings want to have ideals for which they can devote their lives.[310] With this reality in mind, he suggests that "[…] liberal democracies should take care to inculcate in their citizens a certain irrational thymotic pride in their political system and way of life, rather than relying for stability on their capacity to deliver economic prosperity and equal rights".[311] In other words, he insists that *megalothymia* "[…] must continue to have a place in a vibrant liberal democratic state, albeit in a tamed form that does not lead to violence. However, there is no good reason to believe, as he does, that liberalism will be able to tame these megalithymotic impulses".[312] He is thus forced "to give scope to *megalothymia* within liberal

[306] M C Lemon, *Philosophy of History: A Guide for Students* (Routledge, Oxon 2003) 396
[307] Francis Fukuyama, *The End of History and the Last Man* (Free Press, New York 2006) 190
[308] Ibid 190
[309] Ibid 310
[310] Ibid 314
[311] M C Lemon, *Philosophy of History: A Guide for Students* (Routledge, Oxon 2003) 404
[312] Mark D Gismondi, *Ethics, Liberalism and Realism in International Relations* (Routledge, Oxon 2008) 99

democracy"[313], especially because of the current reappearance of *megalothymia* on an unprecedented scale. Hereby, he admits that thymotic individuals have been seeking other forms of contentless activities that can give them recognition. This is because the traditional forms of struggle are no longer possible, while material prosperity has made such struggles within the economic realm superfluous.[314]

We can discern this, for instance, in today's democratic societies where people "[...] are not content to merely congratulate themselves on their broadmindedness, but who would like to 'live within a horizon'. That is, [as he acknowledges,] they want to choose a belief and commitment to 'values' deeper than mere liberalism itself, [such as traditional values] offered by [e.g.] traditional religions".[315] Thus, it is questionable whether liberal democracy is even *in theory* universal, and whether this theory is vital and vigorous enough to compete with (traditional) civilizations encompassing both 'culture' and 'religion'. Because of the impossibility of unleashing *megalothymia* by means of satisfaction of desire through material abundance and mere rational recognition, it results, *de facto*, in an even greater reappearance and resurgence of *megalothymian* horizons, i.e. traditional ways of life. This shows, in fact, the impotence and deficit of the universalist thesis of liberal democracy in coping with such contradiction.[316] Thus, liberal democracy is not completely satisfactory to man, since, as Huntington argues, people are not likely to find in political principles the deep emotional content and meaning provided, for example, by kith and kin, blood and belonging, culture and nationality.[317] These ties do not need to have factual bases for satisfying the deep human need for belonging to a meaningful community. Hence, the presumption that we are all liberal democratic believers in the American Creed – containing liberty, equality, democracy, civil rights, nondiscrimination, and the rule of law – which is, *mutatis mutandis*, held to be self-evident in other Western European democracies, is unlikely to satisfy that need.[318]

Fukuyama is, thus, aware of the impossibility for liberal democracy to solve the problem of *megalothymia*. He even considers the reappearance of *megalothymia*, in the form of alternative ways of life, as a barrier and challenge to democracy, yet not serious enough to constitute an existential threat to it. In other words, as regards the notion of 'culture' in its broadest sense, Fukuyama acknowledges that "[...] the form of resistance to the transformation of certain traditional values to those of democracy [culture] constitutes an obstacle to

[313] Shadia B Drury, *Alexandre Kojève: The Roots of Postmodern Politics* (Palgrave Macmillan, New York 1994) 188
[314] Francis Fukuyama, *The End of History and the Last Man* (Free Press, New York 2006) 319, 332
[315] Ibid 307
[316] Ibid 314
[317] Samuel P Huntington, *Who Are We? The Challenge to America's National Identity* (Simon & Schuster, New York 2004) 339
[318] Ibid

democratization"[319], but he does not consider it capable enough to undermine this process. And it is, *inter alia*, in this same context that he considers religion as one of the forms of cultural obstacles to democracy.[320] Yet, it is worth noting that it is "Samuel Huntington [who] did the world [finally] an enormous service by changing the subject from comparative social system to civilizations based on religion".[321] Moreover, besides the dissolution of existing identities and boundaries, there is the inadequacy of liberal democracy itself to not only leave man's *megalothymian* longings unsatisfied, but even to disunite the objective material and subjective aesthetic harmony that is so vital to human fulfillment and wholeness.[322] This forms the main reason for the (re-)appearance of genuinely (new) ways of life[323], i.e. civilizations that led to the rise of – often antidemocratic – *megalothymian* movements, since unlike liberal democracy the traditional civilizations provide man with alternatives for the fulfillment of his *megalothymian* longings. An example of such an alternative which is fostered by the *megalothymian* deficit of liberal democracy concerns the recurrence of the Islamic way of life that manifests itself in various movements. For it presents alternatives for bridging the gap between the objective material and subjective aesthetic harmony in man. Thus, 'man' in 'liberal democracy' is merely reduced to a self-interested rational consumer, whereby not his *megalothymian* longings but only his needs for rational recognition and satisfaction of desire are fulfilled. And that in spite of the fact that he has a deeper spiritual essence, which is "intrinsically equipped with the necessary qualifications to see beyond his self-interest, and is therefore responsible, guided by revelation, for creating structures reflective of this understanding".[324]

Another, more practical, reason why alternative ways of life manifest themselves in *megalothymian* movements is because "[...] private associational life is much more immediately satisfying than mere citizenship in a large modern democracy [since] recognition by the state is necessarily impersonal; community life, by contrast, involves a much more individual sort of recognition from people who share one's interests, and often one's values, religion, ethnicity, and the like".[325] This implies that "[...] in contrast to liberal societies, communities sharing 'languages of good and evil' are more likely to be bound together by a strong glue than those based merely on shared self-interest".[326] It is why Fukuyama acknowledges that life in contemporary liberal democracies, in which various civilizations meet, "[...] is one in which cultural or group identities are

---

319 Francis Fukuyama, *The End of History and the Last Man* (Free Press, New York 2006) 215
320 Ibid 216
321 David P Goldman, *It's Not the End of the World, It's Just the End of You: The Great Extinction of the Nations* (RVP Publishers, New York 2011) 347
322 Amr G E Sabet, *Islam and the Politics: Theory, Governance and International Relations* (Pluto Press, London 2008) 34
323 Kenneth Jowitt, 'After Leninism: The New World Disorder' (1991) 2 (1) JoD 11, 15
324 Amr G E Sabet, *Islam and the Politics: Theory, Governance and International Relations* (Pluto Press, London 2008) 166
325 Francis Fukuyama, *The End of History and the Last Man* (Free Press, New York 2006) 323
326 Ibid 325

being continually asserted, reasserted, and sometimes invented out of whole cloth. This is an area in which the original theories of modern liberalism do not provide us with much useful guidance. [...] In modern liberal societies, individuals organize themselves into cultural groups that assert group rights against the state and limit the choice of individuals within those groups".[327] As such, he argues that "[...] democracy is not likely to emerge in a country where the nationalism or ethnicity of its constituent groups is so highly developed that they do not share a sense of nation or accept one another's rights. A strong sense of national unity is necessary prior to the emergence of stable democracy".[328] Thence, we can state that the resurgence of *megalothymian* movements constitutes an obstacle to the creation of a stable democracy.

Therefore, although Fukuyama contends that the realm of politics is autonomous from that of culture, he is, nonetheless, forced to admit that, due to the aforementioned theoretical deficit, "liberal democracies [...] are not self-sufficient: the community life on which they depend must ultimately come from a source different from liberalism itself".[329] To put it differently, "rational recognition is not self-sustaining, but must rely on pre-modern, non-universal forms of recognition to function properly [meaning that] stable democracy requires a sometimes irrational culture [...]".[330] Thus, the fact that liberal democracy is not self-sufficient and self-sustaining puts the claim to universality of liberal democracy into perspective and makes the incorporation of a *thymotic* pride within it ineluctable. This is why, as noted above, he argues that for a proper functioning of democracy an irrational *thymotic* pride has to be developed[331], which he denotes as the 'democratic' or 'civic culture'. In other words, he himself employs the notion of *megalothymia* for solving the deficit of democracy regarding the satisfaction of spiritual longings, enfranchisement of various groups within society, and the defense of democracy against civilizations with an excess of *megalothymia.*[332] By incorporating *megalothymia* in his thesis in order to develop an irrational culture, he uses the theory of George Wilhelm Friedrich Hegel.[333] According to this philosopher, "[...] the ultimate crucible of citizenship [...] is the willingness to die for one's country: [thence] the state would have to require military service and continue to fight wars.' [Fukuyama adopts this option of waging war for incorporating *megalothymia* within his thesis which he, accordingly, substantiates by contending that] 'a liberal democracy that could fight a short and decisive war every generation or so to defend its own liberty and independence would be far healthier and more satisfied than one that experienced nothing but continuous peace".[334]

---

327 Ibid 344-345
328 Ibid 216
329 Ibid 220, 326
330 Ibid 334
331 Ibid 215
332 Ibid 326, 219, 324-325
333 Allen W Wood (ed), *Hegel: Elements of the Philosophy of Right* (CUP, Cambridge 1991)
334 Francis Fukuyama, *The End of History and the Last Man* (Free Press, New York 2006) 329

Thus, for the satisfaction of citizens' spiritual longings, we need to incorporate ideals that are not always rational, especially for the newly enfranchised groups, since the liberal principles alone are found inadequate for protecting liberal democratic societies.[335] Accordingly, Huntington points out that civilizational diversity challenges our belief in the universal relevance of Western culture which, with the current civilizational clashes, suffers from the following three problems: it is false; it is immoral; and it is dangerous.[336] In addition, he argues that civilizational diversity, i.e. "multiculturalism at home, threatens the United States and the West; universalism abroad threatens the West and the world. Both deny the uniqueness of Western culture".[337] Thus, Huntington does not conceive Western civilization as universal, but only as something unique within this current multicivilizational world. Subsequently, the survival of this unique civilization depends on American reaffirmation of their Western identity and Westerners' acceptance of the uniqueness of their civilization. Therefore, "the principal responsibility of Western leaders [...] is not to attempt to reshape other civilizations in the image of the West, which is beyond their declining power, but to preserve, protect, and renew the unique qualities of Western civilization".[338] In order to defend this uniqueness, Huntington also incorporates the *megalothymian* factor within his theory. In so doing, in the case of America – as the forerunner of Western civilization – he proposes a nationalism based on religion as the alternative to cosmopolitanism and imperialism.[339]

In the same vein, but in a different mode, others argue that "[...] there are more grounds on which to oppose the Islamists than simply a religious "clash of civilizations". While religion is probably the most powerful force in determining a culture's strength, it is not the only one. Love for country, loyalty to a homeland and a way of life, even hatred of other ways, are also powerful cultural forces around which to rally".[340] But Huntington seems to put the emphasis more on religion when he argues that "in a world in which religion shapes the allegiances, the alliances, and the antagonisms of people on every continent, it should not be surprising if Americans again turn to religion to find their national identity and their national purpose".[341] Others plead also for the incorporation of similar *megalothymian* ideals, by warning that "[...] countries that have abandoned nationalism, religion, and ideology in favor of the milquetoast administration of daily affairs – for example, the Europeans – suffer from the

[335] Ibid 219, 324-325
[336] Samuel P Huntington, *The Clash of Civilizations and the Remaking of World Order* (Simon & Schuster, London 2002) 310
[337] Ibid 318
[338] Ibid 311
[339] Samuel P Huntington, *Who Are We? The Challenge to America's National Identity* (Simon & Schuster, New York 2004) 364-365
[340] Tony Blankley, *The West's Last Chance: Will We Win the Clash of Civilizations?* (Regnery Publishing, Washington 2005) 194
[341] Samuel P Huntington, *Who Are We? The Challenge to America's National Identity* (Simon & Schuster, New York 2004) 365-366

most dreadful psychic symptom of all"[342] as regards their identity. This leads to the question whether Europe has turned irredeemably secular and, if it has, then, whether a secular Europe can rally around any sustainable value for which it is willing to fight and die in order to survive.[343] The menace of this becomes particularly dire when we take note of "the absence of a native secularism in Islam, and the widespread Muslim rejection of an imported secularism inspired by Christian example, [which] may [accordingly] be attributed to certain profound differences of belief and experience in the two religious cultures".[344] Especially when due allowance is made for the fact that "a whole series of Islamic radical and militant movements, loosely and inaccurately designated as "fundamentalist," share the objective of undoing the secularizing reforms of the last century, abolishing the imported codes of law and the social customs that came with them, and returning to the Holy Law of Islam and an Islamic political order".[345] In this regard, we can argue that, "broadly speaking, Muslim fundamentalists are those who feel that the troubles of the Muslim world at the present time are the result of not insufficient modernization but of excessive modernization, which they see as a betrayal of authentic Islamic values. For them the remedy is a return to true Islam, including the abolition of all the laws and other social borrowings from the West and the restoration of the Islamic Holy Law, the shari'a, as the effective law of the land".[346]

Thus, we can assert that this "[...] 'indigenisation perspective' falls into the very trap of cultural globalisation against which it wants to stand up: the claim for cultural and scientific authenticity in local traditions is in itself a production of modernity. To reject modernity and to search for alternatives in traditions already presupposes participation in a knowledge of modern culture".[347] This shows the reciprocity of the current antagonism. Cognizant of this, Huntington and those who follow him champion the uniqueness of Western civilization in a milieu of cooperation and understanding within a multicivilizational world order.[348] On the other hand, Fukuyama advocates war which he considers legitimate for universalizing liberal democracy and for keeping it healthy. This conveys the impression that this ideology and its triumph are used as *jus victoriae*. And so, based on Samuel von Pufendorf, we can describe the solution of Fukuyama as an attempt to make business out of war for personal interests,

---

[342] David P Goldman, *It's Not the End of the World, It's Just the End of You: The Great Extinction of the Nations* (RVP Publishers, New York 2011) 14

[343] Tony Blankley, *The West's Last Chance: Will We Win the Clash of Civilizations?* (Regnery Publishing, Washington 2005) 190

[344] Bernard Lewis, *What Went Wrong? The Clash Between Islam and Modernity in the Middle East* (Harper Perennial, New York 2003) 100

[345] Ibid 106

[346] Bernard Lewis, *The Crisis of Islam: Holy War and Unholy Terror* (Phoenix, London 2004) 115

[347] Mona Abaza and George Stauth, 'Occidental Reason, Orientalism, Islamic Fundamentalism: A Critique' (1988) 3 Int Sociol 343, 353

[348] Samuel P Huntington, *The Clash of Civilizations and the Remaking of World Order* (Simon & Schuster, London 2002) 321

and as the promotion if not imposition of one's own ideals and ideologies, e.g. by waging war in the name of peace (*si vis pacem para bellum*). Besides, it is questionable whether this bellicose solution indemnifies the *megalothymian* deficit of liberal democracy, and whether it can compete with alternative civilizations with an excess of *megalothymia*. This belligerent solution rather fuels the *megalothymia* of other civilizations that consequently resist the Western concepts, which, as noted above, are conceived as a new form of imperialism.

Based on the foregoing, we can infer that liberal democracy is not self-sufficient and self-sustaining, that is, not satisfactory to man, since it does not accommodate and conciliate the ineluctable *megalothymian* demand of society. Also, the solutions provided for bridging this *megalothymian* gap are not viable enough to compete with civilizations that have an established, if not excessive, *megalothymia*. Most perilous in this is a naive faith in the universality of liberal democracy, for the frailty and tenuousness of this globalizing political theory lies in its denial and negligence of the concept of civilization. This means that the notion of *megalothymia* is not taken into account within the framework of 'liberal democracy' and, because of that, it fails to elaborate on the demeanor of this latter towards excessively *megalothymian* civilizations. The preclusion of the concept of civilization, and by that the neglect of the inevitable concept of *megalothymia*, becomes even lethal for this universalizing thesis, once we make due allowance for its resurgence, which is fostered by globalization. However, this has also not escaped Fukuyama's attention – as the main advocate of the universality thesis of liberal democracy – and has even forced him to relativize his thesis by asserting, for instance, that "[...] the problem of jihadist terrorism will not be solved by bringing modernization and democracy to the Middle East. Modernization and democracy are good things in their own right, but in the Muslim world they are likely to increase, not dampen, the terror problem in the short run".[349] In other words, the *megalothymian* dilemma has, in fact, forced Fukuyama to face the significance of the notion of civilization and to relativize his globalist theory. Thus, while he argues that irrational forms of recognition are replaced by rational ones in the universal and homogeneous state[350], he, nevertheless, admits that there is on a sub-political level, that is, on the level of cultural identities, a resistance to homogenization[351] and competition between different cultures.[352]

Hence, he relativizes his *Pax Democratica* thesis and acknowledges, as regards the notion of 'culture' in the broadest sense of the term, that "[...] at the end of the modernization process, nobody wants cultural uniformity; in fact, issues of cultural identity come back with a vengeance"[353], since, at the sub-

[349] Francis Fukuyama, 'A question of identity' *The Australian* (Sydney 3 February 2007) <http://www.theaustralian.com.au/news/a-question-of-identity/story-e6frg6n6-1111112933880> accessed 3 January 2013

[350] Francis Fukuyama, *The End of History and the Last Man* (Free Press, New York 2006) 259

[351] Ibid 244

[352] Ibid 234

[353] Ibid 344

political level, local cultures have also taken on renewed vigor and significance in the form of political movements in order to promote local culture and local identity. In the post-Cold War world, as the rise of fundamentalist movements suggests, culture in the broadest sense of the word, i.e. civilization, has often replaced ideology in politics.[354]

This is why Fukuyama has been subsequently forced to acknowledge that "Samuel Huntington is correct when he says that we will never live in a world in which we have cultural uniformity, the global culture of what he calls 'Davos Man' ".[355] Thus, as we elaborated above, Fukuyama, in agreeing with Huntington, has been compelled to concede that "[...] culture remains an irreducible component of human societies, and that you cannot understand development and politics without a reference to cultural values".[356] Hence, given the aforementioned deficits and shortcomings, his theory of political globalization, that is, universalization of liberal democracy, cannot be said to be universally accepted as a normative value – as empirically confirmed by resistance from traditional *megalothymian* civilizations. This means that his globalist thesis, which in fact obliterates the concept of civilization and, by that, cultural diversity[357], does not lead to a global political monoculturalism as long as the concept of civilization is not taken into account. Especially when one has regard for the fact that globalization has rather the potential to foster cultures in the broadest sense of the term, i.e. civilization, which have to become rigid in order to protect themselves from external influences. This can, however, imperil the universal appeal of various fundamental concepts, such as fundamental human rights that transcend both concepts of 'politics' and 'culture'. Thus, "one world culture is a euphemism for westernization of people's way of life on a global scale"[358] which, as some observe, is "eroding cultural authenticity in order to encourage similar aspirations and greater uniformity of lifestyles"[359], i.e. the homogenization of cultures.

The conclusion that we can draw from the preceding discussion is that globalism's disdain for the notion of civilization is rightly opposed by the skeptics, since the neglect of this notion has created the ground for cultures to resurge and resist the imposition of globalism's civilizational concepts. On the one hand, the attempt to universalize the Western political civilization erodes other civilizations, and fosters polarization and antagonism due to its neglect of the concept of civilization and the proposed bellicose solution to indemnify the *megalothymian* deficit for defending itself against civilizations with an excess of *megalothymia*. On the other hand, the universalization of Western notions and,

---

[354] UN Development Programme, 'Globalization with a Human Face' (1999)

[355] Francis Fukuyama, *The End of History and the Last Man* (Free Press, New York 2006) 344

[356] Ibid 344

[357] E Osei Kwadwo Prempeh, Joseph Mensah, and Senyo B-S K Adjibolosoo (eds), *Globalization and the Human Factor: Critical Insights* (Ashgate Publishing, Hampshire 2004) 84

[358] Ibid 69

[359] Paul Hopper, *Understanding Cultural Globalization* (Polity Press, Cambridge 2007) 88

by that, the disregard for the relevance of other civilizations lead to a dichotomous antagonism which relativizes and imperils essential concepts such as fundamental human rights and freedoms. In sum, globalism's disdain for the notion of civilization has hastened the emergence of antagonism, which endangers fundamental human rights and freedoms by repudiating and opposing them along with the rejection of globalism's universal claims to its relative concepts.[360] Although the menace of this neglect for fundamental rights and freedoms has been briefly discussed, for the sake of better understanding the perilous challenges the world is currently facing, it is imperative to make due allowance, in the next paragraph, for the rise of antagonism towards the West which is fostered, if not brought about, by globalism. It is thus exigent to note that this perilous antagonism does not stop at a mere opposition and criticism of the West but, as we will see below, goes so far as to become apologetic of illegitimate oppositions that, in essence, aim to annihilate and intimidate the West as well as to undermine fundamental rights and freedoms in general and the fundamental right to freedom of expression in particular.

1.5. The Fundamental Menace of Antagonism

The concept of civilization, as the underpinning tenet of dichotomous antagonism (that is, the clashes between Orientalism and Occidentalism), cannot be trivialized and neglected, for, as we have seen before, it is much too ingrained within globalized world affairs. Especially when we are cognizant of the fact that the neglect of this human dimension of the process of globalization is used as a means for opposing the West, which goes further than just criticism. Therefore, it is important to elucidate the aforementioned disdain which has fueled the current antagonism that does not stop at a mere skeptical critique of the West, but poses an existential threat to fundamental rights and freedoms.

In this regard, and as noted in our elaboration of Said's thoughts, the current image of the West in general and the United States in particular is traced back to an era called 'classical imperialism'. What is more, this image is conceived to be underpinned by Orientalism with a civilizational mission at the heart. Heretofore, we also noted that Said is of the view that this attitude has continued to exert considerable influence in modern Orientalism that, respectively, undergirds modern imperialism. According to him, there is, however, a major difference between these two periods. Whereas previously the supremacy of Western civilization was acclaimed, since the twentieth-century the concept of civilization is used to convey an ironic sense of how vulnerable the West is.[361] In his view, this irony is, for instance, discernible from the Western rhetoric concerning

---

[360] In this regard, reference can be made to the doubt raised by Paul Cliteur as to "whether democratic values are ripe for export" in Paul Cliteur, *The Secular Outlook: In Defense of Moral and Political Secularism* (Wiley-Blackwell, West Sussex 2010) 131

[361] Edward W Said, *Culture & Imperialism* (Vintage, London 1994) 229

terrorism in its generality.[362] It is also in this context that, according to him, "[...] the American mainstream media use the rhetoric of terrorism to disparage anything that does not meet the approval of the American government".[363] And as regards the content of news coverage, he contends that "the fear and terror induced by the overscale images of 'terrorism' and 'fundamentalism' – call them the figures of an international or transnational imaginary made up of foreign devils – hasten the individual's subordination to the dominant norms of the moment.' [...] 'Thus to oppose the abnormality and extremism embedded in terrorism and fundamentalism [...] is also to uphold the moderation, rationality, executive centrality of a vaguely designed 'Western' [...] ethos'; [...] 'this dynamic imbues 'us' with a righteous anger and defensiveness in which 'others' are finally seen as enemies, bent on destroying our civilization and way of life".[364] It seems, however, that Said downplays, if not underestimates, the magnitude of terrorism when he, in his animadversion of Huntington, argues that "the carefully planned and horrendous, pathologically motivated suicide attack and mass slaughter by a small group of deranged militants has been turned into proof of Huntington's thesis".[365] As we can see, antagonism does not stop at a mere criticism of the West and global consumerism of Western cultural products. For it goes so far as to underestimate the magnitude of terrorism and to label the vulnerability of the West and phenomena such as terrorism as mere ironic imaginations of Western imperialism.

The paradox of this view is that Said, as noted above, reproaches the West for upholding the vaguely designed Western ethos, while he himself is entrapped in this prejudiced rhetoric underpinned by his apparent animosity towards the West. In other words, as we have observed heretofore, "Said's discourse analysis does not itself escape the all-inclusive "Occidentalism" he specifically rejects as an alternative to Orientalism".[366] In the same vein, Shireen T. Hunter, who follows Said in this line of thought, albeit implicitly, repudiates the existence of any dichotomous antagonism and asserts that the conflict between the West and Islam is not civilizational, but rather a matter of power, that is, "[...] specific Western policies coupled with the overall disequilibrium in power relationships between the West and the Islamic world are more responsible for the anti-Western dimensions of the Islamists' thinking and behavior than is mere civilizational incompatibility".[367] Yet, what is striking is Said's contention that the American world, representing the West, and the Arab world are two distinct

---

[362] Reference can, for instance, be made to: Edward W Said, *The Politics of Dispossession: The Struggle for Palestinian Self-Determination 1969-1994* (Chatto and Windus, London 1994) 257

[363] Valerie Kennedy, *Edward Said: A Critical Introduction* (Polity Press, Cambridge 2000) 57

[364] Edward W Said, *Culture & Imperialism* (Vintage, London 1994) 376

[365] Edward W Said, 'The Clash of Ignorance' *The Nation* (New York 4 October 2001) <http://www.thenation.com/article/clash-ignorance?page=full> accessed 25 July 2012

[366] James Clifford, *The Predicament of Culture: Twentieth-Century Ethnography, Literature, and Art* (HUP, Cambridge 1988) 271

[367] Shireen T Hunter, *The Future of Islam and the West: Clash of Civilizations or Peaceful Coexistence?* (The Center for Strategic and International Studies, Westport 1998) 19, 115

worlds. And what distinguishes one from the other is, firstly, the lack of contact between the Western nations and their Eastern counterparts, and, secondly, the barrier of language and religion that differentiates them.[368] However, although Said is cognizant of this, he, nonetheless, seems to trivialize the magnitude of the aforementioned perilous outrages, and considers the menace emanating from the Islamic worldview to be negligible, and a product of inflated Western imagination. To reinforce this, he adds that "[…] into this vicious cycle feed a few groups like bin Laden's and the people he commands, whether they are in Saudi Arabia or Yemen or anywhere else. [But] They're magnified and blown up to insensate proportions that have nothing to do with their real power and the real threat they represent. This focus obscures the enormous damage done by the United States, whether militarily, environmentally, or economically, on a world scale, which far dwarfs anything that terrorism might do".[369]

What is more, "Uncountable are the editorials in every American and European newspaper and magazine of note adding to vocabulary of gigantism and apocalypse, each use of which is plainly designed not to edify but to inflame the reader's indignant passion as a member of the 'West', and what we need to do".[370] Thus, while Said has never condoned terrorism, he, nevertheless, minimizes, if not underestimates, the devastating magnitude of it by antagonizing and upbraiding the West for the aforementioned contingencies, and blaming it for the demonization of the perpetrators. And again, in order to condone the Islamic reaction to the West, he considers the West itself to be the cause of this antagonism by asserting that Muslims "[…] in their idioms and from within their own threatened localities, attack the West, or Americanization, or imperialism, with little more attention to detail, critical differentiation, discrimination, and distinction than has been lavished on them by the West".[371] This ought to be understood in the same way as the Orientalist feature that Said elaborates, according to which, the knowledge of the Orientalist about the Oriental is what paves the way for the creation of the identity of the former but which, subsequently, becomes the breeding ground for the latter to establish respectively *his* identity according to that same imposed Orientalist knowledge.

Thus, his thesis does not only hold the West amenable for the antagonizing reactions, but it even upbraids the West for the imposition of an identity on the 'other', whereas, in his own deductive and constructivist[372] theory, "the Orient is never seen as an actor, an agent with free will or designs or ideas of its own".[373]

---

[368] David Barsamian, *Culture and Resistance: Conversations with Edward W. Said* (Pluto Press, London 2003)

[369] David Barsamian, 'They call all resistance "terrorism"' [2001], Issue 19, *International Socialist Review*

[370] Edward W Said, 'The Clash of Ignorance' *The Nation* (New York 4 October 2001) <http://www.thenation.com/article/clash-ignorance?page=full> accessed 25 July 2012

[371] Edward W Said, *Culture & Imperialism* (Vintage, London 1994) 376

[372] James Clifford, *The Predicament of Culture: Twentieth-Century Ethnography, Literature, and Art* (HUP, Cambridge 1988) 257

[373] Ibn Warraq, *Defending the West: A Critique of Edward Said's Orientalism* (Prometheus Books, New York 2007) 28, 246

In addition, two paradoxical issues are discernible from Said's line of thought. First, while he opposes the dichotomy of East and West by perceiving it as a Western imperialistic and ignorant creation[374] that has no objective existence[375], he himself deploys this dichotomy. He does this by arguing that the Western and Arab world are two distinct worlds. And what distinguishes them is, firstly, the lack of contact between the Western nations and their Eastern counterparts, and, secondly, the barrier of language and religion that differentiates them from one another.[376] Second, Said attempts to convey the impression that the notion of terrorism is a fictitious Western invention[377] in order to create this dichotomy. This is, however, a flagrant trivialization of the very existence of terrorism, and an egregious blurring of the devastations – both in human and material terms – that this phenomenon brings about. And while Peter Berkowitz places it in a broader perspective in order "[...] to demonstrate that the Orient and the West are 'supreme fictions', Said cavalierly effaces the vital distinction between terrorist attacks on civilians and wars by liberal democracies against terrorist organizations and ruthless dictators: The suicide bombing phenomenon has appeared with all its hideous damage, none more lurid and apocalyptic of course than the events of September 11 and their aftermath in the wars against Afghanistan and Iraq".[378]

The elaboration above leads us, thus far, to the inevitable conclusion that Said's *ex parte* bearing is paradoxically entrapped in a prejudiced horizon as regards the West. And it goes even so far as to almost condone phenomena such as terrorism, despite his own assertion that a 'rhetoric of blame' undermines the potential for social change. Accordingly, Mona Abaza and Georg Stauth are right in criticizing Said's concept of knowledge-power interplay, and in conceiving it as "[...] a reductionist Foucaultian discourse on epistemes of cultural classification of the Other, [for] his paradigm of knowledge/power and attempts at better and deeper understanding of the Other, and thus of doing less injustice to the local, indigenous people, brings about a false framework of indigenous culture and religion which denies a long history of productive cultural exchange".[379] It also leads to 'Orientalism in reverse', i.e. 'going native', which

[374] Edward W Said, 'The Clash of Ignorance' *The Nation* (New York 4 October 2001) <http://www.thenation.com/article/clash-ignorance?page=full> accessed 25 July 2012

[375] Robert Irwin, *Dangerous Knowledge: Orientalism & Its Discontents* (Overlook Press, Woodstock 2006) 288

[376] David Barsamian, *Culture and Resistance: Conversations with Edward W. Said* (Pluto Press, London 2003)

[377] For instance, Said asserts that "terrorism has become a sort of screen created since the end of the Cold War by policymakers in Washington, as well as a whole group of people, like Samuel Huntington and Steven Emerson, who have their ticket in that pursuit. It is fabricated to keep the population afraid and insecure, and to justify what the United States wishes to do globally. [...] the whole history of terrorism has a pedigree in the policies of imperialists". David Barsamian, 'They call all resistance "terrorism"' [2001], Issue 19, *International Socialist Review*

[378] <http://www.hoover.org/publications/policy-review/article/5664> accessed 8 March 2012

[379] Mona Abaza and George Stauth, 'Occidental Reason, Orientalism, Islamic Fundamentalism: A Critique' (1988) 3 Int Sociol 343, 344

is manifested by an apologetic attitude towards Islamic fundamentalism[380] that fails, above all, to put historical facts into perspective or to mention them all unselectively.[381]

The menace of Said's *ex parte* antagonism becomes also tangible once we take into consideration the way he endeavors to explain the cause of the extraneous Western representation of 'others'. According to him, the imperialistic Western representation of the Orient and Islam, as briefly touched upon above, is explainable against the background of the fact that "if the mind must suddenly deal with what it takes to be a radically new form of life [...] the response on the whole is conservative and defensive".[382] Additionally, he asserts that in general, "[...] all cultures impose corrections upon raw reality, changing it from free-floating objects into units of knowledge'. [...] 'It is perfectly natural for the human mind to resist the assault on it of untreated strangeness; therefore cultures have always been inclined to impose complete transformations on other cultures, receiving these other cultures not as they are but as, for the benefit of the receiver, they ought to be".[383] Said applies this reasoning, which actually makes the reciprocity of antagonism evident merely to Occidentals by stating that "[...] the Orientalist makes it his work to be always converting the Orient from something into something else: he does this for himself, for the sake of his culture [...]"[384] which deems to have led to misrepresentations of the Orient and Islam in the West.

What is, thus, lopsided in this is the fact that Said wittingly fails to acknowledge and apply the same reasoning concerning the human mind and culture to the representation of the West by 'others'. The aim of this is to hold the West amenable and to depict these others as the victims, whereas this same reasoning concerning the human mind and culture is, *mutatis mutandis*, applicable to the perception of the West by 'others'. This is relevant as regards the aforementioned causative root of antagonism, which is said to be embedded in the Western agency. However, as stated above, one of the inconsistencies of his thesis is the fact that "at several points in his book, Said contends that the Orient had no objective existence. In other places he seems to imply that it did exist, but that the Orientalists systematically misrepresented [and misinterpreted[385]] it"[386], while in other instances he himself depicts the East and

---

[380] Ibid. Martin Albrow and Elizabeth King (eds), *Globalization, Knowledge and Society* (SAGE Publications, London 1990) 210

[381] Bill Ashcroft and Pal Ahluwalia, *Edward Said* (Routledge, London 2001) 80

[382] Edward W Said, *Orientalism* (Penguin Books, London 2003) 59

[383] Ibid 67

[384] Ibid

[385] For instance, Said contends that international luminaries have pontificated about Islam's troubles in Edward W Said, 'The Clash of Ignorance' *The Nation* (New York 4 October 2001) <http://www.thenation.com/article/clash-ignorance?page=full> accessed 25 July 2012

[386] Robert Irwin, *Dangerous Knowledge: Orientalism & Its Discontents* (Overlook Press, Woodstock 2006) 288

West along linguistic and religious lines as two distinct worlds[387] by deliberately omitting the Orientals for representing themselves. And as Irwin rightly points out, "if indeed the Orient did not exist, it should not be possible to misrepresent it".[388] But "for Said, however, they seem to exist [yet] only when Orientalists write about them. Surely that is a truly 'Orientalist' position, by Said's own pejorative definition. Orientals could not be autonomous individuals or moral subjects with their own desires, in charge of their destiny, but only passive subjects or helpless victims of Western conspiracies. Said could not acknowledge that they were actively and politically engaged with the world, for it would destroy the main thrust of his argument".[389] Furthermore, he does not only consider the West itself as the cause of antagonism, and is not only silent about perceptions regarding the Occident held by Occidentalists, but he rebuts even an autonomous existence of a corresponding equivalent of Orientalism in the Orient.[390] And whenever he sporadically touches upon the phenomenon of 'Occidentalism', as noted above, he blames the Orientalist for making the Oriental into the Occidental cultural figure he would become. For he argues that the Orientalist, by emphasizing the difference between Eastern ancient tradition and Western modernity[391], maintains even the prejudices against and the inherent fear of Islam[392] and menace of *jihad*[393]; not a fear of "[...] destruction of Western civilization but rather the destruction of barriers that kept East and West from each other".[394]

Accordingly, in his apologetic trivialization[395], Said argues that "[...] Western society did not face a significant threat from terrorists of an Islamic fundamentalist persuasion. The real danger in the encounter between the East and West arose from Western misrepresentation of Islam".[396] Thus, as far as he does not deny the very existence of the concept of Occidentalism, he considers it to be the antithetical byproduct of Orientalism itself, and this is why Buruma and Margalit, who share Said's view that Occidentalism is a Western invention, are also erring by contending that "[...] Occidentalism, like capitalism, Marxism, and many other modern isms, was born in Europe, before it was transferred to other parts of the world".[397] However, this perception that the first Occidentalists

---

[387] David Barsamian, *Culture and Resistance: Conversations with Edward W. Said* (Pluto Press, London 2003)

[388] Robert Irwin, *Dangerous Knowledge: Orientalism & Its Discontents* (Overlook Press, Woodstock 2006) 291

[389] Ibn Warraq, *Why the West Is Best: A Muslim Apostate's Defense of Liberal Democracy* (Encounter Books, New York 2011) 143-144

[390] Edward W Said, *Orientalism* (Penguin Books, London 2003) 50, 204

[391] Ibid 269

[392] Ibid 253-254

[393] Ibid 287

[394] Ibid 263

[395] Aijaz Ahmad, *In Theory: Classes, Nations, Literatures* (Verso, London 2008) 198

[396] Robert Irwin, *Dangerous Knowledge: Orientalism & Its Discontents* (Overlook Press, Woodstock 2006) 306

[397] Ian Buruma and Avishai Margalit, *Occidentalism: A Short History of Anti-Westernism* (Atlantic Books, London 2005) 6

were Europeans[398] is not shared by everyone and is even contested by others like Alastair Bonnett who argues that "[...] the West is not merely a Western creation but something that many people around the world have long been imagining and stereotyping, employing and deploying' [and hence] '[...] far from being merely a response to Western images of 'self' and 'other', it has often exhibited novel and influential ways of defining the West [and thus contrary to Said and those who share his view] it was the non-West that invented the West".[399] Even with regard to radical Islamism, which Bonnett perceives to have come into being in the context of Western dominance, he, nevertheless, argues that we ought to comprehend this phenomenon in its own terms, since its relationship to the West has been one that 'others' the West in order to give shape and force to Islamic revival and to suppress the political and religious traditions of Islamic societies.[400] However, a further discussion of this ongoing question as to whether antagonism is caused by the West itself concerns an altercation which is yet to be settled. Therefore, any further engagement in this agitation is falling prey to this vicious circle that reaches beyond the scope of this research. More important is recognizing the undeniability of this civilizational clash which has occurred as a consequence of the dichotomous antagonism that has been fostered by pluralism of this age of globalization.

Hence, the foregoing has clarified that disregard for the concept of civilization by globalism in apprehending the current civilizational antagonism can result in existential menaces with unprecedented repercussions that, based on that same neglected concept, not only contain criticism towards the West, but go so far as to condone the animosities and outrages. This is why, in antagonizing the West and rendering it culpable of any opposition to it, Said tends to conceive the operation of ideology in others' narratives and conceptions of truth except in his own[401], which means thus that he himself is entrapped in the ideological dichotomy of Orientalism and Occidentalism[402], that is, the East-West paradox from which the force of his entire ontological and epistemological polemic ensues.[403] This implies that "the reverse side of his 'Orientalism' is [inevitably] an 'Occidentalism' whereby his analysis of 'the West' follows precisely the same Enlightenment malpractices which he criticizes in the latter's approaches to 'the East'. He represents European culture in ways which essentialize, objectify, demean, de-rationalize, and de-historicize it".[404] What is more, as we saw

---

[398] Ibid 22

[399] Alastair Bonnett, *The Idea of the West: Culture, Politics and History* (Palgrave Macmillan: New York 2004) 1-2

[400] Ibid 151

[401] Valerie Kennedy, *Edward Said: A Critical Introduction* (Polity Press, Cambridge 2000) 78

[402] James Clifford, *The Predicament of Culture: Twentieth-Century Ethnography, Literature, and Art* (HUP, Cambridge 1988) 271

[403] Aijaz Ahmad, *In Theory: Classes, Nations, Literatures* (Verso, London 2008) 182. Ibn Warraq, *Defending the West: A Critique of Edward Said's Orientalism* (Prometheus Books, New York 2007) 32

[404] Robin W Winks (ed), *Oxford History of the British Empire: Historiography* (OUP, Oxford 1999) 197

already, "[...] the kind of essentializing procedure which Said associates exclusively with 'the West' is by no means a trait of the European alone; any number of Muslims routinely draw epistemological and ontological distinctions between East and West, the Islamicate and Christendom, and when [for instance] Ayatollah Khomeini did it he hardly did so from an Orientalist position".[405] This is why some scholars have soundly argued that "Said's work, with its strident anti-Westernism, has made the goal of modernization of Middle Eastern societies that much more difficult. His work, wherein all the ills of Middle Eastern societies are blamed on the wicked West, has rendered much-needed self-criticism by Muslims, Arab, and non-Arab alike, nearly impossible".[406]

The preceding discourse leads us to the conclusion that the aforementioned dichotomous antagonism does not stop at a mere criticism of the West but, as has become evident, it goes so far as to condone perilous discontent that, in essence, aims to annihilate and intimidate the West and, subsequently, to undermine the fundamental rights and freedoms in general and the fundamental right to freedom of expression in particular. As to this perilous aim, Paul Cliteur rightly observes that one can distinguish two phases regarding the limitation of this fundamental right. Before 1989, the only constraints of this right stemmed from the legislations of the nation-state. After this period, violent networks and individuals also confine this fundamental right.[407] Examples of this include the Rushdie affair[408], the assassination of the Dutch filmmaker, Theo Van Gogh, death threats at the address of Dutch politician, Geert Wilders, and when this failed, his continued persecution through the Dutch criminal law.[409] The underlying aim of such actions is not only the restriction of the freedom of expression of the person in question but – through an attack on the person – to create a sense of fear that leads, in general, to appeasement and self-censorship[410], i.e. curtailment of the freedom of expression. In this regard, it is worth noting that due to globalization, and thus "thanks to [among others] the rapid development of the media, and especially of television, the more recent forms of terrorism are aimed not at specific and limited enemy objectives but at world opinion. Their primary purpose is not to defeat or even to weaken the enemy militarily but to gain publicity and to inspire fear – a psychological

[405] Aijaz Ahmad, *In Theory: Classes, Nations, Literatures* (Verso, London 2008) 183-184
[406] Ibn Warraq, *Defending the West: A Critique of Edward Said's Orientalism* (Prometheus Books, New York 2007) 54
[407] Paul Cliteur, 'Van Rushdie tot Jones: over geweld en uitingsvrijheid' in Afshin Ellian, Gelijn Molier and Tom Zwart (eds), *Mag ik dit zeggen? Beschouwingen over de vrijheid van meningsuiting* (Boom Juridische Uitgevers, Den Haag 2011) 67-87
[408] Daniel Pipes, *The Rushdie Affair: The Novel, the Ayatollah, and the West* (Transaction Publishers, New Brunswick 2003)
[409] This was done through the so-called 'Article 12 Sv-procedure', that is, Article 12 of the Dutch Code of Criminal Procedure
[410] Paul Cliteur, 'Godslastering en zelfcensuur na de moord op Theo van Gogh' (2004) NJB 45, 2328-2335

victory".[411] This sense of fear has thus resulted in the fact that "[...] many liberals in the West, from government officials to academics and journalists, have failed to stand up for our fundamental liberties [...] but instead have engaged in appeasement and self-censorship".[412] In addition, the sense of guilt that runs through Western liberalism can produce a corrosive self-hatred which is destructive for the West. This is why it can be argued that we need to ascertain our Western values and confirm their superiority in order to preserve our culture[413], viz. we need to (re-)affirm the uniqueness of Western civilization.[414]

In other words, the fear of violence creates two types of reactions from within the West and among Occidentals, leading to the suspension of fundamental rights in general and the freedom of expression in particular. There is, namely, an unconditional expression of solidarity with those who are offended, and a sweeping disqualification of those who exercise their freedom of expression.[415] And the influence of theories, like "the influence of Said, has [firstly] resulted in the deliberate obfuscation or ignoring of the evidence, where the empirical data are forced into the Procrustean bed prepared by historians afraid of seeming to endorse anything smacking of racism, colonialism, and imperialism"[416], since the "Post-World War II Western intellectuals and leftists [have been] consumed by guilt for the West's colonial past and continuing colonialist present, and they wholeheartedly [have embraced] any theory or ideology that voiced or at least seemed to voice the putatively thwarted aspirations of the peoples of the third world".[417] Thus, at the heart of the Western response is, among others, a political correctness but also a psychological negation, as will be seen in the course of this survey, of the nature and magnitude of the radical Islamist menace.[418] And so, it can be inferred that our contemporary epoch, which is underpinned by the process of globalization with its pluralism, has not only had positive sides, but also unforeseeable negative impacts on human life that are not always recognized. It is then also the undeniable presence of this human dimension which is mainly underplayed while, at the same time, it has actually been the main source of antagonism that has fostered, if not brought about, civilizational clashes.

---

[411] Bernard Lewis, *The Crisis of Islam: Holy War and Unholy Terror* (Phoenix, London 2004) 125

[412] Ibn Warraq, *Why the West Is Best: A Muslim Apostate's Defense of Liberal Democracy* (Encounter Books, New York 2011) 185

[413] Ibn Warraq, *Why the West Is Best: A Muslim Apostate's Defense of Liberal Democracy* (Encounter Books, New York 2011) 202, 203

[414] Samuel P Huntington, *The Clash of Civilizations and the Remaking of World Order* (Simon & Schuster, London 2002) 20-21

[415] Paul Cliteur, 'Van Rushdie tot Jones: over geweld en uitingsvrijheid' in Afshin Ellian, Gelijn Molier and Tom Zwart (eds), *Mag ik dit zeggen? Beschouwingen over de vrijheid van meningsuiting* (Boom Juridische Uitgevers, Den Haag 2011) 67-87

[416] Ibn Warraq, *Defending the West: A Critique of Edward Said's Orientalism* (Prometheus Books, New York 2007) 168

[417] Ibid 246

[418] Tony Blankley, *The West's Last Chance: Will We Win the Clash of Civilizations?* (Regnery Publishing, Washington 2005) xii

As it has been elaborated in the course of our inquiry, this has especially imperiled the fundamental rights and freedoms in general and the fundamental right to freedom of expression in particular. Accordingly, this confining menace posed to the fundamental right to freedom of expression underpins the following part of our research. More concrete, in the second part of our study, an attempt will be made to assess, from a legal perspective, this limiting impact of antagonism that emanates from this accelerated pluralism as far as this fundamental right is concerned. But before doing so, an attempt will be made to explain why exactly this fundamental right is at risk of being confined, which we subsequently aim to scrutinize.

Part II

Freedom of Expression

2. Freedom of Expression: An Introduction

In this second part of our research, due allowance will be made for the *de jure* limitation that tends to be imposed on the fundamental right to freedom of expression by the dichotomous antagonism that is being fostered, if not brought about, by pluralism that characterizes our globalized age. However, before assaying this *de jure* limitation, it is exigent to apprehend why, among all the fundamental rights and freedoms, precisely the fundamental right to freedom of expression is being imperiled by pluralism, and why it is important to assess its impact on this particular right. Accordingly, in what follows, an attempt will be made to elucidate and conceptualize as to why, among all the fundamental rights, exactly the fundamental right to freedom of expression is being threatened in culturally diverse societies, before examining the *de jure* impact of pluralism on this fundamental right.

To this end, the theory of Hannah Arendt concerning the notion of speech is deployed, prior to our scrutiny of the extent of the threat being posed to the fundamental right to freedom of expression by the civilizational clashes. By taking her theory concerning speech within the public realm as our point of departure, it will be argued that pluralism is not only an undeniable reality, but is even the prerequisite for possessing fundamental rights and freedoms, the denial of which would, however, result in 'alienation' and 'worldlessness', with deprivation of rights and freedoms as its consequence. This is because speech, as an authentic political action, cannot take place in isolation, but is ineluctably dependent on plurality and *vice versa*. According to Arendt, speech is the actualization of that same human condition of plurality, that is, appearance as a distinct and unique being among equals. The enquiry below will, thus, make apparent the ineluctability of speech and the freedom to it as the prerequisite for societal intersubjectivity. The inevitability of this pluralism for freedom in general and freedom of speech in particular will also become evident. Nevertheless, as we have been witnessing in recent years, civilizational pluralism tends to confine speech and the freedom to it. The limiting effect of this cultural pluralism makes it ineluctable to grasp the theoretical limitation of speech and the freedom to it, before scrutinizing the *de jure* impact of this pluralism on the right to freedom of expression. And for this theoretical assessment, the philosophy of John Stuart Mill has been found ineluctable.

Subsequently, as to the foregoing discussion on the importance of freedom of speech and its eventual limitations in a theoretical sense, we will proceed with our assessment of the *de jure* impact of pluralism on the fundamental right to freedom of expression at the following three distinct levels of the public realm that are underpinned by this multiplicity: the international, European, and national levels.

2.1. Freedom of Expression and Pluralism

Before examining the *de jure* impact of pluralism on the fundamental right to freedom of expression, it is important to grasp why precisely this particular right is imperiled by the contemporary civilizational clashes within the pluralist society at the international, European and national levels. For this conceptualization, the theory of Hannah Arendt on speech and freedom will be deployed as a guide. The essence of Arendt's theory from her book '*The Human Condition*' lies in the foundation of the notion of *vita activa* which encompasses the three fundamental human activities of work, labor, and action, all of which are interrelated with birth and death, i.e. natality and mortality. Yet, as we will see hereinafter, action has the closest affinity with natality, for "the new beginning inherent in birth can make itself felt in the world only because the newcomer possesses the capacity of beginning something anew, that is, of acting".[419] This book forms the basis of her other works that, for the sake of argument and a thorough comprehension of her theory, are additionally discussed here. Amongst all the human conditions mentioned in this book, it is the human activity of 'action' that undergirds her entire line of thought, which is, above all, the only political condition *par excellence* that also underpins our study. This is because, as she puts it, "action, the only activity that goes on directly between men without the intermediary of things or matter [and which is thus the exclusive prerogative of man[420]] corresponds to the human condition of plurality, to the fact that men, not Man, live on the earth and inhabit the world. [Thus] while all aspects of the human condition are somehow related to politics, this plurality is specifically *the* condition – not only the *conditio sine qua non*, but the *conditio per quam* – of all political life".[421]

Accordingly, it is *ad rem* to observe from the very outset that, as Arendt contends, the *human condition* has not to be confused with *human nature*, which is often designated with notions such as reason and thought.[422] This is important to grasp, because Arendt's understanding of freedom is "[...] the very opposite of [the metaphysical] 'inner freedom', the inward space into which men may escape from external coercion and *feel* free. This inner feeling remains without outer manifestation and hence is by definition politically irrelevant".[423] On this internal realm, she states that if we, indeed, have a nature or essence, then only a deity can know and define it. For so doing, the first condition would be that he has to be able to speak about a 'who' as though it were a 'what'.[424] Contemporarily, we witness similar avoidance and purgation of ontological discourses, one of the most plain examples of which is the theory of Michael Ignatieff who asserts that any metaphysical proposition and foundation is

[419] Hannah Arendt, *The Human Condition* (2nd edn UCP, Chicago 1958) 9
[420] Ibid 22
[421] Ibid 7
[422] Ibid 193
[423] Hannah Arendt, *Between Past and Future* (Penguin Books, New York 2006) 145
[424] Hannah Arendt, *The Human Condition* (2nd edn UCP, Chicago 1958) 10

idolatry which we ought to forgo and to base human rights merely on their functionality for human beings[425], for "while the foundations for human rights belief may be contestable, the prudential grounds for believing in human rights protection are much more secure. Such grounding as modern human rights require [...] is based on what history tells us: that human beings are at risk of their lives if they lack a basic measure of free agency; [...] A prudential – and historical – justification for human rights need not make appeal to any particular idea of human nature. Nor should it seek its ultimate validation in a particular idea of the human good. [...] a universal regime of human rights protection ought to be compatible with moral pluralism. That is, it should be possible to maintain regimes of human rights protection in a wide variety of civilizations, cultures, and religions, each of which happens to disagree with others as to what a good human life should be".[426]

As touched upon heretofore, Arendt's contention is that "the inward space where the self is sheltered against the world must not be mistaken for the heart or the mind, both of which exist and function only in interrelationship with the world. Not the heart and not the mind, but inwardness as a space of absolute freedom within one's own self was discovered in late antiquity by those who had no place of their own in the world and hence lacked a worldly condition which [...] was unanimously held to be a prerequisite for freedom".[427] But this inner space is actually not freedom, for one cannot *be* as long as one is not among peers, and the negligence or denial of this plurality is a denial of the very historicity [428] of the human person and personhood that leads rather to

[425] However, later Ignatieff admits that it is impossible to do without some understanding of intrinsic dignity to sustain belief in human rights which he, nevertheless, links to his notion of agency; Michael Ignatieff, *Human Rights: As Politics and Idolatry* (PUP, Princeton 2001) 5, 53-54, 82-83, 164

[426] Michael Ignatieff, *Human Rights: As Politics and Idolatry* (PUP, Princeton 2001) 55-57. Yet, this is the case, as the example of the European Convention on Human Rights with its notion of 'margin of appreciation' makes evident. For further information about this notion, reference can, for instance, be made to Yutaka Arai-Takahashi, *The Margin of Appreciation Doctrine and the Principle of Proportionality in the Jurisprudence of the ECHR* (Intersentia, Oxford 2001). Howard Charles Yourow, *The Margin of Appreciation Doctrine in the Dynamics of European Human Rights Jurisprudence* (Martinus Nijhoff Publishers, Dordrecht 1996). Eva Brems, *Human Rights: Universality and Diversity* (Martinus Nijhoff Publishers, Den Haag 2001). Ignatieff is, however, criticized for mixing the metaphysical thesis with the epistemological one into one single theory; see Johannes Morsink, *Inherent Human Rights: Philosophical Roots of the Universal Declaration* (UPP, Philadelphia 2009) 8

[427] Hannah Arendt, *Between Past and Future* (Penguin Books, New York 2006) 145

[428] According to Hannah Arendt, although natality, in which action is ontologically rooted, corresponds to a new beginning whereby every human being inserts himself into the human world through action and speech, yet, nobody is the author of his life story, but is entrapped in the overall story and remembrance of life that has no author. Hannah Arendt, *The Human Condition* (2nd edn UCP, Chicago 1958) 184, 193. This means that Arendt conceives 'life' as being a 'narrative' "[...] because [as Julia Kristeva brings to attention] a story is a memory of an action that is itself a birth and a foreignness that endlessly begin anew in the public space, and whose ontological possibilities are established in the initial fact of our birth". Julia Kristeva, *Hannah Arendt: Life Is a Narrative* (UTP, Toronto 2001) 25, 48. Henceforth, "that

superfluousness which is, *ipso facto*, interwoven with world alienation and loneliness, i.e. not belonging to the world at all.[429] This is why Arendt is right when she asserts that "the fundamental deprivation of human rights is manifested first and above all in the deprivation of a place in the world which makes opinions significant and action effective".[430] This deprivation is designated by Arendt as the deprivation from the right to have rights[431], for no human life can be possible without a world of appearance, that is, a world wherein, directly or indirectly, the presence of other human beings is evident to whom one can appear.[432] In other words, as the etymology of the verb *to act* indicates, "the two Greek words [for this verb] are *ἄρχειν*: to begin, to lead, and finally, to rule; and *πράττειν*: to carry something through. The corresponding Latin verbs are *agere*: to set something in motion; and *gerere*, which is hard to translate and somehow means the enduring and supporting continuation of past acts whose results are the *res gestae*, the deeds and events we call historical. In both instances action occurs in two different stages; its first state is a beginning by which something new comes into the world. The Greek word *ἄρχειν* which covers beginning, leading, ruling, that is the outstanding qualities of the free man, bears witness to an experience in which being free and the capacity to begin something new coincided. [...] The manifold meaning of *ἄρχειν* indicates the following: only those could begin something new who were already rulers [...] and had thus liberated themselves from the necessities of life for enterprises in distant lands or citizenships in the polis. [...] In Latin, to be free and to begin are also interconnected, though in a different way. Roman freedom was a legacy bequeathed by the founders of Rome to the Roman people; their freedom was tied to the beginning their forefathers had established by founding the city,

---

human beings are born for freedom means that their actions are fit subjects for stories, which alone give full measure to their contingency, their spontaneity, and their unpredictability" in Dana Villa (ed), *The Cambridge Companion to Hannah Arendt* (CUP, Cambridge 2000) 117

429 Serena Parekh, *Hannah Arendt and the Challenge of Modernity: A Phenomenology of Human Rights* (Routledge, New York 2008) 4. Furthermore, Arendt defines loneliness as political isolation, and isolation is, she explains, "[...] that impasse into which men are driven when the political sphere of their lives, where they act together in the pursuit of a common concern, is destroyed". To put it differently, she argues that the "isolated man who lost his place in the political realm of action is deserted by the world of things as well, if he is no longer recognized as *homo faber* but treated as an *animal laborans* whose necessary "metabolism with nature" is of concern to no one. Isolation then becomes loneliness" in Hannah Arendt, *The Origins of Totalitarianism* (Harcourt, Orlando 1968) 474, 475

430 Hannah Arendt, *The Origins of Totalitarianism* (Harcourt, Orlando 1968) 296

431 "The right to have rights entails, politically, the right to belong to a state or some kind of organized human community. But it also means, ontologically, the right to a place in the world where one can speak and act meaningfully" in Serena Parekh, *Hannah Arendt and the Challenge of Modernity: A Phenomenology of Human Rights* (Routledge, New York 2008) 12. Thus, being deprived of the right to have rights means to lose one's place in the world. For an elaborated discussion of this notion of 'the right to have rights', reference can be made to Alison Kesby, *The Right to Have Rights: Citizenship, Humanity and International Law* (OUP, Oxford 2012)

432 Hannah Arendt, *The Human Condition* (2nd edn UCP, Chicago 1958) 22

whose affairs the descendants had to manage, whose consequences they had to bear, and whose foundations they had to "augment". All these together are the *res gestae* of the Roman republic".[433]

Hence, the Arendtian comprehension of the faculty of freedom is the capacity to begin, that is, to act, for action and beginning are essentially the same.[434] This outward freedom ought to be distinguished from the aforementioned inward freedom, for as Arendt argues, "men *are* free – as distinguished from their possessing the gift for freedom – as long as they act, neither before nor after; for to *be* free and to act are the same".[435] Thus, action is the only human activity that depends exclusively on plurality, i.e. the constant presence of others[436] who are one's equals in their uniqueness and to whom one can appear. To put it differently, "plurality is the condition of human action because we are all the same, that is, human, in such a way that nobody is ever the same as anyone else who ever lived, lives, or will live".[437] Yet this is not to say that freedom is not something that belongs to every human individual as a natural birthright, but, again, it is merely made in the world by means of intersubjective interactions.[438] And this intersubjectivity, which is the plurality of human beings, has significance only in the public realm where one can appear as equal[439], and not within the private realm which is by definition prepolitical, because it is only in equal intersubjectivity characterizing the former realm – as the only sphere of freedom – that we can become conscious of freedom or its very opposite.[440]

Arendt distinguishes the second realm, *oikos*, from the former space, *polis*, the unequivocal condition for which the human being is conceived as *homo politicus* is the *appearance* which, in following Aristotle, can be found in two activities: action (*praxis*) and speech (*lexis*). This is because, as she observes, the concept of freedom, as a political phenomenon, was coeval with the rise of the Greek city-states[441], albeit not in the physical sense but the sheer organization, that is, the intersubjectivity of people stemming from acting and speaking together[442] which is thus a space of appearance. Hence, "the field where freedom has always been known [...] as a fact of everyday life, is the political realm. And even today, whether we know it or not, the question of politics and the fact that man is a being endowed with the gift of action must always be present to our mind when we speak of the problem of freedom; for action and politics, among

---

433 Hannah Arendt, *Between Past and Future* (Penguin Books, New York 2006) 164-165
434 Ibid 168
435 Ibid 151
436 Hannah Arendt, *The Human Condition* (2nd edn UCP, Chicago 1958) 23
437 Ibid 8
438 Simon Swift, *Hannah Arendt* (Routledge, London 2009) 22. However, it is worth remarking that within the realm of international human rights law, freedom *is* conceived as the birthright of every human being just as we see in the Preamble of the 1956 Supplementary Convention on the Abolition of Slavery, the Slave Trade, and Institutions and Practices Similar to Slavery
439 Hannah Arendt, *The Human Condition* (2nd edn UCP, Chicago 1958) 32
440 Hannah Arendt, *Between Past and Future* (Penguin Books, New York 2006) 147
441 Hannah Arendt, *On Revolution* (Penguin Books, New York 1965) 20
442 Hannah Arendt, *The Human Condition* (2nd edn UCP, Chicago 1958) 198

all the capabilities and potentialities of human life, are the only things of which we could not even conceive without at least assuming that freedom exists […]".[443] Thus, in considering the concept of freedom, a distinction has to be made between the two forms of intersubjectivity – *oikos* and *polis* – for, as she rightly points out, "[…] not every form of human intercourse and not every kind of community is characterized by freedom. Where men live together but do not form a body politic – as, for example, in tribal societies or in the privacy of the household – the factors ruling their actions and conduct are not freedom but the necessities of life and concern for its preservation".[444]

Based on the foregoing, we can infer, thus far, that plurality is the inevitable requisite of action and speech by means of which one can appear and, thus, *be* free[445] for freedom "[…] is actually the reason that men live together in political organization at all. Without it, political life as such would be meaningless. The *raison d'être* of politics is freedom, and its field of experience is action"[446] in general and speech as *the* authentic political action in particular. To clarify this, reference can be made to her aforementioned Aristotelian line of thought whereupon she grounds this theory. In this, as we previously observed, she asserts that "for man, to the extent that he is a political being, is endowed with the power of speech. The two famous definitions of man by Aristotle, that he is a political being and a being endowed with speech, supplement each other and both refer to the same experience in Greek *polis* life".[447] In addition, it is important to clarify the interrelationship between the aforementioned notions of action and speech, about which she contends that "if action as beginning corresponds to the fact of birth, if it is the actualization of the human condition of natality [from which togetherness is driven], then speech corresponds to the fact of distinctness and is the actualization of the human condition of plurality, that is, of living as a distinct and unique being among equals".[448] In this regard, it has to be borne in mind that, as she explains it, "the very idea of equality as we understand it, namely that every person is born as an equal by the very fact of being born and that equality is a birthright, was utterly unknown prior to the modern age".[449] Thus, equality which is oftentimes conceived to imperil freedom is, in fact, identical with it, yet not in the sense of equivalency in conditions but the equality among those who form a body of peers within the political realm where they gather as citizens and not as private persons.[450]

It is important to take this line of thought into account since it is this that undergirds her critique regarding the 1789 Declaration of the Rights of Man and Citizens. On this declaration, she asserts that "since the Rights of Man were

---

[443] Hannah Arendt, *Between Past and Future* (Penguin Books, New York 2006) 144-145
[444] Ibid 147
[445] Hannah Arendt, *The Human Condition* (2nd edn UCP, Chicago 1958) 175
[446] Hannah Arendt, *Between Past and Future* (Penguin Books, New York 2006) 145
[447] Hannah Arendt, *On Revolution* (Penguin Books, New York 1965) 9
[448] Hannah Arendt, *The Human Condition* (2nd edn UCP, Chicago 1958) 178
[449] Hannah Arendt, *On Revolution* (Penguin Books, New York 1965) 30
[450] Ibid 20-21

proclaimed to be "inalienable", irreducible to and undeducible from other rights or laws, no authority was invoked for their establishment; Man himself was their source as well as their ultimate goal".[451] Based on this, she argues that the men of the French Revolution "[...] believed that they had emancipated nature itself, as it were, liberated the natural man in all men, and given him the Rights of Man to which each was entitled, not by virtue of the body politic to which he belonged but by virtue of being born. In other words, [in her point of view] by the unending hunt for hypocrites and through the passion for unmasking society, they had, albeit unknowingly, torn away the mask of the *persona* as well, so that the Reign of Terror eventually spelled the exact opposite of true liberation and true equality [...]".[452] Thus, "the trouble with these rights has always been that they could not but be less than the rights of nationals, and that they were invoked only as a last resort by those who had lost their normal rights as citizens".[453] In contrast, she argues that "the American version actually proclaims no more than the necessity of civilized government for all mankind; the French version, however, proclaims the existence of rights independent of and outside the body politic, and then goes on to equate these so-called rights, namely the rights of man *qua* man, with the rights of citizens".[454]

The two notions of action and speech become materialized only within the web of human interactions that take place within the public realm, whereas, as stated before, the loss of human rights entails the very opposite of this, that is, the deprivation of a place within the world that makes opinions significant and actions effective. In other words, "the state of absolute rightlessness for Arendt is [precisely] a state of being deprived, not of the freedom to do what you want, but the right to action, not the right to think what you want, but the right to form an opinion".[455] The eradication of speech as *the* authentic political action[456] is to individualize[457], i.e. to alienate, especially when we bear in mind that action and speech[458] cannot take place in isolation but are dependent on plurality, that is, the web[459] of acts and words of others.[460] Thus, "[...] wherever the man-made world

---

[451] Hannah Arendt, *The Origins of Totalitarianism* (Harcourt, Orlando 1968) 291

[452] Hannah Arendt, *On Revolution* (Penguin Books, New York 1965) 98

[453] Ibid 140

[454] Ibid

[455] Serena Parekh, *Hannah Arendt and the Challenge of Modernity: A Phenomenology of Human Rights* (Routledge, New York 2008) 29; as Parekh also brings to attention, Arendt "[...] claims that the loss of the rights to meaningful speech and action represents the most fundamental kind of deprivation because they are part and parcel of the human condition"

[456] Dana Villa (ed), *The Cambridge Companion to Hannah Arendt* (CUP, Cambridge 2000) 133

[457] Arendt rightly asserts that "totalitarian movements are mass organizations of atomized, isolated individuals" in Hannah Arendt, *The Origins of Totalitarianism* (Harcourt, Orlando 1968) 323

[458] According to Arendt, "A life without speech and without action [...] is literally dead to the world; it has ceased to be a human life because it is no longer lived among men" in Hannah Arendt, *The Human Condition* (2nd edn UCP, Chicago 1958) 176

[459] "The metaphor of the 'web' indicates the invisible, gossamerlike ties, networks, and contexts of human relationships that constitute the 'horizon' of human affairs. The term *horizon* in phenomenology suggests the ever-present but never quite fully transparent presuppositions,

does not become the scene for action and speech [...] freedom has no worldly reality. Without a politically guaranteed public realm, freedom lacks the worldly space to make its appearance".[461] Put alternatively, being deprived of a place within the web of human intersubjectivity entails lacking a world reality that only exists in the presence of others and the appearance to all which is called 'Being'.[462] In addition, it is important to take note of the fact that this elimination is not only an eradication of freedom as such, but of the very source of freedom which is given with the birth of man and resides in his capacity to make a new beginning.[463]

Through the foregoing survey of Arendt's theory, it has become clear as to why precisely the fundamental right to freedom of expression is central to the pluralist realm. This is deduced from her notion of speech within the public realm which has been taken as our point of departure. According to her theory, speech, as the authentic political action, cannot take place in isolation, but is ineluctably dependent on the plurality of the public realm and *vice versa*. For it is only in this realm that one can appear and thus be free. More concrete, it is thus on the basis of this assessment that we can infer that, among all the fundamental rights and freedoms, it is precisely the fundamental right to freedom of expression that stands at the center of civilizational pluralism. However, in recent years we have seen that pluralism not only fosters the freedom of speech, as the theory of Arendt suggests, but that it even tends to confine speech in the broadest sense of the term and the freedom to it. In other words, in our contemporary globalized world, freedom of speech is deemed to be imperiled by pluralism instead of being fostered by it. Thus, pluralism does not only advance freedom of speech but also imposes a limitation on it. Before scrutinizing the *de jure* impact of pluralism on the right to freedom of expression, the question arises as to what extent limitations on speech and the freedom to it are allowable when we consider it from a theoretical standpoint. This is the question with which the following section will be concerned and upon which the philosophy of John Stuart Mill will shed light.

2.2. Theoretical Boundaries of the Freedom of Expression

As previously observed, pluralism does not only foster freedom of speech, but tends rather to confine it. Delineation is possible because speech and the freedom to it are not absolute. The question that arises is, then, what the permissible scope

contexts, and referential networks that we must always also take for granted when we are in the world. [...] For Hannah Arendt, the "web" of human relationships and enacted stories constitutes the horizon, in the phenomenological sense, of human affairs" in Seyla Benhabib, *Modernity & Political Thought: The Reluctant Modernism of Hannah Arendt* (Rowman & Littlefield Publishers, Lanham 2000) 112

460 Hannah Arendt, *The Human Condition* (2nd edn UCP, Chicago 1958) 188

461 Hannah Arendt, *Between Past and Future* (Penguin Books, New York 2006) 147

462 Hannah Arendt, *The Human Condition* (2nd edn UCP, Chicago 1958) 199

463 Hannah Arendt, *The Origins of Totalitarianism* (Harcourt, Orlando 1968) 464, 466

of this confinement may be. In assessing this, the prime theory that comes to the fore is that of John Stuart Mill, which is discussed hereinafter. In other words, prior to elucidating *de jure* confinements, it is important to pay attention to the theoretical limitations of the freedom of expression, based on the theory of Mill. Over the significance of this freedom, Mill asserts that "were an opinion a personal possession of no value except to the owner; if to be obstructed in the enjoyment of it were simply a private injury, it would make some difference whether the injury was inflicted only on a few persons or on many. But the peculiar evil in silencing the expression of an opinion is, that it is robbing the human race; posterity as well as the existing generation; those who dissent from the opinion, still more than those who hold it. If the opinion is right, they are deprived of the opportunity of exchanging error for truth: if wrong, they lose, what is almost as great a benefit, the clearer perception and livelier impression of truth, produced by its collision with error".[464]

What is conspicuous in this exposition is the essential role of this freedom for humanity and, particularly, for the development of the human person. In order to further ground the importance and ineluctability of this fundamental freedom, Mill discusses its vital role in the determination of the truth itself by stating that even "truth, in the great practical concerns of life, is so much a question of reconciling and combining of opposites, that very few have minds sufficiently capacious and impartial to make the adjustment with an approach to correctness, and it has to be made by the rough process of a struggle between combatants fighting under hostile banners".[465] According to Mill, this is because on any matter about which different opinions can be fostered, the truth depends inevitably on the balance that we need to strike between the conflicting views.[466] This is why some argue that "the mutual recognition of each other's claims to truth and truthfulness is a fundamental principle of civil society. An open society is a dynamic public space wherein perspectives frequently alter".[467] Hence, even the truth requires a diversity of opinions[468], regarding which Mill distinguishes four: "First, if any opinion is compelled to silence, that opinion may, for aught we can certainly know, be true. To deny this is to assume our own infallibility. Secondly, though the silenced opinion be an error, it may, and very commonly does, contain a portion of truth; and since the general or prevailing opinion on any subject is rarely or never the whole truth, it is only by the collision of adverse opinions that the remainder of the truth has any chance of being supplied. Thirdly, even if the received opinion be not only true, but the whole truth; unless it is suffered to be, and actually is, vigorously and earnestly contested, it will, by most of those who receive it, be held in the manner of a prejudice, with little comprehension or feeling of its rational grounds. And not

---

[464] Stefan Collini (ed), *J. S. Mill: On Liberty and Other Writings* (CUP, Cambridge 2010) 20
[465] Ibid 49
[466] Ibid 38
[467] Afshin Ellian, 'Van Janmaat tot El Moumni: De Discriminatie tussen gewone en heilige meningen' [2003] *Justitiële verkenningen* 29, 3 [own translation]
[468] Stefan Collini (ed), *J. S. Mill: On Liberty and Other Writings* (CUP, Cambridge 2010) 52

only this, but, fourthly, the meaning of the doctrine itself will be in danger of being lost, or enfeebled, and deprived of its vital effect on the character and conduct: the dogma becoming a mere formal profession, inefficacious for good, but cumbering the ground, and preventing the growth of any real and heartfelt conviction, from reason or personal experience".[469]

Accordingly, Mill's view deviates from Arendt's theory regarding the actualization of this fundamental freedom, for he goes a step further to argue that an unfettered liberty has to be allotted to both 'expression' and 'thought' because of the following reasons: "first, expression is so closely related to thought that the control of expression would become in effect a control on thought. Second, he asserts that the claim to the right to limit freedom of expression, that is, the claim to the right to silence the expression of opinions in society, presupposes infallibility on the part of those who make the claim. Mill's belief is that no one can legitimately claim infallibility, and hence no one can legitimately claim the right to suppress any opinion. On the contrary, society has everything to gain and nothing to lose by absolute freedom of discussion".[470] Yet, in spite of this vigorous advocacy for the freedom of opinion and the expression thereof, a further reading reveals that Mill considers the limitation of expression inevitable. The core principle in this consideration, which can also be said to be the *locus dassicus* for contemporary pluralist societies, is his 'harm principle'. Simply put, this principle declares that harm to others is *the* legitimate ground for intervening and delineating the freedom of the perpetrator. Thus, as Mill asserts, we should not forget "that the only purpose for which power can be rightfully exercised over any member of a civilized community, against his will, is to prevent harm to others"[471] which, *inter alia*, does not need to entail harm in the actual sense for a mere imminent risk suffices as meeting this condition. Furthermore, as regards responsibility towards society, Mill encumbers the individual with two obligations. Firstly, the obligation to respect the rights of others, and, secondly, the obligation to defend society against external intruders. It is also in this context that the distinction between 'harm' and 'offense' ought to be taken into account, especially when it concerns the boundaries of expression. On this, Mill contends that such demarcation is hard to determine for if the test would be mere offense to those whose opinion is attacked, such offense is given whenever the attack is telling and powerful, especially if the person concerned is strongly touched by the subject.[472] And while he discourages offensive speech and is, simultaneously, cautious about the bounds of speech, he is, nonetheless, perspicuous about the restraints of action[473] by contending that "no one pretends

---

[469] Ibid 54

[470] Leo Strauss and Joseph Cropsey (eds), *History of Political Philosophy* (3rd edn UCP, Chicago 1987) 798

[471] Stefan Collini (ed), *J. S. Mill: On Liberty and Other Writings* (CUP, Cambridge 2010) 13

[472] Ibid 54

[473] The comprehension of the notion of 'action' as deployed by Mill is not to be confused with Arendt's understanding of this notion that we have discussed throughout this research, which comes down to the political activity that corresponds to our plurality as distinct beings. Thus, in Arendt's view, action corresponds to the human condition of plurality which is, accordingly,

that action should be as free as opinions. On the contrary, even opinions lose their immunity, when the circumstances in which they are expressed are such as to constitute their expression a positive instigation to some mischievous act. [...] Acts, of whatever kind, which, without justifiable cause, do harm to others, may be and in the more important cases absolutely require to be, controlled by the unfavorable sentiments, and when needful, by the active interference of mankind. The liberty of the individual must be thus far limited; he must not make himself a nuisance to other people. But if he refrains from molesting others in what concerns them, and merely acts according to his own inclination and judgment in things which concern himself, the same reasons which show that opinion should be free, prove also that he should be allowed, without molestation, to carry his opinions into practice at his own cost".[474]

Henceforth, the scope of free expression is considered to be absolute in so far as it does not infringe the freedom of others, i.e. cause harm to them. As mentioned already, this is apparent from his reasoning according to which we have to be cognizant of "[...] those who say, that the free expression of all opinions should be permitted, on condition that the manner be temperate, and do not pass the bounds of fair discussion. [Hence, Mill comments that] much might be said on the impossibility of fixing where these supposed bounds are to be placed; for if the test be offence to those whose opinion is attacked, I think experience testifies that this offence is given whenever the attack is telling and powerful, and that every opponent who pushes them hard, and whom they find it difficult to answer, appears to them, if he shows any strong feeling on the subject, and intemperate opponent".[475] Thus we must be reticent about premature limitations. In this light, he reminds us of the fact that, as aforesaid, "in general, opinions contrary to those commonly received can only obtain a hearing by studied moderation of language, and the most cautious avoidance of unnecessary offence, from which they hardly ever deviate even in a slight degree without

---

the condition of all political life. To the contrary, Mill's understanding has to be taken at its face value which, subsequently, can be best comprehended through the following explanation that he provides: "a volition is not an efficient, but simply a physical cause. Our will causes our bodily actions in the same sense, and in no other, in which cold causes ice, or a spark causes an explosion of gunpowder. The volition, a state of our mind, is the antecedent; the motion of our limbs in conformity to the volition, is the consequent. This sequence I conceive to be not a subject of direct consciousness, in the sense intended by the theory. The antecedent, indeed, and the consequent, are subjects of consciousness. But the connection between them is a subject of experience. I can not admit that our consciousness of the volition contains in itself any a priori knowledge that the muscular motion will follow. If our nerves of motion were paralyzed, or our muscles stiff and inflexible, and had been so all our lives, I do not see the slightest ground for supposing that we should ever (unless by information from other people) have known any thing of volition as a physical power, or been conscious of any tendency in feelings of our mind to produce motions of our body, or of other bodies" in John Stuart Mill, *A System of Logic, Ratiocinative and Inductive, Being a Connected View of the Principles of Evidence, and the Methods of Scientific Investigation* (8th edn Harper & Brothers Publishers, New York 1882) 437-438

[474] Stefan Collini (ed), *J. S. Mill: On Liberty and Other Writings* (CUP, Cambridge 2010) 56-57

[475] Ibid 54

losing ground: while unmeasured vituperation employed on the side of the prevailing opinion, really does deter people from professing contrary opinions, and from listening to those who profess them. For the interest, therefore, of truth and justice, it is far more important to restrain this employment of vituperative language than the other".[476] Hence, in this line of reasoning, he tends to advocate even the delineation of prevailing opinions that are vituperative and warns against hostility towards opinions that are not popular and not shared by the majority – regardless of how they are expressed. However, although the scope of harm seems to be determined by injurious acts, a further reading of Mill reveals that this scope is defined in a much broader sense. This is, for instance, evident from his assertion that "[...] there are many acts which, being directly injurious only to the agents themselves, ought not to be legally interdicted, but which, if done publicly, are a violation of good manners, and coming thus within the category of offences against others, may rightfully be prohibited. Of this kind are offences against decency; on which it is unnecessary to dwell, the rather as they are only connected indirectly with our subject [...]".[477] Thus, the threshold tends to be public manners, even though he made no further discussion of this, perhaps because of the aforementioned fears that he has regarding unnecessary limitation. What is more, the application of this modified threshold tends to go even further, for he argues that "[...] the manner of asserting an opinion, even though it be a true one, may be very objectionable, and may justly incur severe censure".[478] Thus it is not the content of the opinion that matters here, but the manner in which it is uttered. Accordingly, although Mill acknowledges that it is hard to determine the bounds of offense, he is, nevertheless, of the view that free expression in public has to meet the civilized conditions of interaction which he terms as 'the morality of public discussion'. However, as mentioned above, he avoids a further elucidation of this by simply stating, among others, that offenses of this nature are almost impossible to convict.[479]

To recapitulate, he is thus of the view that "while there must be freedom to discuss all opinions, however immoral they may be considered, 'the manner of asserting an opinion, even though it be a true one, may be very objectionable', and the use of 'intemperate discussion, namely, invective, sarcasm, personality, and the like' may 'justly incur severe censure'. But it is 'obvious that law and authority have no business with restraining' this type of expression. Essentially, Mill is here demanding what amounts to good manners in the way an opinion is expressed. But such a restriction on discussion must be enforced by public opinion, not by law, because to give the legal power of censorship to anybody is to give the power of control which can be used and abused in a manner which is potentially without limit. So, while the content of any opinion should never be silenced [...] the mode of expression can and should at all times be regulated by

[476] Ibid 55
[477] Ibid 98
[478] Ibid 54
[479] Ibid

the force of public opinion".[480] However, it is imperative to note that it is, in the first place, the person himself who has to rely on his moral capacity and development prior to any social impediment or legal coercion. And so, it is supposed that "[...] he *ought* to choose to obey laws and customs which most people think are reasonable means of governing other-regarding conduct (even if he thinks better rules might be devised). He *ought* to suppress, by means of his own moral will power (which must be developed), those of his desires and impulses which, if he acted upon them, would harm other people in unreasonable ways. He *ought* to develop his capacity to recognize when he is likely to cause serious injury to others, and he ought to develop a sufficiently strong conscience, or desire to do right, that he chooses to respect their rights [...]. Society has legitimate authority to coerce the individual (if need be) to follow whichever rules of other-regarding conduct are in the majority's estimation generally expedient. No person is infallible – nobody is absolutely sure what an ideal code looks like in this respect. But, provided complete liberty of discussion of the alternatives is guaranteed, the majority is warranted in establishing such laws and customs as it (at least tacitly) considers reasonable".[481]

The obedience to social rules in the case of 'other-regarding' ought to be understood in terms of Mill's utilitarianism.[482] In this regard, he states: "Though society is not founded on a contract, and though no good purpose is answered by inventing a contract in order to deduce social obligations from it, every one who receives the protection of society owes a return for the benefit, and the fact of living in society renders it dispensable that each should be bound to observe a certain line of conduct towards the rest. This conduct consists first, in not injuring the interest of one another; or rather certain interests, which, either by express legal provision or by tacit understanding, ought to be considered as rights; and secondly, in each person's bearing his share [...] of the labours and sacrifices incurred for defending the society or its members from injury and molestation. These conditions society is justified in enforcing at all costs to those who endeavor to withhold fulfilment. Nor is this all that society may do. The acts of an individual may be hurtful to others, or wanting in due consideration for their welfare, without going the length of violating any of their constituted rights. The offender may then be justly punished by opinion, though not by law. As soon as any part of a person's conduct affects prejudicially the interests of others,

[480] K C O'Rourke, *John Stuart Mill and Freedom of Expression: The genesis of a theory* (Routledge, London 2001) 137-138

[481] 80

[482] Some rightly designate this as 'the social authority principle'. "The authority principle says that society has legitimate power to enforce rules of other-regarding conduct. The individual has no right to choose as he pleases with respect to conduct which is harmful to others, in the sense that it directly causes them perceptible damage beyond their mere dislike. Rather, he ought to obey the general rules accepted by the majority, and is justifiably subject to coercion for that purpose" in K C O'Rourke, *John Stuart Mill and Freedom of Expression: The genesis of a theory* (Routledge, London 2001) 111

society has jurisdiction over it, and the question whether the general welfare will or will not be promoted by interfering with it, becomes open discussion".[483]

As discussed above, although Mill warns us about interference from the majority and even seems to plead in favor of the delineation of prevailing opinions rather than minority ones, his utilitarian approach tends to permit the involvement of the former in determining the manners for the society to which opinions have to accord. It is pertinent to note that, as elucidated in the course of this research, it is precisely this very approach that forms the limitation of free speech. This is also evident from Mill's reasoning whereby "those who do not live up to the rules of the game have no such rights; they must be restrained in the same way as those whose actions harm others in society. The implicit principle here is that as long as discussion remains discussion, it ought to be permitted absolute freedom; but once it passes beyond discussion to action, it ought to be treated as action".[484] Thus, the foregoing discussion might convey the impression that, at the surface, hate speech ought to be allowed so that the truthfulness of it can be attested and judged by reality itself. Yet, a thorough reading of Mill's theory leads to the inference that, although hate speech seems to be allowable at first sight, it, nevertheless, ought to be restrained for it does not meet the morality of public discussion and is deemed to pass beyond it, due to which it ought to be treated as a harmful act.[485] Some commentators interpret this merely in the light of the harm principle by contending that "[...] speech that instigates the inflicting of physical harm, either to certain persons or groups, needs to be removed from the protection of the Free Speech Principle".[486] Yet this is a partial reading of Mill's theory for, as elaborated hitherto, he provides a refined threshold for the morality of public discourse which blurs, or better merges, the borderline between speech and action as such.

This nuance becomes persuasive especially when Mill's utilitarianism[487] is taken into account which comes down to his 'greatest happiness principle'. When it is applied to our contemporary world affairs, it can be interpreted in the sense that freedom of expression which does not meet the morality of public discussion in the eyes of the majority can easily be curtailed since, as Jeremy Bentham plainly explains it in terms of this paradigm, one has to strive for the greatest happiness of the greatest number which is, thus, the measure of right and wrong.[488] Currently, we also witness the reversal of this principle whereby multicivilizationalism is deemed to have reversed the morality of public discourse from *majoritarianism* to *minoritarianism*. Despite anything to the contrary, this shift has resulted in the fact that, for instance, contiguous to the

---

483 Stefan Collini (ed), *J. S. Mill: On Liberty and Other Writings* (CUP, Cambridge 2010) 75-76

484 Leo Strauss and Joseph Cropsey (eds), *History of Political Philosophy* (3rd edn UCP, Chicago 1987) 799

485 Stefan Collini (ed), *J. S. Mill: On Liberty and Other Writings* (CUP, Cambridge 2010) 55

486 Clifford G Christians and John C Merrill (eds), *Ethical Communication: Moral Stances in Human Dialogue* (UMP, Missouri 2009) 31

487 John Stuart Mill, *Utilitarianism* (Longmans, London 1879); In particular, chapter five of this survey has to be taken into account in reading Mill's '*On Liberty*'

488 Ross Harrison (ed), *Bentham: A Fragment on Government* (CUP, Cambridge 1988)

stated curtailments, this latter category considers it justified to impose extrajudicial limitations on the fundamental right to freedom of expression.

The preceding discourse on the boundaries of speech leads us to the conclusion that the freedom to it is not absolute, but subject to limitations that emanate from the very notion of pluralism. Thus, after having conceptualized the fundamental right to freedom of expression in the preceding paragraph – which has made the ineluctability of it within the contemporary world order tangible – in this section, an attempt has been made to elucidate the permissible limitations of this right within a pluralistic society. This has been done through the thinking of John Stuart Mill that takes 'plurality' as its point of departure. This is important to grasp, especially if we take serious note of the fact that, in recent years, pluralism has not only fostered the freedom of speech, but that it seems to have rather confined speech and the freedom to it. However, most attention has been drawn, thus far, by the extrajudicial constraints, i.e. *de facto* limitations. This has had very little thought, as a consequence, being bestowed upon the *de jure* delineations that are imposed on this fundamental right by the acceleration of multicivilizationalism. Accordingly, with the preceding theoretical discussion in mind, an attempt will be made to explore the *de jure* limitations of this fundamental freedom, which are deemed to be fostered by the accelerated pluralism at the global, regional, and domestic level. That is, in the following sections of our research, an attempt will be made to elaborate on the central question over the extent to which pluralism has had *de jure* effects on the fundamental right to freedom of expression at the international, European, and national level.

2.3. The Right to Freedom of Expression at the International Level

After having conceptualized the significance of the fundamental right to freedom of expression within currently pluralistic society and determined the theoretical boundaries of this right, it is pertinent to proceed with the examination of the question as to what the *de jure* impact, if any, of pluralism has been on this fundamental right at the three distinct levels of the public realm that are underpinned by this multiplicity. This we will assess in the remaining part of this research. The first level at which the civilizational clashes emanating from this pluralism tend to confine the fundamental right to freedom of expression is the international level. Accordingly, the question over the extent to which this delineation has taken place at this level will be addressed hereinafter.

In order to be able to conduct this survey, we, firstly, need to apprehend the fundamental right to freedom of expression and its legal limitations at the global level, before we can analyze the delineation deemed to be imposed on it by contemporary world affairs. In so doing, the primordial international legal instrument, in which the freedom of expression has been ingrained, is the

Universal Declaration of Human Rights (UDHR).[489] This Declaration was adopted by the United Nations General Assembly[490] on 10 December 1948[491] in Paris and is part and parcel of the International Bill of Human Rights. The Bill of Rights contains also the following major legal tools: the International Covenant on Civil and Political Rights with its two Optional Protocols, and the International Covenant on Economic, Social and Cultural Rights.[492] Although the Declaration is considered to be part of customary international law, the fact remains that it is not a legally binding instrument. Still, its significance is not to be underrated for this document has functioned as the foundation and inspiration[493] of, among others, the sequent Covenants and, later, other regional legal instruments such as the Convention for the Protection of Human Rights and Fundamental Freedoms. As regards the freedom of expression[494], it is pertinent to recall that this freedom is expounded in Article 19 of this Declaration which reads as follows:

"Everyone has the right to freedom of opinion and expression; this right includes freedom to hold opinions without interference and to seek, receive and impart information and ideas through any media and regardless of frontiers"

At first sight, this Article conveys the impression that this right is subject to no restraints. However, as elaborated hitherto, social existence inevitably carries within it duties towards others which are necessary for making peaceful coexistence possible. For this, the threshold can be drawn at different levels, ranging from refrainment from causing harm to taking up duties and responsibilities. This ineluctable curtailment inherent to social existence becomes evident once this provision is read in conjunction with Article 29 of the UDHR[495] which, on the one hand, ensures duties towards the community to which one belongs and, on the other, restrains the exercise of rights and freedoms as determined by law for the purpose of securing due recognition and respect for the

---

[489] For a further discussion on the historical background, reference can be made to, e.g., Johannes Morsink, *The Universal Declaration of Human Rights: Origins, Drafting & Intent* (UPP, Pennsylvania 1999)

[490] The General Assembly is the plenary organ of the UN which is composed of all the Members of this organization ex. Article 9 UN Charter. For further elaboration on the powers and composition of this organ, reference can be made to chapter IV of the Charter of the United Nations. For a thorough discussion, reference can also be made to Philippe Sands and Pierre Klein, *Bowett's Law of International Institutions* (5th edn Sweet & Maxwell, London 2001)

[491] This day is annually commemorated <http://www.un.org/en/events/humanrightsday/> accessed 15 June 2013

[492] For a historical overview, reference can be made to <http://www.un.org/Depts/dhl/udhr/> accessed 15 June 2013

[493] Eva Brems, *Human Rights: Universality and Diversity* (International Studies in Human Rights, Martinus Nijhoff Publishers, The Hague 2001)

[494] It is worth remarking that the expressions 'freedom of speech' and 'freedom of expression' are oftentimes used as synonyms due to which in this inquiry these two expressions are used interchangeably

[495] Gudmundur Alfredsson and Asbjorn Eide (eds), *The Universal Declaration of Human Rights: A Common Standard of Achievement* (Martinus Nijhoff Publishers, The Hague 1999) 403

rights and freedoms of others and of meeting the just requirements of morality, public order and the general welfare in a democratic society.[496] Accordingly, this entails that rights and freedoms may not be exercised contrary to the purposes and principles of the United Nations, just as we can read in Article 5(1) of the ICCPR which asserts that *"nothing in the present Covenant may be interpreted as implying for any state, group or person any right to engage in any activity or perform any act aimed at the destruction of any of the rights and freedoms recognized herein or at their limitation to a greater extent than is provided for in the present Covenant"*.

Henceforth, the relevance of Article 19 to this inquiry is beyond doubt for it contains several vital aspects, the most important of which for our research are the following. Firstly, like all fundamental rights, not the *possession* of the right to freedom of expression but only the *exercise* of it is subject to limitations. And that is because it takes place in relation to and in coexistence with others, which encumbers one with duties and responsibilities towards them. Secondly, the boundaries of freedoms and rights in general and of the freedom of expression in particular are determined by the aforementioned communal interactions against which the rights and freedoms are kept in equilibrium, that is, the limits of one's freedoms and rights are there where the rights and freedoms of others begin, which is thus in line with the philosophy of John S. Mill. Furthermore, as to the communal responsibility, reference is made to the democratic makeup of society. The prime reason why human rights and freedoms are inevitably brought into connection with governance is because, as the Federalist Papers rightly assert, "if men were angels, no government would be necessary. If angels were to govern men, neither external nor internal controls on government would be necessary. In framing a government which is to be administered by men over men, the great difficulty lies in this: you must first enable the government to control the governed, and in the next place oblige it to control itself. A dependence on the people is, no doubt, the primary control on the government; but experience has taught mankind the necessity of auxiliary precautions".[497]

This leads us to the next reason as to why, among all forms of governance, preference has been given to democracy for protecting human rights and freedoms. The answer lies within the concept of democracy itself, for as we will elaborate hereafter, when people reign themselves, their rights and interests are deemed to be protected in the best possible way. In other words, etymologically the notion of 'democracy' is made up of the term *δῆμος* (people) and *κράτος*

[496] The so-called second generation of human rights has a more relaxed regime for the limitation of rights as it is apparent from Article 4 ICESCR which reads as follows: "The States Parties to the present Covenant recognize that, in the enjoyment of those rights provided by the State in conformity with the present Covenant, the State may subject such rights only to such limitations as are determined by law only in so far as this may be compatible with the nature of these rights and solely for the purpose of promoting the general welfare in a democratic society". UNCHR Res 23 (1999) UN Doc E/CN.4/RES/1999/167

[497] James Madison, Alexander Hamilton and John Jay, *The Federalist Papers* (Penguin Books, London 1987) 319-320

(power). Democracy is posited on the freely expressed will of people[498] to determine their own political, economic, social and cultural systems as well as their full participation in all aspects of their lives.[499] This means that '*the will of the people*' has to be the basis of authority of government as it is expressed, among others, in periodic and genuine elections by free voting procedures.[500]For the underpinning purpose of this mode of governance is that "everyone has the right to take part in the government of his country, directly or through freely chosen representatives" (Article 21 of the UDHR). This participatory right is further clarified in Article 25 of the International Covenant on Civil and Political Rights (ICCPR) which reads as follows:

"Every citizen shall have the right and the opportunity, without any of the distinctions mentioned in article 2 and without unreasonable restrictions:

(a) To take part in the conduct of public affairs, directly or through freely chosen representatives;

(b) To vote and to be elected at genuine periodic elections which shall be by universal and equal suffrage and shall be held by secret ballot, guaranteeing the free expression of the will of the electors;

(c) To have access, on general terms of equality, to public service in his country".

What is conspicuous in this axiomatic participatory form of governance is the notion of 'citizenship' for only a citizen has the right to participate in the polity and can, therefore, be the bearer of rights and freedoms. Subsequently, democracy is perceived as the "basic right of citizenship to be exercised under conditions of freedom, equality, transparency and responsibility, with due respect for the plurality of views, and in the interest of the polity".[501] This is why "the freedom of everyone to exercise their own mind in the manner they choose and to express the resulting views and beliefs has been a stated flagship of Western democracies. But a feature of human rights that has caused much controversy and inconsistent applications within all societies. Such freedom has the clear ability, in a number of ways more than other rights, to impact upon the natural tension between the interests of the individual and the society within which he or she lives".[502] For that reason, in a democratic society, the individual is restricted in the exercise of his rights and freedoms by the duties that he has towards the community[503], that is, for the purpose of securing due recognition and respect for

---

[498] "Democracy is a system of government which embodies, in a variety of institutions and mechanisms, the ideal of political power based on the will of the people"; (1) An Agenda for Democratization

[499] I(8) of the Vienna Declaration and Programme of Action

[500] Article 21(3) of the Universal Declaration of Human Rights. Declaration on Criteria for Free and Fair Elections

[501] Principle (1) of the Universal Declaration on Democracy

[502] Alex Conte and Richard Burchill, *Defining Civil and Political Rights: The Jurisprudence of the United Nations Human Rights Committee* (2nd edn Ashgate Publishing Limited, Surrey 2009) 76

[503] Article 29(1) of the Universal Declaration of Human Rights

the rights and freedoms of others[504] and of meeting the just requirements of morality, public order and the general welfare.[505] The belief that human rights and freedoms define relationships between individuals and power structures is based on the notion that they delimit State power and, at the same time, require the State to take positive measures for ensuring an environment that enables all people to enjoy their human rights[506], meaning that human rights and freedoms are susceptible to delimitation. And delimitation is believed to be permissible so long as it is *reasonable* and based on *objective criteria.* However, both criteria are vague and subject to the interpretation of the State which makes human rights and freedoms vulnerable and puts them at risk of arbitrariness.

What is more, fundamental rights and freedoms in their modern version are the fruits of the French Revolution. The document that promulgated them was "the French Declaration of the Right of Man [and of the Citizen], [that] as the Revolution came to understand it, was meant to constitute the source of all political power, to establish not the control but the foundation-stone of the body politic. The new body politic was supposed to rest upon man's natural rights, upon his rights in so far as he is nothing but a natural being [...] And these rights were not understood as prepolitical rights that no government and no political power has the right to touch and to violate, but as the very content as well as the ultimate end of government and power".[507] As the name of this document as well as the contemporary human rights tools indicate, fundamental rights and freedoms are, due to the aforementioned form of governance, inevitably politicized. This is why Arendt is right when she asserts that "the trouble with these rights has always been that they could not but be less than the rights of nationals, and that they were invoked only as a last resort by those who had lost their normal rights as citizens".[508]

Yet, it is imperative to recall that while her critique is sound, her own concept of 'the right to have rights', as elaborated above, is, nevertheless, not at variance with this citizenly comprehension, that is, to belong to a political community. Being revolutionary in this regard has solely been the creation of the European Court of Human Rights that supersedes and transcends this relativized politicization of human rights and freedoms by detaching it from national sovereignty and politics.[509] Although democracy is not the ultimate and perfect

[504] "In particular, the rights of others are undermined when deep-rooted hatred is manifested and expressed under certain circumstances" in UNHRC, 'Report of the Special Rapporteur on the Promotion and protection of the right to freedom of opinion and expression' (2012) UN Doc A/67/357

[505] Article 29(2) of the Universal Declaration of Human Rights

[506] UN Inter-Parliamentary Union, "Human Rights: A Handbook for Parliamentarians", No.5, 2005, 1

[507] Hannah Arendt, *On Revolution* (Penguin Books, New York 1965) 99

[508] Ibid 140

[509] Although the creation of this Court is a unique and unprecedented achievement, it still has the shortcoming that it is merely an *ultimum remedium* tool ex Article 35 of the European Convention for the Protection of Human Rights and Fundamental Freedoms. What is more striking as regards the dependency of fundamental rights and freedoms on politics and thus the

form of governance[510] as we have seen in the number of critiques[511] and despite the fact that "the definition of democracy is an increasingly important subject of debate within and among societies, the practice of democracy is increasingly regarded as essential to progress on a wide range of human concerns and to the protection of human rights" [512] i.e. the possibility for the full exercise of fundamental freedoms and rights is believed to exist only within democratic systems. [513] In other words, "democracy remains the best hope for securing human dignity and rights"[514] for it is "an always-perfectible [self-correcting[515]]

(menace of) politicization of them is the notion of 'margin of appreciation' as invented and applied by this Court. For further reading on this notion, see Yutaka Arai-Takahashi, *Margin of Appreciation Doctrine and the Principle of Proportionality in the Jurisprudence of the ECHR* (Intersentia, Antwerp 2001), Howard Charles Yourow, *The Margin of Appreciation Doctrine in the Dynamics of European Human Rights Jurisprudence* (Martinus Nijhoff Publishers, Dordrecht 1996). The dependency of fundamental rights and freedoms on politics comes also to the fore in the UN's respect of national sovereignty whereby it states that "[...] to address the subjects of democratization and democracy does not imply a change in the respect that the United Nations vows for the sovereignty of States or in the principle of non-intervention in internal affairs set out in Article 2, para 7, of the Charter of the United Nations"; An Agenda for Democratization. The same reasoning is reiterated in other documents such as the Universal Declaration on Democracy in which it is stated that, although democracy is conceived as a universally recognized ideal, nevertheless, as a mode of government it has to be applied in accordance with modalities which mirror the diversity of experiences and cultural particularities without, however, any derogations from internationally recognized principles, norms and standards whereby "each State has the sovereign right, freely to choose and develop, in accordance with the will of its people, its own political, social, economic and cultural systems without interference by other States in strict conformity with the United Nations Charter". It is, however, interesting to remark that while Human Rights Committee underlines the existence of a margin of discretion, especially in case of public moral, it, nonetheless, asserts that it cannot accept that moral issues are exclusively a matter of domestic concern; see *Toonen v Australia*, Communication No. 488/1992, UN Doc CCPR/C/50/D/488/1992 (1994)

[510] UNCHR, Fifty-ninth session 'Civil and Political Rights. Continuing dialogue on measures to promote and consolidate democracy. Report of the High Commissioner for Human Rights submitted in accordance with Commission resolution 2001/41' (27 January 2003) UN Doc E/CN.4/2003/59

[511] The most famous one is the phraseology "tyranny of the majority" which was employed by John Adams in 1788 but also by Alexis de Tocqueville in 1835 and John Stuart Mill in 1859. And it is this latter philosopher who also explicitly warns against this by stating that tyranny of the majority is "[...] among the evils against which society is required to be on its guard"; in Stefan Collini (ed), *J. S. Mill: On Liberty and other writings* (CUP, Cambridge 2010) 8

[512] (3) An Agenda for Democratization

[513] UNCHR Res 47 (2000) UN Doc E/CN.4/RES/2000/47

[514] UNCHR, Fifty-ninth session 'Civil and Political Rights. Continuing dialogue on measures to promote and consolidate democracy. Report of the High Commissioner for Human Rights submitted in accordance with Commission resolution 2001/41' (27 January 2003) UN Doc E/CN.4/2003/59. This is also apparent from the wording of Article 25 of the ICCPR the drafters of which seem to "[...] have taken the view that the enjoyment of human rights is dependent upon the existence of a democratic government based on the consent of the people" in Alex Conte and Richard Burchill, *Defining Civil and Political Rights: The Jurisprudence of the United Nations Human Rights Committee* (2nd edn Ashgate Publishing, Surrey 2009) 97

process that should be measured by the degree to which its principles, norms, standards and values are given effect and contributes to the full realization of all human rights".[516] But to what extent this can be achieved depends on a variety of political, social, economic, and cultural factors.[517]

It is rather democracy itself that gains legitimization and avails of certain advantages from fundamental rights and freedoms by considering them as its essence.[518] Particularly, the fundamental right to freedom of expression is considered to be a critical foundation of democracy.[519] Thus, the opinion is widely cherished that, in general, democracy and respect for human rights and fundamental freedoms are inseparable[520], indissoluble[521], interdependent[522], and mutually reinforcing.[523] And based on this, and with regard to the freedom of

---

[515] Principle (3) of the Universal Declaration on Democracy

[516] UNCHR Res 36 (2003) UN Doc E/CN.4-RES/2003/36

[517] Principle (2) of the Universal Declaration on Democracy

[518] UNCHR, Fifty-ninth session 'Civil and Political Rights. Continuing dialogue on measures to promote and consolidate democracy. Report of the High Commissioner for Human Rights submitted in accordance with Commission resolution 2001/41' (27 January 2003) UN Doc E/CN.4/2003/59

[519] UNHRC, 'Report of the Special Rapporteur on the Promotion and protection of the right to freedom of opinion and expression' (2012) UN Doc A/67/357

[520] Principle (6), (7) of the Universal Declaration of Democracy

[521] UNCHR Res 57 (1999) UN Doc E/CN.4/RES/1999/57. UNCHR Res 60 (1995) UN Doc E/CN.4/RES/1995/60

[522] UNCHR Res 36 (2003) UN Doc E/CN.4-RES/2003/36

[523] See, for instance, Vienna Declaration and Programme of Action (A/CONF.157/23), adopted on 25 June 1993 by the World Conference on Human Rights. UNCHR Res 57 (1999) UN Doc E/CN.4/RES/1999/57. I(8), II(C)(74) of the Vienna Declaration and Programme of Action. The 1993 World Plan of Action on Education for Human Rights and Democracy; the 1995 UNESCO Integrated Framework of Action on Education for Peace, Human Rights and Democracy. UNCHR Res 47 (2000) UN Doc E/CN.4/RES/2000/47. UNCHR Res 46 (2002) UN Doc E/CN.4/RES/2002/46. The 2000 Warsaw Declaration: Toward a Community of Democracies. Principle (6) of the Universal Declaration on Democracy. Nonetheless, politicization of the fundamental freedoms and rights put them rather at risk and limits them than fostering and promoting them. In other words, the fundamental rights and freedoms are oftentimes at the advantageous disposal of politics and modes of governances. The most recent and, so far, innocent form of this limiting effect of democracy on fundamental rights and freedoms is the so-called 'militant democracy'. Such militant demeanor at the international level comes also to the fore in Article 4 of the International Covenant on Economic, Social and Cultural Rights which states that "the States Parties to the present Covenant recognize that, in the enjoyment of those rights provided by the State in conformity with the present Covenant, the State may subject such rights only to such limitations as are determined by law only in so far as this may be compatible with the nature of these rights and solely for the purpose of promoting the general welfare in a democratic society". Thence, the fundamental rights and freedoms do foster this mode of governance, but the opposite cannot be said to be always the case. This is why detachment of the fundamental freedoms and rights from politics and politicization ought, as far as possible, to be applauded; many examples can be mentioned of this detaching development such as the creation of the European Court of Human Rights, the UN individual complaint procedure, and the concept of 'responsibility to protect' within the international law which is an innovation, if not revolution, once we bear in mind the required respect for the sovereignty of States and the principle of non-intervention in internal affairs as

expression, it is argued that "[...] the exercise of the right to freedom of opinion and expression is one of the essential foundations of a democratic society, [which] is enabled by a democratic environment, [that] offers, inter alia, guarantees for its protection, is essential to full and effective participation in a free and democratic society, and is instrumental to the development and strengthening of effective democratic systems".[524] In addition, within this mode of governance, that is, "in a liberal democracy, [which remains the best hope for securing and facilitating human dignity and rights[525]] freedom of opinion and expression serves both the personal autonomy and self-realization of the individual and guarantees the democratic process of the society. A free responsible citizen is protected from any outside intervention in order to enable him/her to form and express his/her opinions without any outside threat or coercion. Freedom of expression and opinion is a typical "first generation" human rights with very classical individual emphasis".[526] Thus, "the right to freedom of opinion and expression as proclaimed in article 19 of the UDHR constitutes a cornerstone of democratic society. This is the reason why many human rights instruments adopted by the UN bodies since 1984 elaborate principles set out in this article".[527] As has been previously brought to attention, this provision is further elaborated in the International Covenant on Civil and Political Rights (ICCPR) whereby "the state of democracy presupposes freedom

---

set out in Article 2(7) of the Charter of the United Nations in addition to which this organization stresses that "the United Nations is, by design and definition, universal and impartial. While democratization is a new force in world affairs, and while democracy can and should be assimilated by all cultures and traditions, it is not for the United Nations to offer a model of democratization or democracy or to promote democracy in a specific case. Indeed, to do so could be counter-productive to the process of democratization which, in order to take root and to flourish, must derive from the society itself. Each society must be able to choose the form, pace and character of its democratization process. Impositions of foreign models not only contravenes the Charter principle of non-intervention in internal affairs, it may also generate resentment among both the Government and the public, which may in turn feed internal forces inimical to democratization and to the idea of democracy"; (10) An Agenda for Democratization. Detachment can also be found, for instance, in the 1985 Declaration on the Human Rights of Individuals Who Are Not Nationals of the Country in Which They Live, according to which human rights and fundamental freedoms have to be universally respected and observed. This is also reiterated in, among others, the International Convention on the Elimination of All Forms of Racial Discrimination. Despite all this, the interrelationship between human rights and democracy is embedded in Article 21 of the Universal Declaration of Human Rights and reiterated in many international legal tools. For example in the II(C)(74) of the Vienna Declaration and Programme of Action

[524] UNHRC Res 12/16, 'Promotion and Protection of All Human Rights, Civil, Political, Economic, Social and Cultural Rights, Including the Right to Development' (2 October 2009) UN Doc A/HRC/RES/12/16

[525] UNCHR Res 60 (1995) UN Doc E/CN.4/RES/1995/60

[526] Gudmundur Alfredsson and Asbjorn Eide (eds), *The Universal Declaration of Human Rights: A Common Standard of Achievement* (Martinus Nijhoff Publishers, The Hague 1999) 394

[527] Ibid 404

of opinion and expression"[528] but, as we will see hereinafter, it, simultaneously, imposes a confinement on this fundamental freedom. This is because, as it is oftentimes contended, democracy cannot be indifferent to its own fundamental principles.[529] In the case of Article 19, this means that while this provision does not contain the grounds on the basis of which this freedom can be constrained, it has, nevertheless, not to be forgotten that in the light of human coexistence – about which Article 29 UDHR[530] restrains the exercise of rights and freedoms for the purpose of securing due recognition and respect for the rights and freedoms of others and of meeting the just requirements of morality, public order and the general welfare – this fundamental right can be limited through primarily but not exclusively the principle of non-discrimination that undergirds, among others, this Declaration and particularly this provision. Yet, in considering the delineation of the fundamental right to freedom of expression, we need to inquire farther into the sequent legal tool within the International Bill of Rights – the 1966 International Covenant on Civil and Political Rights – wherein this fundamental right and its legal limitations are outlined more elaborately. We can find the right to freedom of expression in Article 19[531] of this Covenant which reads as follows:

"*1. Everyone shall have the right to hold opinions without interference.*
2. Everyone shall have the right to freedom of expression; this right shall include freedom to seek, receive and impart information and ideas of all kinds, regardless of frontiers, either orally, in writing or in print, in the form of art, or through any other media of his choice.
3. The exercise of the rights provided for in paragraph 2 of this article carries with it special duties and responsibilities. It may therefore be subject to certain restrictions, but these shall only be such as are provided by law and are necessary:[532]

[528] Principle (21) of the Universal Declaration on Democracy

[529] Afshin Ellian, 'Op de grens van vrijheid: ketterij in de vrije samenleving' in Afshin Ellian, Gelijn Molier and Tom Zwart (eds), *Mag ik dit zeggen? Beschouwingen over de vrijheid van meningsuiting* (Boom Juridische Uitgevers, The Hague 2011) 222

[530] Gudmundur Alfredsson and Asbjorn Eide (eds), *The Universal Declaration of Human Rights: A Common Standard of Achievement* (Martinus Nijhoff Publishers, The Hague 1999) 403

[531] Although not explicitly mentioned in Article 4 of ICCPR, this right is, nonetheless, a non-derogable right. In other words, "the only right which is expressed in absolute language but is not either expressly or impliedly included in the list of non-derogable rights is article 19(1), concerning the right to hold opinions without interference. While it seems illogical at face value, it should be noted that the right to hold opinions is given effective protection during states of emergency since the freedom of thought (protected under article 18(1) of the ICCPR) *is* non-derogable under article 4(2)" in Alex Conte and Richard Burchill, *Defining Civil and Political Rights: The Jurisprudence of the United Nations Human Rights Committee* (2nd edn Ashgate Publishing, Surrey 2009) 42

[532] "There were two schools of thought on the question of how the limitations or restrictions should be written. One school was of the opinion that the limitations clause should be a brief statement of general limitations [...]; the other school maintained that it should be a full catalogue of specific limitations. Consequently, several texts of a general clause were proposed

(a) For respect of the rights or reputations of others;
(b) For the protection of national security or of public order (ordre public), or of public health or morals".[533]

The interpretation and monitoring of the implementation of this Covenant is conducted by an organ consisting of independent experts called the Human Rights Committee that publishes its findings in the form of general comments. In the same vein, freedom of expression as contained in the aforementioned provision is elucidated in General Comment No. 10. As regards to the right 'to hold opinions without interference', as contained in the first paragraph of this Article, this General Comment states that the Covenant permits no exceptions and restrictions. It is only the *expression* of opinions that is confined to certain limitations [534] which are expounded in (domestic) laws about which the Committee explains that "it is the interplay between the principle of freedom of expression and such limitations and restrictions which determines the actual scope of the individual's right".[535] And what underpins this is the fact that "[...] the exercise of the right to freedom of expression carries with it special duties and responsibilities[536] and for this reason certain restrictions on the right are permitted which may relate either to the interests of other persons or to those of the community as a whole".[537] However, such restrictions may not undermine and jeopardize this fundamental right itself and must meet the legal prerequisites mentioned in this provision.

Notwithstanding its relevance, it is worth noting that the aforementioned General Comment had been replaced by the General Comment No. 34 during the 102nd session of 2011. This General Comment makes a distinction between the 'freedom of opinion' and 'freedom of expression'[538] without, however, providing

---

while at the same time more than thirty specific limitations were suggested" in Marc J Bossuyt, *Guide to the 'travaux préparatoires' of the International Covenant on Civil and Political Rights* (Martinus Nijhoff Publishers, Dordrecht 1987) 387

533 It is worth noting that the *travaux préparatoires* of this provision contains more grounds for limitations as they were submitted by the states, but only few were chosen as one can read in this provision. Also, the Third Committee's observation during the 16th Session (1961) bears witness to this through the assertion that "there was general agreement on the fundamental important of freedom of opinion and expression. Difference arose primarily over the extent and forms of any limitations that might be allowed". For the further legal history of this, see Marc J Bossuyt, *Guide to the 'travaux préparatoires' of the International Covenant on Civil and Political Rights* (Martinus Nijhoff Publishers, Dordrecht 1987)

534 The limitations that may be imposed on this freedom, according to the third paragraph of this provision, must be provided by law and have to be necessary for the respect of the rights and reputations of others, or for the protection of national security or of public order, or of public health and morals

535 ICCPR General Comment No. 10, par. 3

536 Interesting in this regard is the Declaration on the Right and Responsibility of Individuals, Groups and Organs of Society to Promote and Protect Universally Recognized Human Rights and Fundamental Freedoms

537 ICCPR General Comment No. 10, par. 4

538 Not a definition but only a description of these two rights is provided. The freedom of opinion encompasses all forms of opinion including opinions of a scientific, political, historical, religious and moral nature, and the freedom of expression comprises, as the

any further clarification or explanation of either notion. But as referred to already, the freedom of opinion can be put forth as the unconditional right inherent to the human person whereas the materialization, that is, the expression of it is confined to certain conditions just as this General Comment also elucidates in stating that "the two freedoms are closely related, with freedom of expression providing the vehicle for the exchange and development of opinions".[539] This can be comprehended in the light of the preceding philosophical elaboration as regards the absolute nature of this right which is inherent to the human person[540], and thus indispensable for the full development and cultivation of personhood, without leaving any room for exception or restriction [541] which entails also its independence from any form of governance.[542] For instance, General Comment No. 25 bears witness to it[543] by explaining that "whatever form of constitution or government is in force, the Covenant requires states to adopt such legislative and other measures as may be necessary to ensure that citizens have an effective opportunity to enjoy the rights it protects". Hence, "[...] freedom of speech does not derive its raison d'être from democracy. Before being a necessary element of self-government of a nation, free speech is a necessary element of individual self-determination and personal

---

General Comment No. 34 states, the expression and receipt of communications of every form of idea and opinion capable of transmission to others entailing political discourse, commentary on one's own, public affairs, canvassing, discussion of human rights, journalism, cultural and artistic expression, teaching, religious discourse, and eventually commercial advertising. See *Mika Miha v Equatorial Guinea*, Communication No. 414/1990, *Fernando v Sri Lanka*, Communication No. 1189/2003, *Coleman v Australia*, Communication No. 1157/2003, *Velichkin v Belarus*, Communication No. 1022/2001, *Mavlonov and Sa'di v Uzbekistan*, Communication No. 1334/2004, *Shin v Republic of Korea*, Communication No. 926/2000, *Ross v Canada*, Communication No. 736/97

[539] ICCPR General Comment No. 34, par. 2

[540] As the ICCPR General Comment No. 34 asserts, "[...] a reservation to paragraph 1 [of Article 19] would be incompatible with the object and purpose of the Covenant. Furthermore, although freedom of opinion is not listed among those rights that may not be derogated from pursuant to the provisions of article 4 of the Covenant, it is recalled that "in those provisions of the Covenant that are not listed in article 4, paragraph 2, there are elements that in the Committee's opinion cannot be made subject to lawful derogation under article 4". Freedom of opinion is one such element, since it can never become necessary to derogate from it during a state of emergency"

[541] ICCPR General Comment No. 34, par. 9; it is asserted that "it is incompatible with paragraph 1 to criminalize the holding of an opinion"; *Faurisson v France*, Communication No. 550/93

[542] This comes also to the fore in the legal history of this provision whereby, during the drafting of it, it was asserted that "the right to freedom of expression was not to be limited within the confines of any political or territorial entity; it was to be exercised 'regardless of frontiers'" in Marc J Bossuyt, *Guide to the 'travaux préparatoires' of the International Covenant on Civil and Political Rights* (Martinus Nijhoff Publishers, Dordrecht 1987) 381-382. Also, the ICCPR General Comment No. 25 brings this to the fore by stating that "Whatever form of constitution or government is in force, the Covenant requires States to adopt such legislative and other measures as may be necessary to ensure that citizens have an effective opportunity to enjoy the rights it protects"

[543] ICCPR General Comment No. 25

dignity, which is at the centre of the idea of fundamental rights".[544] Accordingly, as regards this fundamental freedom, the "Special Rapporteur reiterated that violations of the right to freedom of opinion and expression may occur in all regions and countries, whatever their system". [545] Thus, the attempt to *materialize*, i.e. to express, this right subjects it simultaneously to delineations and social and societal conditions[546] irrespective of the mode of body politic concerned. This is also mirrored in the legal history of this provision as elucidated by the Commission on Human Rights during the 5th Session (1949), 6th Session (1950), and 8th Session (1952) whereby it had been stated that the "[...] freedom of opinion and freedom of expression were not of the same character: the former was purely a private matter, belonging as it did to the realm of the mind, while the latter was a public matter, or a matter of human relationship, which should be subject to legal as well as moral restraint. [...] Although it was recognized that a person was invariably conditioned or influenced by the external world, it was generally agreed that no law could regulate his opinion and no power could dictate what opinion he should or should not entertain. [...] The decision was made, therefore, to treat the right to freedom of opinion separately from the right to freedom of expression [...]"[547], the latter being the only one of the two that may be subjected to delineations. Hence, after apprehending the content of this fundamental right as formulated at the international level, both in the Universal Declaration and the International Covenant, it is imperative to note the limitations to which this right may be subjected. In so doing, an attempt will be made to comprehend, in the following section, the boundaries (that is, the legal limitations) that can be imposed on this fundamental human right.

---

[544] Ivan Hare and James Weinstein (eds), *Extreme Speech and Democracy* (OUP, Oxford 2009) 12

[545] <http://daccess-dds-ny.un.org/doc/UNDOC/GEN/G03/171/69/PDF/G0317169.pdf?OpenElement> accessed 20 June 2013

[546] Further elaboration on this can be found in the ICCPR General Comment No. 25. Relevant in this regard is also Article 25 of the ICCPR which reads as follows: "Every citizen shall have the right and the opportunity, without any of the distinctions mentioned in article 2 and without unreasonable restrictions:

(a) To take part in the conduct of public affairs, directly or through freely chosen representatives;

(b) To vote and to be elected at genuine periodic elections which shall be by universal and equal suffrage and shall be held by secret ballot, guaranteeing the free expression of the will of the electors;

(c) To have access, on general terms of equality, to public service in his country"

[547] Marc J Bossuyt, *Guide to the 'travaux préparatoires' of the International Covenant on Civil and Political Rights* (Martinus Nijhoff Publishers, Dordrecht 1987) 378

2.3.1. Limitations of Freedom of Expression at the International Level

In this part of our inquiry, an attempt will be made to examine the legally determined boundaries of the right to freedom of expression at the international level as far as it is pertinent to the present study. The two relevant provisions containing this fundamental right at the global level have been mentioned in the preceding section and shall, accordingly, be taken as our point of departure in determining the scope of limitations imposed on this fundamental right. The first provision covering this fundamental right is, as mentioned, Article 19 of the Universal Declaration which does *not* provide for the legal limitations in this same Article. And the second provision is Article 19 of the International Covenant on Civil and Political Rights which *does* contain the legal boundaries of this freedom in the same provision. Although the legal limitations are not mentioned in Article 19 of the Universal Declaration, it should not be forgotten that, as stated before, this provision "[...] must be read in conjunction with other provisions of the UDHR, and especially with the conditions on duties and limitations laid down in article 29 of the Declaration. Quite often states are referring specifically to article 19 when making reservations or interpretative declarations to other human rights treaties".[548] For example, we can refer to the reservations made in Article 4 of the International Convention on the Elimination of All Forms of Racial Discrimination.[549] This means that the freedom of expression limits the non-discrimination principle but, reversely, also this principle, as one of the inevitable prerequisites, confines this fundamental freedom even though Article 19 of the UDHR itself does not explicitly provide for the limitation of this right.[550]

---

[548] Gudmundur Alfredsson and Asbjorn Eide (eds), *The Universal Declaration of Human Rights: A Common Standard of Achievement* (Martinus Nijhoff Publishers, The Hague 1999) 403

[549] Article 4 of the International Convention on the Elimination of All Forms of Racial Discrimination reads as follows: "*States Parties condemn all propaganda and all organizations which are based on ideas or theories of superiority of one race or group of persons of one colour or ethnic origin, or which attempt to justify or promote racial hatred and discrimination in any form, and undertake to adopt immediate and positive measures designed to eradicate all incitement to, or acts of, such discrimination and, to this end, with due regard to the principles embodied in the Universal Declaration of Human Rights and the rights expressly set forth in article 5 of this Convention, inter alia:*
(a) Shall declare an offence punishable by law all dissemination of ideas based on racial superiority or hatred, incitement to racial discrimination, as well as all acts of violence or incitement to such acts against any race or group of persons of another colour or ethnic origin, and also the provision of any assistance to racist activities, including the financing thereof;
(b) Shall declare illegal and prohibit organizations, and also organized and all other propaganda activities, which promote and incite racial discrimination, and shall recognize participation in such organizations or activities as an offence punishable by law;
(c) Shall not permit public authorities or public institutions, national or local, to promote or incite racial discrimination".

[550] As stated already in this inquiry, limitations of the fundamental rights and freedoms, as contained in the Universal Declaration, can be found in Article 29 of this same Declaration

However, as stated already, "unlike article 19 of the UDHR, article 19(3) of the CCPR expressly allows for restrictions and limitations upon the freedom of expression. According to paragraph 3, the exercise of the right provided for in paragraph 2 carries with it special duties and responsibilities and may therefore be subjected to certain restrictions. [This should be seen in the light of the fact that] these limitations [are] doubtlessly drawn on article 29(1) of the UDHR [...]".[551] According to Article 19 of the ICCPR, the limitations imposed on this fundamental right have to be prescribed by law, need to be a requirement for respecting the rights and reputations of others, and for protecting one of the legitimate objectives mentioned in this Article[552], but they also cannot be discriminatory in nature. What is more, according to the Siracusa Principles on the Limitation and Derogation of Provisions in the International Covenant on Civil and Political Rights, "whenever a limitation is required in the terms of the Covenant to be "necessary", this term implies that the limitation: (a) is based on one of the grounds justifying limitation recognized by the relevant article of the Covenant, (b) responds to a pressing public or social need, (c) pursues a legitimate aim, and (d) is proportionate to that aim", i.e. showing the need for a limitation that encompasses "[...] a reasonably mechanical exercise whereby a State will point to permitted objectives and draw links between the limiting measures and those objectives. [However] the establishing of such a relationship does not provide the State with the ability to limit the right or freedom to whatever extent it wishes. The limiting measures must also be shown to be proportionate, such that the State may not use more restrictive means than are required to achieve the purpose of the limitation".[553]

What has also to be taken into account in the assessment of these prerequisites in general, and the principle of proportionality in particular, especially with regard to the freedom of expression, is the significance of public debate within a democratic society.[554] The latter prerequisite means that the scope of limitations, despite the margin of discretion which will be discussed below, may not be interpreted in a disadvantageous way so that it would jeopardize the essence of the right in question. Furthermore, what is meant by being 'prescribed by law', according to the Siracusa Principles, is that: "15. No limitation on the exercise of human rights shall be made unless provided for by national law of general application which is consistent with the Covenant and is

---

which are, above all, in accordance with the limitations that are prescribed and provided in the ICCPR

[551] Gudmundur Alfredsson and Asbjorn Eide (eds), *The Universal Declaration of Human Rights: A Common Standard of Achievement* (Martinus Nijhoff Publishers, The Hague 1999) 404

[552] For further clarification of these criteria, see the Siracusa Principles on the Limitation and Derogation of Provisions in the International Covenant on Civil and Political Rights

[553] Alex Conte and Richard Burchill, *Defining Civil and Political Rights: The Jurisprudence of the United Nations Human Rights Committee* (2nd edn Ashgate Publishing, Surrey 2009) 49

[554] This has become evident in the Communications of the Committee, an example of which is *Bodrožić v Serbia and Montenegro*, Communication No. 1180/2003, UN Doc CCPR/C/85/D/1180/2003 (2006)

in force at the time the limitation is applied. 16. Laws imposing limitations on the exercise of human rights shall not be arbitrary or unreasonable. 17. Legal rules limiting the exercise of human rights shall be clear and accessible to everyone. 18. Adequate safeguards and effective remedies shall be provided by law against illegal or abusive imposition or application of limitations on human rights". What is more, it is clear that Article 19 of the ICCPR, unlike Article 29 of the UDHR, does not base the necessity of a limitation upon the prerequisite of a 'democratic society' by making no reference to this latter notion. This ought to be perceived in the same light as our preceding scrutiny of the fact that this fundamental freedom does not need to be ineluctably dependent on this or any other mode of governance which rather tends to restrain this fundamental freedom than it would guarantee it. And we have been cognizant of this, e.g. from the modern shape that democracy has adopted which is oftentimes denoted by the notion of 'militant democracy'. However, although no reference is made in this provision to democracy, it should not be forgotten that the Committee still relates freedom of expression to this mode of governance, by, for instance, asserting that this right is of paramount importance in any democratic society in which limitations imposed on the exercise of this right must meet strict tests of justification.[555]

Besides the legal prerequisites that are expounded in this provision for preventing arbitrary usage of power by the government on the one hand, and providing citizens with legal security against this power on the other, it is pertinent to take the following notion into consideration, especially when the limitation of rights and freedoms is, nonetheless, entrusted to the discretion of the state to decide on them as it sees fit. This notion, as mentioned above, is the 'the margin of discretion', also denoted as the 'margin of appreciation' at the European level. The first guarantee – although very vague – against any abuse of this discretion is that, as pointed out, the scope of a limitation imposed by the state authorities who are, in principle, conceived to be in a better position to assess the domestic needs, may not be interpreted in a way that it would jeopardize the essence of the right in question. For instance, in the case of public morals being one of the limiting grounds, it is asserted that: "27. Since public morality varies over time and from one culture to another, a state which invokes public morality as a ground for restricting human rights, while enjoying a certain margin of discretion, shall demonstrate that the limitation in question is essential to the maintenance of respect for fundamental values of the community. 28. [Yet it is imperative to note that] the margin of discretion left to states does not apply to the rule of non-discrimination as defined in the Covenant".[556]

In other words, this discretion and, hence, limiting measures may not be exerted when they would be at odds with this fundamental principle. This brings us therefore to the next pertinent prerequisite which is the non-discrimination principle that can be considered as the fourth condition for limiting fundamental

---

[555] *Shchetko v Belarus*, Communication No. 1009/2001, UN Doc CCPR/C/87/D/1009/2001 (2006)

[556] Siracusa Principles on the Limitation and Derogation of Provisions in the International Covenant on Civil and Political Rights

rights in general and the right to freedom of expression in particular. At the international level, this principle is, in the first place, to be found in Article 1 of the UDHR which states that "*all human beings are born free and equal in dignity and rights. They are endowed with reason and conscience and should act towards one another in a spirit of brotherhood*". Subsequently, this principle can, in its generality, be found in Article 2 of the UDHR which asserts that "*everyone is entitled to all the rights and freedoms set forth in this Declaration, without distinction of any kind, such as race, color, sex, language, religion, political or other opinion, national or social origin, property, birth or other status. Furthermore, no distinction shall be made on the basis of the political, jurisdictional or international status of the country or territory to which a person belongs, whether it be independent, trust, non-self-governing or under any other limitation of sovereignty*". Thus, as Article 7 of the UDHR explicates, infringement of the notion of equality, i.e. discrimination or incitement to discrimination on the basis of the aforementioned grounds, is prohibited by law.[557]

Although the Universal Declaration forms the basis of the international human rights law, it has no legally binding force. Therefore, we have to seek farther for a better comprehension of the principle of non-discrimination. This pursuance brings us to the International Covenant on Civil and Political Rights whereby, as stated below, the non-discrimination principle implicitly undergirds this Covenant and is explicitly mentioned, firstly, in its Article 2 which obliges the states to respect and ensure to all individuals within their territories and subject to their jurisdiction the rights recognized by this Covenant, without any distinction of any kind, such as race, color, sex, language, religion, political or other opinion, national or social origin, property, birth or other status. This principle can, secondly, be found in Article 4 of the ICCPR which is concerned with derogations from the rights and freedoms, provided that such derogatory measures are consistent with the obligations under international law and are not discriminatory on the mere grounds of race, color, sex, language, religion or social origin. Although the non-discrimination principle and the grounds on which it can be based are mentioned in this provision, a further discussion of this Article will, nevertheless, not fall within the scope of the present scrutiny since this inquiry is not concerned with cases of public emergency.

Be that as it may, this provision is relevant to the current research as far as it concerns the prohibition of discrimination and the grounds on which it can be based. Furthermore, this principle can be found in Articles 20, 24 and 26 of this Covenant. Article 24 is concerned with the rights of the child against whom it is forbidden to discriminate based on the aforementioned grounds that are reiterated in this provision, to which national origin, property and birth are added.

[557] Article 7 of the UDHR reads as follows: "All are equal before the law and are entitled without any discrimination to equal protection of the law. All are entitled to equal protection against any discrimination in violation of this Declaration and against any incitement to such discrimination"

However, since our study is not concerned with specific categories or realms, a further discussion of this provision will not fall within the scope of our scrutiny.

As regards Article 26, it can be noted that this provision is, in essence, a reiteration of Article 7 of the UDHR concerning the equality of all persons before the law but also the prohibition of and protection against any form of discrimination[558] whereby, in addition to the aforementioned grounds, the 'political or other opinion' is added. "The Committee both in General Comment 18 and in its jurisprudence has identified article 26 as an autonomous right, that is, a general right of non-discrimination which exists independently and not, as in the case of article 2(1), a parasitic right which is dependent upon the existence of other substantive rights in the Covenant".[559] Furthermore, it is notable that in this provision – besides the provided grounds on which discrimination can take place – through the phraseology 'other status', the opportunity is left open for future grounds to be decided on an *ad hoc* basis about which the drafters had, at the moment of codification, been benighted.[560] This means that the provided grounds on which discrimination can take place are not limitative and exhaustive but merely illustrative. It is also pertinent to reiterate that the non-discrimination principle is not limited to these few provisions but, as the General Comment No. 18 asserts: "1. Non-discrimination, together with equality before the law and equal protection of the law without any discrimination, constitute a basic and general principle relating to the protection of human rights".[561] Although this principle underpins the protection of human rights and freedoms, it has to be borne in mind that, as the Committee also acknowledges, the Covenant neither defines the term 'discrimination' nor indicates what it constitutes. For further clarification, reference is made, among others, to the International Convention on the Elimination of All Forms of Racial Discrimination which will be discussed hereinafter.

Against this background, the Committee concludes that – despite the lack of a definition – it "[...] believes that the term "discrimination" as used in the Covenant should be understood to imply any distinction, exclusion, restriction or preference which is based on any ground such as race, colour, sex, language, religion, political or other opinion, national or social origin, property, birth or other status, and which has the purpose or effect of nullifying or impairing the recognition, enjoyment or exercise by all persons, on an equal footing, of all rights and freedoms'. [Notwithstanding that it draws attention to] 'the enjoyment of rights and freedoms on an equal footing, however, [it] does not mean identical

---

[558] ICCPR General Comment No. 18

[559] Alex Conte and Richard Burchill, *Defining Civil and Political Rights: The Jurisprudence of the United Nations Human Rights Committee* (2nd edn Ashgate Publishing, Surrey 2009) 294

[560] It should be borne in mind that "[...] in order to fall within the definition of 'other status', one must belong to a group which is marked out by some inherent identifying factor which is not susceptible to change" in Alex Conte and Richard Burchill, *Defining Civil and Political Rights: The Jurisprudence of the United Nations Human Rights Committee* (2nd edn Ashgate Publishing, Surrey 2009) 307

[561] ICCPR General Comment No. 18

treatment in every instance".[562] Moreover, besides the aforementioned specific provisions wherein this principle is expounded and "outside the context of Article 4, the principle of non-discrimination becomes involved in the limitation of rights through concepts such as arbitrariness and proportionality"[563], which we have explicated in the context of the legal prerequisites prescribed by Article 19 of the ICCPR for imposing limitations on the right to freedom of expression.

Yet, before continuing, it is important to rehears another provision we have previously mentioned wherein the principle of non-discrimination is also enclosed and which is ineluctable in our exposition on the limitations of the freedom of expression. This concerns Article 20 of the ICCPR, according to which: "*1. Any propaganda for war shall be prohibited by law. 2. Any advocacy of national, racial or religious hatred that constitutes incitement to discrimination, hostility or violence shall be prohibited by law*". The prohibitions as contained in this provision are, in the Committee's point of view, "[...] fully compatible with the right of freedom of expression as contained in article 19, the exercise of which carries with it special duties and responsibilities. The prohibition under paragraph 1 extends to all forms of propaganda threatening or resulting in an act of aggression or breach of the peace contrary to the Charter of the United Nations, while paragraph 2 is directed against any advocacy of national, racial or religious hatred that constitutes incitement to discrimination, hostility or violence, whether such propaganda or advocacy has aims which are internal or external to the State concerned. The provisions of article 20, paragraph 1, do not prohibit advocacy of the sovereign right of self-defense or the right of peoples to self-determination and independence in accordance with the Charter of the United Nations".[564]

In other words, any propaganda for war and any advocacy of national, racial or religious hatred that constitutes incitement to discrimination, hostility or violence is prohibited[565] and can form a justified basis for limiting the freedom of expression for it is conceived to comprise 'hate speech'. In continuing with our discussion of the key principle of non-discrimination in the context of the present inquiry on the freedom of expression, it is imperative to state that, as noted,

---

562 Ibid

563 Alex Conte and Richard Burchill, *Defining Civil and Political Rights: The Jurisprudence of the United Nations Human Rights Committee* (2nd edn Ashgate Publishing, Surrey 2009) 51

564 ICCPR General Comment No. 11

565 In this same vein, (incitement to) genocide (or any order to this end ex Article 33) has to be borne in mind as it is encompassed in the Rome Statute of the International Criminal Court. According to Article 6 of this Statute, genocide entails the following acts committed with the intent to destroy, in whole or in part, a national, ethnical, racial or religious group: a) killing of members of the group; b) causing serious bodily or mental harm to members of the group; c) deliberately inflicting on the group conditions of life calculated to bring about its physical destruction in whole or in part; d) imposing measures intended to prevent births within the group; e) forcibly transferring children of the group to another group. It goes, hence, without saying that incitement to genocide is *par excellence* not covered by the right to freedom of speech for it is, as a serious crime of concern to the international community as a whole (Article 5(a)), inherently unlawful and thus punishable ex Article 25(e) of the Statute

notwithstanding the fact that no universal definition of the principle of non-discrimination is available, the Human Rights Committee attempts to define this principle through a reference to other legal instruments that exclusively deal with it. One of the two instruments referred to is the Convention on the Elimination of All Forms of Discrimination against Women which states in its first provision that "*for the purposes of the present Convention, the term "discrimination against women" shall mean any distinction, exclusion or restriction made on the basis of sex which has the effect or purpose of impairing or nullifying the recognition, enjoyment or exercise by women, irrespective of their marital status, on a basis of equality of men and women, of human rights and fundamental freedoms in the political, economic, social, cultural, civil or any other field*". The other legal instrument which is directly concerned with the prohibition of discrimination in general and confinement of hate speech in particular, and to which the Committee also refers, is the International Convention on the Elimination of All Forms of Racial Discrimination (CERD). This Convention was adopted by General Assembly Resolution 2106 (XX) of 21 December 1965 and entered into force on 4 January 1969. It is supervised by the Committee on the Elimination of Racial Discrimination whose recommendations are employed for further clarification of the provisions that are discussed below.

Discrimination is in this Convention defined in the context of race in the broadest sense of the term. Article 1(1) of the CERD declares that " *'racial discrimination' shall mean any distinction, exclusion, restriction or preference based on race, color, descent, or national or ethnic origin which has the purpose or effect of nullifying or impairing the recognition, enjoyment or exercise, on an equal footing, of human rights and fundamental freedoms in the political, economic, social, cultural or any other field of public life*".[566] What is more, this Convention distinguishes four main categories of hate speech that are contained in Article 4. This Article states that, besides the general obligation that the States Parties have to condemn all propaganda and all organizations involved in racial hatred and discrimination, and to adopt immediate and positive measures designed to eradicate all incitement to, or acts of, such discrimination[567], they

[566] However, as Article 1(2) CERD asserts, this Convention does not "[…] apply to distinctions, exclusions, restrictions or preferences made by a State Party to this Convention between citizens and non-citizens". And, according to paragraph 3 of this provision, "Nothing in this Convention may be interpreted as affecting in any way the legal provisions of States Parties concerning nationality, citizenship or naturalization, provided that such provisions do not discriminate against any particular nationality". Nonetheless, one must "11. Take steps to address xenophobic attitudes and behaviour towards non-citizens, in particular hate speech and racial violence, and to promote a better understanding of the principle of non-discrimination in respect of the situation of non-citizens; 12. Take resolute action to counter any tendency to target, stigmatize, stereotype or profile, on the basis of race, colour, descent, and national or ethnic origin, members of "non-citizen" population groups, especially by politicians, officials, educators and the media, on the Internet and other electronic communications networks and in society at large" in the CERD General Recommendation No. 30

[567] It is worth reminding that, in general, the Human Rights Committee "[…] wishes to point out that the principle of equality sometimes requires States parties to take affirmative action in order to diminish or eliminate conditions which cause or help to perpetuate discrimination

"*shall declare an offence punishable by law all dissemination of ideas based on racial superiority or hatred, incitement to racial discrimination, as well as all acts of violence or incitement to such acts against any race or group of persons of another color or ethnic origin, and also the provision of any assistance to racist activities, including the financing thereof*".[568] These categories are again treated in the General Recommendation No. 15 which asserts that "Article 4 (a) requires States parties to penalize four categories of misconduct: (i) dissemination of ideas based upon racial superiority or hatred; (ii) incitement to racial hatred; (iii) acts of violence against any race or group of persons of another color or ethnic origin; and (iv) incitement to such acts".[569] In addition, the Committee explicitly confirms that, as we have also extensively elaborated hitherto, "[...] the prohibition of the dissemination of all ideas based upon racial superiority or hatred is compatible with the right to freedom of opinion and expression. This right is embodied in article 19 of the Universal Declaration of Human Rights and is recalled in article 5 (d) (viii) of the International Convention on the Elimination of All Forms of Racial Discrimination. Its relevance to article 4 is noted in the article itself. The citizen's exercise of this right carries special duties and responsibilities, specified in article 29, paragraph 2, of the Universal Declaration, among which the obligation not to disseminate racist ideas is of particular importance. The Committee wishes, furthermore, to draw to the attention of States parties article 20 of the International Covenant on Civil and Political Rights, according to which any advocacy of national, racial or religious hatred that constitutes incitement to discrimination, hostility or violence shall be prohibited by law".[570] In addition, it ought to be kept in mind that any restriction has to be justified by the tripartite test provided in Article 19(3) of the ICCPR.[571]

It is worth recalling that, as noted above, the International Convention on the Elimination of All Forms of Racial Discrimination is concerned solely with the ground of race whereupon discrimination can be based. In this regard, it is imperative to take the legal history of this Convention into consideration. During its preparatory phase, the GA Third Committee had already made a distinction between religion and race by adopting two different resolutions concerning the preparation of a draft declaration and a draft convention. One is based on the

prohibited by the Covenant"; ICCPR General Comment No. 18, General Comment No. 3, General Comment No. 4

[568] The state parties can, *nota bene*, not only declare discrimination in the broadest sense of the term based on race an offence punishable by law but they can, according to the sequent paragraphs of this provision, declare "(b) illegal and prohibit organizations, and also organized and all other propaganda activities, which promote and incite racial discrimination, and shall recognize participation in such organizations or activities as an offence punishable by law; [and they] (c) shall not permit public authorities or public institutions, national or local, to promote or incite racial discrimination"

[569] CERD General Recommendation No. 15

[570] Ibid

[571] This comes to the fore in various communications, an example of which is the *Ross v Canada* Communication No. 736/1997 rendered on 18 October 2000

elimination of all forms of religious intolerance[572] and the other on the elimination of all forms of racial discrimination.[573]

Hence, from the very beginning, various grounds for discrimination have been identified. "The decision to separate the instruments on religious intolerance from those on racial discrimination is considered a compromise solution, intended to overcome the opposition to a joint instrument, emanating primarily from Arab delegations eager to displace the question of anti-Semitism, and from Communist representatives, who did not consider religious discrimination an important matter".[574] While a distinction has been made between race and religion since the former is, unlike the latter, unchangeable, nonetheless, it is imperative to recognize "[...] the importance of the intersection of religion and race and that instances can arise of multiple or aggravated forms of discrimination on the basis of religion and other grounds, such as race, color, descent or national or ethnic origin".[575] This is why it needs to be reaffirmed that General Recommendation No. 15, in which the Committee stipulates that the prohibition of dissemination of ideas based on racial superiority or hatred is compatible with the freedom of opinion and expression, is equally applicable to the questions concerning incitement to religious hatred.[576]

Nevertheless, the bearing of the Arab delegations is ambiguous since, as elaborated hereafter, they have been willing to adopt legal instruments to not only combat discrimination against persons based on their religion, but also to protect religion and religious symbols against offensive incitements – even if their emphasis has also been solely on Islam. However, in the aforementioned discourse on discrimination, the accent remained on the concept of race and, in this light, Resolution 1780 (XVIII) charged the Economic and Social Council with the preparation of a draft declaration and international convention on the elimination of all forms of racial discrimination, both to be respectively submitted to the eighteenth and nineteenth session. The Declaration on the Elimination of all Forms of Racial Discrimination was adopted by means of Resolution 1904 (XVIII) on 20 November 1963 and the Convention was adopted through Resolution 2106 (XX) on 21 December 1965. As regards the endeavors concerning religious discrimination, no further progress has been made except the adoption of the Declaration on the Elimination of All forms of Intolerance and of Discrimination based on Religion or Belief through UN General Assembly Resolution 36/55 on 25 November 1981.[577]

---

572 UNGA Res 1781 (XVII) (7 December 1962)

573 UNGA Res 1780 (XVII) (7 December 1962)

574 Natan Lerner, *The U.N. Convention on the Elimination of All Forms of Racial Discrimination* (Noordhoff International Publishers, Alphen aan de Rijn 1980) 2

575 UNGA Res 64/156 (8 March 2010) UN Doc A/RES/64/156

576 UNHRC Res 7/19, 'Combating defamation of religions' (27 March 2008) UN Doc A/HRC/RES/7/19. UNGA Res 63/171 (24 March 2009) UN Doc A/RES/63/171, UNHRC Res 10/22, 'Combating defamation of religions' (26 March 2009) UN Doc A/HRC/RES/10/22

577 UNGA Res 36/55 (25 November 1981) UN Doc A/RES/36/55. For the furtherance of this, the UN Commission on Human Rights had established, in the light of UNCHR Res 20 (1986) UN Doc E/CN.4/RES/1986/20, the Special Rapporteur on Religion Intolerance. In 2000, the

Although no other independent and exclusive achievements have been recorded on this particular discriminatory ground[578] – except the attempts in the last decade concerning the defamation of religion as expounded below – the notion of religion[579] has been incorporated into various international human rights laws[580] such as, among others, the Universal Declaration of Human Rights[581], the International Covenant on Civil and Political Rights[582], the Convention on the Elimination of All Forms of Racial Discrimination, and in the Declaration on the Rights of Persons Belonging to National or Ethnic, Religious and Linguistic Minorities. Much can be said about the fundamental right to

---

name of this mandate was changed into Special Rapporteur on Freedom of Religion or Belief which was embraced by the ECOSOC decision 2000/261 and the UNGA Res 55/97 (4 December 2000) UN Doc A/RES/55/97. This Declaration asserts in its Article 2(2) that "for the purposes of the present Declaration, the expression "intolerance and discrimination based on religion or belief" means any distinction, exclusion, restriction or preference based on religion or belief and having as its purpose or as its effect nullification or impairment of the recognition, enjoyment or exercise of human rights and fundamental freedoms on an equal basis". And any "discrimination between human beings on grounds of religion or belief constitutes an affront to human dignity and a disavowal of the principles of the Charter of the United Nations, and shall be condemned as a violation of the human rights and fundamental freedoms proclaimed in the Universal Declaration of Human Rights and elucidated in detail in the International Covenants on Human Rights, and as an obstacle to friendly and peaceful relations between nations" ex Article 3 of this Declaration

578 Natan Lerner, *Group Rights and Discrimination in International Law* (International Studies in Human Rights, 2nd edn Martinus Nijhoff Publishers, The Hague 2003) 84

579 As Jennifer Jackson Preece rightly asserts, and as we can read in the provisions regulating the fundamental right to freedom of religion, "[...] religion has two dimensions: the one private and deeply personal arising out of the innermost convictions of the individual; the other public and resulting from the practical effect of those convictions not only on the individual but also on the community to whom he or she belongs' [and hence] 'While religious belief may be best described as an internal state of mind, the exercise of that belief is to a large extent a social practice sustained by shared doctrines, myths, rituals, sentiments and institutions" in Jennifer Jackson Preece, *Minority Rights* (Polity, Cambridge 2005) 18

580 The fundamental right to freedom of religion is, as Article 4(2) of the ICCPR states, a non-derogable fundamental right

581 Article 18 of the Universal Declaration of Human Rights states: "*Everyone has the right to freedom of thought, conscience and religion; this right includes freedom to change his religion or belief, and freedom, either alone or in community with others and in public or private, to manifest his religion or belief in teaching, practice, worship and observance*"

582 Article 18 of the International Covenant on Civil and Political Rights reads as follows: "*1. Everyone shall have the right to freedom of thought, conscience and religion. This right shall include freedom to have or to adopt a religion or belief of his choice, and freedom, either individually or in community with others and in public or private, to manifest his religion or belief in worship, observance, practice and teaching. 2. No one shall be subject to coercion which would impair his freedom to have or to adopt a religion or belief of his choice. 3. Freedom to manifest one's religion or beliefs may be subject only to such limitations as are prescribed by law and are necessary to protect public safety, order, health, or morals or the fundamental rights and freedoms of others. 4. The States Parties to the present Covenant undertake to have respect for the liberty of parents and, when applicable, legal guardians to ensure the religious and moral education of their children in conformity with their own convictions*"

freedom of religion but since there are books in abundance on this right from innumerable angles, the scope of the current discourse is narrowed to only one facet of it that ought to be taken into consideration. This facet concerns the fact that the right to freedom of thought, conscience and religion aims not to protect the thought, conscience or religion as such but rather the bearer of this right. Therefore, it is prohibited to discriminate against the human person but not against thought, conscience or religion. Although no distinct legal instrument has been adopted for the protection of the human person against discrimination on the basis of religion, it goes without saying that religion is a solid ground on the basis of which discrimination of the human person is prohibited. This is, for instance, evident from the fact that this ground is even recognized in the Convention on the Elimination of All Forms of Racial Discrimination as can be read in its Preamble.[583] Thus, although no legal instrument that exclusively deals with this ground is available and that this Convention, like the Convention on the Elimination of All Forms of Discrimination against Women, does not explicitly deal with it, the term 'discrimination', as elucidated heretofore, has to be conceived in its generality to imply any distinction, exclusion, restriction or preference which is based on grounds such as race, color, sex, language, religion, political or other opinion, national or social origin, property, birth or other status, with the purpose or effect of nullifying or impairing such recognition, enjoyment or exercise by all persons, on an equal footing, of all rights and freedoms.[584]

The grounds whereupon discrimination can be based are oftentimes protected by means of the so-called minority rights. In this context, Article 27 of the ICCPR is pivotal for the comprehension of this sort of rights. This Article asserts that "*in those States in which ethnic, religious or linguistic minorities exist, persons belonging to such minorities shall not be denied the right, in community with the other members of their group, to enjoy their own culture, to profess and practice their own religion, or to use their own language*".[585] By referring to this provision, "the Committee observes that this article establishes and recognizes a right which is conferred on individuals belonging to minority groups and which

[583] Preamble of the International Convention on the Elimination of All Forms of Racial Discrimination

[584] ICCPR General Comment No. 18; it should not be forgotten that "the enjoyment of rights and freedoms on an equal footing does, however, not mean identical treatment in every instance' [and that] 'not every differentiation of treatment will constitute discrimination, if the criteria for such differentiation are reasonable and objective and if the aim is to achieve a purpose which is legitimate under the Covenant". For further elaboration of these conditions, see Alex Conte and Richard Burchill, *Defining Civil and Political Rights: The Jurisprudence of the United Nations Human Rights Committee* (2nd edn Ashgate Publishing, Surrey 2009) 310

[585] As regards 'cultural rights', the ICCPR General Comment No. 23 observes that "[…] culture manifests itself in many forms, including a particular way of life associated with the use of land resources, especially in the case of indigenous peoples". However, as the Committee asserted in *Ilmari Länsman et al. v Finland*, Communication No. 511/1992, UN Doc CCPR/C/52/D/511/1992 (1994), "Article 27 does not only protect traditional means of livelihood of national minorities". It is worth noting that the notion of 'minority rights' and 'cultural rights' are oftentimes used interchangeably as synonyms

is distinct from, and additional to, all the other rights which, as individuals in common with everyone else, they are already entitled to enjoy under the Covenant".[586] Thence, any misunderstanding as regards the question of who the bearer of the right in this provision is has to be avoided since, as it has been clearly asserted, it concerns a right which is conferred[587] to individuals as such, i.e. individuals are the bearers of this right and not the community to which they belong.[588] What is more, this provision is not to be confused with Article 2(1) and Article 26 of the ICCPR albeit interrelated.

As the Committee explains at length, the Covenant "[...] distinguishes the rights protected under article 27 from the guarantees under articles 2.1 and 26. The entitlement, under article 2.1, to enjoy the rights under the Covenant without discrimination applies to all individuals within the territory or under the jurisdiction of the State whether or not those persons belong to a minority. In addition, there is a distinct right provided under article 26 for equality before the law, equal protection of the law, and non-discrimination in respect of rights granted and obligations imposed by the States. It governs the exercise of all rights, whether protected under the Covenant or not, which the State party confers by law on individuals within its territory or under its jurisdiction, irrespective of whether they belong to the minorities specified in article 27 or not. Some States parties who claim that they do not discriminate on grounds of ethnicity, language or religion, wrongly contend, on that basis alone, that they have no minorities. The terms used in article 27 indicate that the persons designed to be protected are those who belong to a group and who share in common a culture, a religion and/or a language. Those terms also indicate that the individuals designed to be protected need not be citizens of the State party. In this regard, the obligations deriving from article 2.1 are also relevant, since a State party is required under that article to ensure that the rights protected under the Covenant are available to all individuals within its territory and subject to its jurisdiction, except rights which are expressly made to apply to citizens, for example, political rights under article 25. A State party may not, therefore, restrict the rights under article 27 to its citizens alone. Article 27 confers rights on persons belonging to minorities which 'exist' in a State party. Given the nature and scope of the rights envisaged under that article, it is not relevant to determine the degree of permanence that the term 'exist' connotes. Those rights simply are that individuals belonging to those minorities should not be denied the right, in community with members of their group, to enjoy their own culture, to practice their religion and speak their language. Just as they need not be nationals

---

[586] ICCPR General Comment No. 23

[587] ICCPR General Comment No. 23 states that "although article 27 is expressed in negative terms, that article, nevertheless, does recognize the existence of a "right" and requires that it shall not be denied. Consequently, a State party is under an obligation to ensure that the existence and the exercise of this right are protected against their denial or violation. Positive measures of protection are, therefore, required not only against the acts of the State party itself, whether through its legislative, judicial or administrative authorities, but also against the acts of other persons within the State party"

[588] *Lovelace v Canada,* Communication No. 24/1977, UN Doc CCPR/C/13/D/24/1977 (1981)

or citizens, they need not be permanent residents. Thus, migrant workers or even visitors in a State party constituting such minorities are entitled not to be denied the exercise of those rights. As any other individual in the territory of the State party, they would, also for this purpose, have the general rights, for example, to freedom of association, of assembly, and of expression. The existence of an ethnic, religious or linguistic minority in a given State party does not depend upon a decision by that State party but requires to be established by objective criteria".[589] The interesting aspect of this provision is that the scope of it is not confined to citizens only, which is crucial if considered in the light of the atrocities of the Second World War whereby, as discussed earlier in this research, the loss of citizenship implied the loss of all human rights. However, it has again to be emphasized that this provision confers rights – without creating more rights[590] – only to individuals and not their communities as, besides the wording of this provision itself, it has also become apparent in terms of the jurisprudence of the Committee.[591]

Furthermore, it is worth noting that in the case of conflict with other fundamental rights, "the Committee observes that none of the rights protected under article 27 of the Covenant may be legitimately exercised in a manner or to an extent inconsistent with the other provisions of the Covenant", but, in the context of contemporary pluralistic societies, as some allege, the more pluralism is accelerated, the more resolute minority groups would be – whereby their ends would justify their means – and the more likely it would be that the freedom of expression will be curtailed through, among others, concessions and negotiations.[592] The reason for this might be found, perhaps, in the thoughts of Jennifer Jackson Preece who posits 'freedom' and 'belonging' as each other's opposites. She argues, namely, that "[...] there is a fundamental paradox implicit within this characterization of the human condition. Freedom and belonging may be equally important for human flourishing but they nevertheless remain mutually incommensurate and potentially competing values. Freedom requires autonomy of action; belonging requires coordination and in some situations subordination of autonomous action to preserve the social relationship on which it is based. Freedom necessitates and indeed perpetuates a diversity of choices and so promotes a variety of values, beliefs and identities; belonging necessitates and indeed perpetuates social cohesion and so constrains choices to preserve a common identity and its concomitant values and beliefs. Freedom encourages innovation; belonging encourages orthodoxy. Freedom creates diversity; belonging creates uniformity. At some point, these values will collide and that collision is likely to foster uncertainty, suspicion, fear and even conflict. It is precisely this collision of values which makes the existence of diversity within

589 ICCPR General Comment No. 23

590 Alex Conte and Richard Burchill, *Defining Civil and Political Rights: The Jurisprudence of the United Nations Human Rights Committee* (2nd edn Ashgate Publishing, Surrey 2009) 264

591 *Lovelace v Canada,* Communication No. 24/1977, UN Doc CCPR/C/13/D/24/1977 (1981)

592 Paul Cliteur, *Het Monotheïstisch Dilemma* (Uitgeverij De Arbeiderspers, Amsterdam 2010) 119-122

humankind, especially that religious, racial, linguistic and ethnic diversity which has long been a hallmark of distinct human communities, a potential source of insecurity and conflict".[593] This we currently witness in the civilizational collisions around the globe in general, and in the Western democratic societies in particular.

The foregoing explication brings us to the conclusion that the right to freedom of expression is not an unlimited right but is rather subject to legal limitations as they are codified in various legal instruments that we have thus far elucidated in this study. Yet beyond the limitations codified in the law, contemporary world affairs leave no doubt about the fact that – as we had scrutinized in the first part of this research – civilizational collisions which take place at the international, European and national level do not leave fundamental human rights in general and freedom of expression in particular unaffected. Limitations stemming from these changing world affairs are, however, not codified and are hardly overseen and measured. This is why the question remains over the extent to which these clashes that we had elaborated earlier in this research are still able to curtail the fundamental right to freedom of expression. Against this background, in the following section, an attempt will be made to elaborate on this question in the light of contemporary legal developments at the first level – the international level – where these collisions take place.

2.3.2. Limitations of Freedom of Expression in a Globalized Age

As pointed out in the preceding paragraph, the fundamental right to freedom of expression is not an absolute right, which means that it can be confined by means of limitations that are prescribed by law. One of the prime means that can restrain this right is the principle of non-discrimination which can be based on various grounds. One of the grounds upon which discrimination is prohibited is 'religion' in the broadest sense of the term, which, however, is not independently codified in a distinct legal instrument. This ground is merely formulated as a right among other rights that, in the case of collision with the right to freedom of expression, can impose a limitation on this latter right. The provisions on the right to freedom of religion protect the individual as the sole bearer of this right in both its internal and external dimension, which may be respectively designated as '*forum internum*' and '*forum externum*'.[594] This means that protection is

[593] Jennifer Jackson Preece, *Minority Rights* (Polity, Cambridge 2005) 5-6

[594] The freedom of religion as contained in Article 18 of the ICCPR is, in principle, a non-derogable right, even in time of public emergency, as it is prescribed in Article 4(2) of the ICCPR and re-emphasized in the General Comment No. 22 and 29. The permissibility of restrictions is, however, independent from the issue of derogability and must be justified on the basis of paragraph 3 of Article 18 ICCPR. It is imperative to note that only the *manifestation* of a religion or belief may be subjected to limitations since, according to Article 20 of the ICCPR and General Comment No. 11, 19, and 22, no manifestation of religion or belief may amount to, among others, discrimination, violence or hostility. Thus, not the '*forum internum*' of religion may be limited, but only its '*forum externum*'

provided to the religious person and not to religion as such. Nevertheless, as we will elaborate hereinafter, in recent years, and by means of defamation laws, an attempt has been made to extend the scope of protection beyond the bearer of this right so that protection would also be provided to the objects and symbols of religion.

This extension can be said to come down to the broadening of the ambit of the external dimension of religion, for not only the mere expression of religious conviction is covered, but also the means through which such conviction is manifested. Such manifestation can adopt the following forms: "(a) To worship or assemble in connection with a religion or belief, and to establish and maintain places for these purposes; (b) To establish and maintain appropriate charitable or humanitarian institutions; (c) To make, acquire and use to an adequate extent the necessary articles and materials related to the rites or customs of a religion or belief; (d) To write, issue and disseminate relevant publications in these areas; (e) To teach a religion or belief in places suitable for these purposes; (f) To solicit and receive voluntary financial and other contributions from individuals and institutions; (g) To train, appoint, elect or designate by succession appropriate leaders called for by the requirements and standards of any religion or belief; (h) To observe days of rest and to celebrate holidays and ceremonies in accordance with the precepts of one's religion or belief; (i) To establish and maintain communications with individuals and communities in matters of religion and belief at the national and international levels".[595] It goes without saying that the endeavor to extend this scope will have the consequence that not only the individual as the bearer of this right will be protected but also 'religion' as such – encompassing doctrines and symbols of veneration – will gain protection, with possible implication(s) for other fundamental rights in general and the right to freedom of expression in particular.

As regards the limitations to fundamental rights and freedoms, particularly the right to freedom of expression, it can be observed that the competence for doing this has always been negatively defined. This negative formulation implies that the enjoyment of rights can take place only when governmental interference is minimized and the government is forced to refrain from any (arbitrary) involvement in the exercise of fundamental rights by its citizens. On the contrary, fundamental rights have also been conceived as containing positive obligation which encompasses not only an active involvement of the government in respecting, protecting and fostering such rights in the conduct of its own functions but it "[...] also requires States parties to ensure that persons are protected from any acts by private persons or entities that would impair the enjoyment of [such rights, particularly] the freedoms of opinion and expression to the extent that these Covenant rights are amenable to application between private persons or entities".[596] This latter is especially interesting in light of

---

[595] Article 6 of the Declaration on the Elimination of All Forms of Intolerance and of Discrimination Based on Religion or Belief

[596] ICCPR General Comment No. 34, and 31; See also *Gauthier v Canada*, Communication No. 633/1995

contemporary developments whereby the fundamental right to freedom of expression is jeopardized not only by the state itself but also by other actors, which Cliteur rightly brings to attention in that "since 1989 the world has become acquainted with a new situation concerning the notion of the freedom of speech. Prior to that time, the most important restriction of this freedom was formed by the *legislation* of the nation-states. After that time, there have also been organized and unorganized *violent networks and individuals* that constrain an effective exercise of the freedom of speech".[597] Notwithstanding this development regarding the extrajudicial confinement of this fundamental right, the official parties involved put the emphasis on the classical limitations imposed by the state, which is also seen in the legal history of this provision.[598] This emphasis on the role of the state, and the menace posed by it, has always been pivotal even after the terrorist attacks on the United States whereby – even though such terrorist outrages are defined as crimes against humanity[599] and their negative impact and challenge to human rights and democracy are regretted[600] – we can observe that "the notion of national security has historically been abused to impose unduly broad limitations on freedom of expression, and this has become a particular problem in the aftermath of the attacks of September 2001, and renewed efforts to combat terrorism"[601], especially when it is kept in mind that "soon after those attacks, and in response to them, the government of President George W. Bush embarked upon a systematic campaign of internationally wrongful acts involving the secret detention, rendition and torture of terrorist suspects"[602]; also the NSA spying scandal under President Barack

[597] Afshin Ellian, Gelijn Molier and Tom Zwart (eds), *Mag ik dit zeggen? Beschouwingen over de vrijheid van meningsuiting* (Boom Juridische Uitgevers, The Hague 2011) 67 [own translation]

[598] "The first drafts of the article contained [already] a clause to the effect that every person should have the right to freedom of opinion and expression without interference by governmental action. [...] As originally proposed, the phrase 'without interference' was followed by the phrase 'by governmental action'. There were [however] two views regarding this point. One was that the article was intended to protect the individual only against governmental interference [...]. The other view was that the article should protect the individual against all kinds of interference [...]." in Marc J Bossuyt, *Guide to the 'travaux préparatoires' of the International Covenant on Civil and Political Rights* (Martinus Nijhoff Publishers, Dordrecht 1987) 378-379

[599] UNCHR, Twenty-second session 'Report of the Special Rapporteur on the promotion and protection of human rights and fundamental freedoms while countering terrorism. Framework Principles for securing the accountability of public officials for gross or systematic human rights violations committed in the context of State counter-terrorism initiatives' (1 March 2013) UN Doc A/HRC/22/52

[600] UNCHR Res 23 (1999) UN Doc E/CN.4/RES/1999/167

[601] UNHRC, Fourteenth session 'Report of the Special Rapporteur on the promotion and protection of the rights to freedom of opinion and expression' (25 March 2010) UN Doc A/HRC/14/23/Add.2

[602] UNCHR, Twenty-second session 'Report of the Special Rapporteur on the promotion and protection of human rights and fundamental freedoms while countering terrorism. Framework Principles for securing the accountability of public officials for gross or systematic human

Hussein Obama has made the freedom of expression, especially in the context of cyberspace, an illusion. Thus, there needs to be a balance between legitimate national security concerns and fundamental freedoms. For it seems that "in the context of the fight against terrorism and the reaction to counter-terrorism measures, defamation of religions becomes an aggravating factor that contributes to the denial of fundamental rights and freedoms of target groups, as well as their economic and social exclusion"[603], without, however, making explicit the opposite impact of terrorist acts, committed by violent networks and individuals, on fundamental rights and freedoms.

Although the wrongful acts committed by the Western democracies can by no means be justified for, as Friedrich Nietzsche rightly stated, "*Wer mit Ungeheuern kämpft, mag zusehn, dass er nicht dabei zum Ungeheuer wird*"[604], the existence of the menace and constraints imposed on this fundamental right stemming from non-state actors is, nevertheless, trivialized, minimized, and mentioned only sporadically without any serious attention being paid, for instance, to the reasoning of the Special Rapporteur on this fundamental right who asserts that "the traditional approach to the negation of the rights that are set out in international human rights instruments is generally confined to the question of violations of rights by Governments and their agents. Rightly, concern is expressed that any attempt to address the actions of non-State actors runs the risk of detracting from the responsibility of States not to violate the rights of citizens and others living within their territories. The Special Rapporteur also notes that the question of non-State actors has been traditionally defined as relating to the duty of States to exercise due diligence and to ensure that individuals and collective private entities respect the law and do not abuse or infringe upon the rights of others. The Special Rapporteur accepts that the primary attention must continue to be focused on the commissions and omissions of Governments which lead to violations of fundamental rights. At the same time, however, he cannot remain indifferent to the fact that, with regard to the rights that are the subject of this mandate, an increasing number of actions by non-State individuals and entities have a marked and severely negative impact on the enjoyment of those rights by others".[605] This reasoning clarifies that whereas the existence of the menace stemming from non-state actors is undeniable,

---

rights violations committed in the context of State counter-terrorism initiatives' (1 March 2013) UN Doc A/HRC/22/52

[603] UNCHR Res 3 (2005) UN Doc E/CN.4/RES/2005/3, UNGA Res 60/150 (20 January 2006) UN Doc A/RES/60/150, UNGA Res 62/154 (6 March 2008) UN Doc A/RES/62/154, UNHRC Res 7/19, 'Combating defamation of religions' (27 March 2008) UN Doc A/HRC/RES/7/19, UNGA Res 63/171 (24 March 2009) UN Doc A/RES/63/171, UNGA Res 64/156 (8 March 2010) UN Doc A/RES/64/156

[604] Rolf-Peter Horstman and Judith Norman (eds), *Nietzsche: Beyond Good and Evil* (CUP, Cambridge 2002) (Aphorism 146: Whoever fights with monsters should see to it that he does not become one himself)

[605] UNCHR 'Civil and Political Rights, Including the Question of Freedom of Expression: Report of the Special Rapporteur on the promotion and protection of the right to freedom of opinion and expression' (13 February 2001) UN Doc E/CN.4/2001/64

nonetheless, no serious attention is paid to this perilous phenomenon while, for example, Article 5(1) ICCPR[606] explicitly emphasizes that "nothing in the present Covenant may be interpreted as implying for any State [but also] *group* or *person* any right to engage in any activity or perform any act aimed at the destruction of any of the rights and freedoms recognized herein or at their limitation to a greater extent than is provided for in the present Covenant".[607]

Still, the current extrajudicial curtailment of this fundamental right takes place because certain individuals and groups in society tend to be offended by utterances about their religion, whereas the right to freedom of expression encompasses also expression that may be regarded as deeply offensive[608], so long as the exercise of this right, which carries with it 'special duties and responsibilities', meets the legal conditions enumerated in Article 19(3) and the limitations elucidated in Article 20[609] of the ICCPR. This implies then that while expressions may be offensive, robust and critical vis-à-vis religious doctrines and practice, even in a harsh manner,[610] they may, nevertheless, not amount to advocacy of hatred that would constitute incitement to discrimination, hostility or violence.[611] As long as this is not the case, as Principle 12(3) of the Camden Principles on Freedom of Expression and Equality provides, "states should not prohibit criticism directed at, or debate about, particular ideas, beliefs or ideologies, or religions or religious institutions". That being said, since 1999, the concept of 'defamation of religion' has been pushed forward within the UN framework by mainly, if not solely, the Organization of the Islamic Conference[612] and, subsequently, in that same year applauded by the Economic

---

[606] The counterpart of this can also be found in Article 17 of the ECHR which reads as follows: "*Nothing in this Convention may be interpreted as implying for any State, group or person any right to engage in any activity or perform any act aimed at the destruction on any of the rights and freedoms set forth herein or at their limitation to a greater extent than is provided for in the Convention*".

[607] ICCPR General Comment No. 34, *Velichkin v Belarus*, Communication No. 1022/2001. The same is reiterated in Article 5 of the ICESCR [emphasis added]

[608] *Ross v Canada* Communication No.736/1997 rendered on 18 October 2000

[609] Article 20 ICCPR reads as follows: "*1. Any propaganda for war shall be prohibited by law. 2. Any advocacy of national, racial or religious hatred that constitutes incitement to discrimination, hostility or violence shall be prohibited by law*". ICCPR General Comment No. 11

[610] UNHRC, 'Report of the Special Rapporteur on the Promotion and protection of the right to freedom of opinion and expression' (2012) UN Doc A/67/357

[611] As the Camden Principles on Freedom of Expression and Equality defines in Principle 12: "The term 'hatred' and 'hostility' refer to intense and irrational emotions of opprobrium, enmity and detestation towards the target group. The term 'advocacy' is to be understood as requiring an intention to promote hatred publicly towards the target group. The term 'incitement' refers to statements about national, racial or religious groups which create an imminent risk of discrimination, hostility or violence against persons belonging to those groups".[611] UNCHR Res 23 (1999) UN Doc E/CN.4/RES/1999/167

[612] This idea was, for the first time, fostered by the Organization of the Islamic Conference by means of a draft resolution submitted by Pakistan to the UN Commission on Human Rights in 1999; UNCHR 'Racism, Racial Discrimination, Xenophobia and all Forms of Discrimination' (20 April 1999) UN Doc E/CN.4/1999/L.40. For further information see Austin Dacey, *The*

and Social Council for addressing it within the context of 'the United Nations Year of Dialogue among Civilizations'.[613] With this concept, an attempt is made to effectively combat defamation of religions and cultures as a means of promoting human rights, social harmony, religious and cultural diversity[614] – considered to be a cherished asset for the advancement and welfare of humanity at large[615] – in order to improve, among others, awareness and understanding of the common values shared by all humankind[616], and to use "religious and cultural diversity in a globalized world as a vehicle for complementary creativity and dynamism, and not as a rationale for a new ideological and political confrontation".[617] This discourse on defamation of religion started with the recognition that hatred, intolerance, acts of (psychological and physical) violence and discrimination *against human beings* on the grounds of religion or belief constitute an affront and offense to human dignity, a disavowal of the principles of the Charter of the United Nations[618], and violation and illicit restriction of

---

Future of Blasphemy: Speaking of the sacred in an age of human rights (Continuum, London 2012)

[613] UNCHR Res 23 (1999) UN Doc E/CN.4/RES/1999/167, UNCHR Res 84 (2000) UN Doc E/CN.4/RES/2000/84. UNCHR Res 4 (2001) UN Doc E/CN.4/RES/2001/4, UNCHR Res 9 (2002) UN Doc E/CN.4/RES/2002/9, The purpose of this is formulated as follows: "that religious and cultural diversity in the globalizing world needs to be used as a vehicle for complementary creativity and dynamism and not as a rationale for a new ideological and political confrontation" in UNCHR Res 4 (2003) UN Doc E/CN.4/RES/2003/4, UNCHR Res 6 (2004) UN Doc E/CN.4/RES/2004/6, UNCHR Res 3 (2005) UN Doc E/CN.4/RES/2005/3, UNGA Res 60/150 (20 January 2006) UN Doc A/RES/60/150, UNGA Res 64/156 (8 March 2010) UN Doc A/RES/64/156

[614] UNCHR Res 4 (2001) UN Doc E/CN.4/RES/2001/4, UNCHR Res 9 (2002) UN Doc E/CN.4/RES/2002/9, UNCHR Res 4 (2003) UN Doc E/CN.4/RES/2003/4, UNGA Res 60/150 (20 January 2006) UN Doc A/RES/60/150. Later on, also ethnic and linguistic diversity is added to this list. See UNGA Res 63/171 (24 March 2009) UN Doc A/RES/63/171, UNHRC Res 10/22, 'Combating defamation of religions' (26 March 2009) UN Doc A/HRC/RES/10/22, UNGA Res 64/156 (8 March 2010) UN Doc A/RES/64/156

[615] UNGA Res 60/150 (20 January 2006) UN Doc A/RES/60/150

[616] UNCHR Res 9 (2002) UN Doc E/CN.4/RES/2002/9, UNCHR Res 4 (2003) UN Doc E/CN.4/RES/2003/4, UNCHR Res 3 (2005) UN Doc E/CN.4/RES/2005/3, UNGA Res 61/164 (21 February 2007) UN Doc A/RES/61/164, UNHRC Res 4/9, 'Combating defamation of religions' (30 March 2007) UN Doc A/HRC/RES/4/9, UNGA Res 62/154 (6 March 2008) UN Doc A/RES/62/154, UNHRC Res 7/19, 'Combating defamation of religions' (27 March 2008) UN Doc A/HRC/RES/7/19, UNGA Res 63/171 (24 March 2009) UN Doc A/RES/63/171, UNHRC Res 10/22, 'Combating defamation of religions' (26 March 2009) UN Doc A/HRC/RES/10/22, UNGA Res 64/156 (8 March 2010) UN Doc A/RES/64/156. The question remains as to what these common values, that are held to be shared by all humankind, amount to

[617] UNCHR Res 6 (2004) UN Doc E/CN.4/RES/2004/6, UNCHR Res 3 (2005) UN Doc E/CN.4/RES/2005/3

[618] UNCHR Res 23 (1999) UN Doc E/CN.4/RES/1999/167, UNCHR Res 84 (2000) UN Doc E/CN.4/RES/2000/84, UNCHR Res 9 (2002) UN Doc E/CN.4/RES/2002/9, UNCHR Res 4 (2003) UN Doc E/CN.4/RES/2003/4, UNCHR Res 6 (2004) UN Doc E/CN.4/RES/2004/6, UNCHR Res 3 (2005) UN Doc E/CN.4/RES/2005/3, UNGA Res 60/150 (20 January 2006) UN Doc A/RES/60/150, UNHRC Dec 1/107, 'Incitement to racial and religious hatred and the

human rights and fundamental freedoms.[619] In this regard, states had been summoned to counter intolerance and related violence based on religion or belief[620] by taking the necessary measures, since it had been considered imperative to create conditions for fostering and encouraging greater harmony, peace, social justice, and tolerance within and among societies – through, among others, interreligious and intercultural dialogue.[621] Here, the aim is to promote mutual understanding and appreciation of religious and cultural diversity and values[622], to ensure *tolerance of and [universal] respect for religion and belief* and their value systems, and, in the same context, to combat attacks on *religious places, [sites, shrines, symbols, and venerated personalities]*.[623] Henceforth, we see the shift in protection from persons to ideologies in the broadest sense of the term, which is still contradictory to the very essence of human rights. Yet, in this endeavor, deep concern is expressed at the negative stereotyping of religions and intensification of the campaign to defame religions[624] in general and Islam in

promotion of tolerance' (30 June 2006) UN Doc A/HRC/DEC/1/107, UNGA Res 61/164 (21 February 2007) UN Doc A/RES/61/164, UNGA Res 62/154 (6 March 2008) UN Doc A/RES/62/154, UNHRC Res 7/19, 'Combating defamation of religions' (27 March 2008) UN Doc A/HRC/RES/7/19, UNGA Res 63/171 (24 March 2009) UN Doc A/RES/63/171, UNHRC Res 10/22, 'Combating defamation of religions' (26 March 2009) UN Doc A/HRC/RES/10/22, UNGA Res 64/156 (8 March 2010) UN Doc A/RES/64/156

[619] UNCHR Res 4 (2001) UN Doc E/CN.4/RES/2001/4, UNGA Res 63/171 (24 March 2009) UN Doc A/RES/63/171 [emphasis added]

[620] UNCHR Res 23 (1999) UN Doc E/CN.4/RES/1999/167

[621] UNHRC Res 4/9, 'Combating defamation of religions' (30 March 2007) UN Doc A/HRC/RES/4/9, UNHRC Res 7/19, 'Combating defamation of religions' (27 March 2008) UN Doc A/HRC/RES/7/19

[622] UNCHR Res 4 (2001) UN Doc E/CN.4/RES/2001/4, UNCHR Res 9 (2002) UN Doc E/CN.4/RES/2002/9, UNCHR Res 4 (2003) UN Doc E/CN.4/RES/2003/4, UNCHR Res 6 (2004) UN Doc E/CN.4/RES/2004/6, UNCHR Res 3 (2005) UN Doc E/CN.4/RES/2005/3, UNGA Res 61/164 (21 February 2007) UN Doc A/RES/61/164, UNHRC Res 4/9, 'Combating defamation of religions' (30 March 2007) UN Doc A/HRC/RES/4/9, UNGA Res 62/154 (6 March 2008) UN Doc A/RES/62/154, UNHRC Res 7/19, 'Combating defamation of religions' (27 March 2008) UN Doc A/HRC/RES/7/19, UNGA Res 63/171 (24 March 2009) UN Doc A/RES/63/171, UNGA Res 64/156 (8 March 2010) UN Doc A/RES/64/156

[623] UNCHR Res 23 (1999) UN Doc E/CN.4/RES/1999/167, UNCHR Res 84 (2000) UN Doc E/CN.4/RES/2000/84, UNCHR Res 4 (2001) UN Doc E/CN.4/RES/2001/4, UNCHR Res 9 (2002) UN Doc E/CN.4/RES/2002/9, UNCHR Res 4 (2003) UN Doc E/CN.4/RES/2003/4, UNCHR Res 6 (2004) UN Doc E/CN.4/RES/2004/6, UNCHR Res 3 (2005) UN Doc E/CN.4/RES/2005/3, UNGA Res 61/164 (21 February 2007) UN Doc A/RES/61/164. Later, also sites, shrines and symbols are added to this list which have to be both respected and protected, especially when they are vulnerable to desecration or destruction. See UNGA Res 63/171 (24 March 2009) UN Doc A/RES/63/171. In addition, in the following resolution also 'venerated personalities' are included: UNHRC Res 10/22, 'Combating defamation of religions' (26 March 2009) UN Doc A/HRC/RES/10/22, UNGA Res 64/156 (8 March 2010) UN Doc A/RES/64/156

[624] UNCHR Res 4 (2003) UN Doc E/CN.4/RES/2003/4

particular by arguing that Islam[625] is frequently and wrongly associated with violence, human rights infringements and terrorism[626], particularly by political parties and associations that incite acts of violence, cultural prejudice[627] and xenophobia (Islamophobia) or related intolerance and discrimination towards Islam and any other religion[628], or proclaim and promote ideological superiority and racist ideologies.[629] It goes, thus, without saying that this shift in approach from protection of the human person to the protection of ideology in the broadest sense of the term has led to the fact that instead of persons, ideologies (including their value systems and institutions) are now being protected. This idea of "defamation of religion requires the state [and finally the judiciary] to determine which ideas are acceptable, as opposed to which facts are true. A fundamental rule of law problem presents itself in the notion of 'defamation of religion', inasmuch as belief cannot be empirically proven true"[630] which makes the arbitrary usage of such laws by the state more probable, while our contemporary multicivilizational world affair, which is being enhanced by globalization, is prone to impose further limitations on the freedom of expression. For it seems that not only aggrieving utterances about the human person are now liable to limitation but also expressions about ideologies in the broadest sense of the term.

---

[625] UNCHR Res 4 (2003) UN Doc E/CN.4/RES/2003/4, UNGA Res 62/154 (6 March 2008) UN Doc A/RES/62/154, UNHRC Res 10/22, 'Combating defamation of religions' (26 March 2009) UN Doc A/HRC/RES/10/22

[626] The fact that emphasis is merely put on Islam is apparent from the following example whereby the Commission on Human Rights "*alarmed* at the impact of the events of 11 September 2001 on Muslim minorities and communities in some non-Muslim countries and the negative projection of Islam, Muslim values and traditions by the media, as well as at the introduction and enforcement of laws that specifically discriminate against and target Muslims" in UNCHR Res 9 (2002) UN Doc E/CN.4/RES/2002/9, UNCHR Res 4 (2003) UN Doc E/CN.4/RES/2003/4, UNCHR Res 6 (2004) UN Doc E/CN.4/RES/2004/6, UNCHR Res 3 (2005) UN Doc E/CN.4/RES/2005/3, UNGA Res 60/150 (20 January 2006) UN Doc A/RES/60/150, UNHRC Res 4/9, 'Combating defamation of religions' (30 March 2007) UN Doc A/HRC/RES/4/9, UNGA Res 62/154 (6 March 2008) UN Doc A/RES/62/154, UNHRC Res 7/19, 'Combating defamation of religions' (27 March 2008) UN Doc A/HRC/RES/7/19. It is asserted that terrorism is not to be associated with any religion, nationality, civilization or ethnic group. See UNGA Res 63/171 (24 March 2009) UN Doc A/RES/63/171, UNHRC Res 10/22, 'Combating defamation of religions' (26 March 2009) UN Doc A/HRC/RES/10/22, UNGA Res 64/156 (8 March 2010) UN Doc A/RES/64/156, UNGA Res 65/224 (11 April 2011) UN Doc A/RES/65/224

[627] UNGA Res 63/171 (24 March 2009) UN Doc A/RES/63/171

[628] UNCHR Res 23 (1999) UN Doc E/CN.4/RES/1999/167, UNCHR Res 84 (2000) UN Doc E/CN.4/RES/2000/84, UNCHR Res 4 (2001) UN Doc E/CN.4/RES/2001/4, UNHRC Res 4/9, 'Combating defamation of religions' (30 March 2007) UN Doc A/HRC/RES/4/9, UNGA Res 62/154 (6 March 2008) UN Doc A/RES/62/154, UNHRC Res 7/19, 'Combating defamation of religions' (27 March 2008) UN Doc A/HRC/RES/7/19

[629] UNGA Res 63/171 (24 March 2009) UN Doc A/RES/63/171, UNGA Res 64/156 (8 March 2010) UN Doc A/RES/64/156

[630] Allen D Hertzke (ed), *The Future of Religious Freedom: Global Challenges* (OUP, Oxford 2013) 70

Nevertheless, in recent years, we can observe a reversal of this development[631] – albeit marginal – for it is acknowledged that, as the Special Rapporteur on the promotion and protection of the right to freedom of opinion and expression asserts, "the right to freedom of religion or belief, as enshrined in relevant international legal standards, does not include the right to have a religion or belief that is free from criticism or ridicule. Indeed, the right to freedom of expression includes the right to scrutinize, debate openly, make statements that offend, shock and disturb, and criticize belief systems, opinions and institutions, including religious ones, provided that they do not advocate hatred that incites hostility, discrimination or violence. At the international level, the Special Rapporteur welcomes the shift from the notion of "defamation of religions" to the protection of individuals against incitement to religious hatred. The Human Rights Council [...] has adopted by consensus a resolution on combating intolerance, negative stereotyping and stigmatization of, and discrimination, incitement to violence and violence against, persons based on religion or belief (resolution 19/25) [under a variety of pretexts relating to security and irregular immigration].[632] In that resolution, the Council condemns any advocacy of religious hatred that constitutes incitement to discrimination, hostility or violence, whether it involves the use of print, audiovisual or electronic media or any other means. It also recognizes that [in this clash of civilizations as we have elaborated upon in this research] open [constructive and respectful[633]] public debate of ideas, as well as interfaith and intercultural dialogue[634], at the local, national and international levels can be among the best protections against religious intolerance and can play a positive role in strengthening democracy and combating religious hatred, convinced that a continuing dialogue on these issues can help overcome existing perceptions".[635]

This reversal of approach is also evident from, for example, General Comment No. 34 wherein it is stated that "prohibitions of displays of lack of respect for a religion or other belief system, including blasphemy laws, are incompatible with the Covenant, except in the specific circumstances envisaged in article 20, paragraph 2, of the Covenant. Such prohibitions must also comply

---

[631] This reversal is also observable from the names of the documents which were changed from 'combating defamation of religions' into 'combating intolerance, negative stereotyping and stigmatization of, and discrimination, incitement to violence and violence against, persons based on religion or belief'; UNGA Res 16/18 (12 April 2011) UN Doc A/HRC/RES/16/18

[632] UNGA Res 65/224 (11 April 2011) UN Doc A/RES/65/224

[633] UNGA Res 64/156 (8 March 2010) UN Doc A/RES/64/156

[634] UNGA Res 65/224 (11 April 2011) UN Doc A/RES/65/224, UNGA Res 16/18 (12 April 2011) UN Doc A/HRC/RES/16/18, UNHRC, Nineteenth session 'Racism, racial discrimination, xenophobia and related form of intolerance, follow-up and implementation of the Durban Declaration and Programme of Action' (16 March 2012) UN Doc A/HRC/19/L.7, UNHRC, Twenty-second session 'Racism, racial discrimination, xenophobia and related form of intolerance, follow-up and implementation of the Durban Declaration and Programme of Action' (18 March 2013) UN Doc A/HRC/22/L.40

[635] UNHRC, 'Report of the Special Rapporteur on the Promotion and protection of the right to freedom of opinion and expression' (2012) UN Doc A/67/357

with the strict requirements of article 19, paragraph 3, as well as such articles as 2, 5, 17, 18 and 26. Thus, for instance, it would be impermissible for any such laws to discriminate in favour of or against one or certain religions or belief systems, or their adherents over another, or religious believers over non-believers. Nor would it be permissible for such prohibitions to be used to prevent or punish criticism of religious leaders or commentary on religious doctrine and tenets of faith".[636] The previous attempt to criminalize blasphemy is reversed and laws restricting blasphemy as such are considered to be incompatible with universal human rights standards.[637] In this way, the endeavor to protect religion as such is overruled by the original intention of the law, namely, the protection of the human person. The return to the original intention of the law, which entails the protection of the human person, is thus, as stated in the course of the present study, evident from the United Nations' documents in the latter years whereby the protection against, among others, intolerance, discrimination and acts of violence directed towards persons belonging to religious minorities has regained the attention it deserves.[638] For instance, great concern is often expressed about "[...] serious instances of intolerance, discrimination and acts of violence based on religion or belief, intimidation and coercion motivated by extremism, religious or otherwise, occurring in many parts of the world, including cases motivated by Islamophobia, Judeophobia and Christianophobia, in addition to the negative projection of certain religions in the media and the introduction and enforcement of laws and administrative measures that *specifically discriminate against and target persons* with certain ethnic and religious backgrounds, particularly Muslim minorities, and that threaten to impede their full enjoyment of human rights and fundamental freedoms".[639]

As is evident in the course of this discourse on blasphemy, great importance has been attached to the situation of Muslims but with one main difference. Before the aforementioned reversal of approach and return to the original intention of the law, special emphasis had been put on the psychological and physical assaults and attacks against places of worship, cultural centers, businesses and properties as well as religious symbols of Muslims.[640] However,

---

[636] ICCPR General Comment No. 34. Concluding observations on the United Kingdom of Great Britain and Northern Ireland-the Crown Dependencies of Jersey, Guernsey and the Isle of Man (CCPR/C/79/Add.119)

[637] Austin Dacey, 'United Nations Affirms the Human Right to Blaspheme', *Religion Dispatches Magazine* (11 August 2011) <http://www.religiondispatches.org/archive/politics/4985/united_nations_affirms_the_human_right_to_blaspheme_%7c_politics_%7c_/> accessed 3 December 2013

[638] See for instance UNGA Res 16/18 (12 April 2011) UN Doc A/HRC/RES/16/18, UNHRC, Nineteenth session 'Racism, racial discrimination, xenophobia and related form of intolerance, follow-up and implementation of the Durban Declaration and Programme of Action' (16 March 2012) UN Doc A/HRC/19/L.7, UNHRC, Twenty-second session 'Racism, racial discrimination, xenophobia and related form of intolerance, follow-up and implementation of the Durban Declaration and Programme of Action' (18 March 2013) UN Doc A/HRC/22/L.40

[639] UNGA Res 65/224 (11 April 2011) UN Doc A/RES/65/224 [emphasis added]

[640] UNCHR Res 9 (2002) UN Doc E/CN.4/RES/2002/9, UNCHR Res 6 (2004) UN Doc E/CN.4/RES/2004/6, UNCHR Res 3 (2005) UN Doc E/CN.4/RES/2005/3, UNGA Res 60/150

with the reversal of approach, vilification is considered to be a serious affront not to religion but to human dignity which can lead to the illicit restriction of the freedom of religion of the *adherents* and incitement to religious hatred and violence. Thus, discrimination on the basis of religion or belief is considered to constitute a violation of human rights that can lead to social disharmony, due to which states are requested to combat this burgeoning trend and the resulting discriminatory practices against *adherents* of all religions.[641] Yet, as we can observe, defamation of religion[642] as such is prone to defame also the adherents of religion, due to which the borderline between hate speech on the one hand, that is, the prohibition of advocating hatred or inciting hostility, discrimination or violence, and on the other the freedom of expression that may go so far as to even offend, shock and disturb, and criticize belief systems, opinions and institutions, including religious ones, is very thin and perilous, and which must be attentively guarded against abuses. This becomes more pressing when the resurgence of hate speech and the lightning speed of its circulation through the mass media and Internet in this globalized world are borne in mind. But also, when we take note of the rising immigration flows and population movements, the declining domestic economies and the emergence of terrorism, which have all fostered a growing tendency to stigmatize specific groups and communities.[643]

However, the acceleration of multicivilizationalism which underpins this discourse ought not to lead to a premature acceptance of bans on hate speech since it has already been determined, during the debate on the question of additional restriction, that the confinement of the freedom of expression should contain as few restrictions as possible.[644] Even in the case of hate speech, it is

(20 January 2006) UN Doc A/RES/60/150, UNGA Res 61/164 (21 February 2007) UN Doc A/RES/61/164, UNHRC Res 4/9, 'Combating defamation of religions' (30 March 2007) UN Doc A/HRC/RES/4/9, UNGA Res 62/154 (6 March 2008) UN Doc A/RES/62/154, UNHRC Res 7/19, 'Combating defamation of religions' (27 March 2008) UN Doc A/HRC/RES/7/19, UNGA Res 63/171 (24 March 2009) UN Doc A/RES/63/171, UNHRC Res 10/22, 'Combating defamation of religions' (26 March 2009) UN Doc A/HRC/RES/10/22, UNGA Res 64/156 (8 March 2010) UN Doc A/RES/64/156 [emphasis added]. This wording is generalized in the later documents wherein, instead of Muslims, reference is made to the adherents of religions in general; See for instance UNGA Res 65/224 (11 April 2011) UN Doc A/RES/65/224 and UNGA Res 16/18 (12 April 2011) UN Doc A/HRC/RES/16/18

641 UNGA Res 65/224 (11 April 2011) UN Doc A/RES/65/224

642 This is evident from, e.g., UNGA Res 65/224 (11 April 2011) UN Doc A/RES/65/224 whereby the states are urged "to take all possible measures to promote tolerance and respect for all religions and beliefs and the understanding of their value systems and to complement legal systems with intellectual and moral strategies to combat religious hatred and intolerance" but also when one "underlines the need to combat vilification of religions, and incitement to religious hatred in general, by strategizing and harmonizing actions at the local" national, regional and international levels through education and awareness-raising

643 UNHRC, 'Report of the Special Rapporteur on the Promotion and protection of the right to freedom of opinion and expression' (2012) UN Doc A/67/357

644 Marc J Bossuyt, *Guide to the 'travaux préparatoires' of the International Covenant on Civil and Political Rights* (Martinus Nijhoff Publishers, Dordrecht 1987) 398. This is especially crucial in the case of incitement to commit genocide as it comes to the fore in Article III (c) of the Convention on the Prevention and Punishment of the Crime of Genocide

crucial to keep in mind that "with regard to the prohibition of any advocacy of national, racial or religious hatred that constitutes incitement to discrimination, hostility or violence established under article 20(2) of the Covenant, it is important to establish a clearer understanding of the terms to prevent any misapplication of the law. This formulation includes three key elements: first, only advocacy of hatred is covered; second, hatred must amount to advocacy which constitutes incitement, rather than incitement alone; and third, such incitement must lead to one of the listed results, namely discrimination, hostility or violence. As such, advocacy of hatred on the basis of national, racial or religious grounds is not an offence in itself. Such advocacy becomes an offence only when it also constitutes incitement to discrimination, hostility or violence, or when the speaker seeks to provoke reactions on the part of the audience".[645] What is more, "(a) Hate speech laws should, at a minimum, conform to the following: (i) No one should be penalized for statements which are true; (ii) No one should be penalized for the dissemination of hate speech unless it has been shown that the perpetrator had the intention to incite discrimination, hostility or violence".[646] Thus, against this background, it is possible to state that the acceptance of bans on hate speech has to be accompanied by the necessary circumspection and reticence.

The inquiry above leads us to the conclusion that, at the international level, the acceleration of multicivilizationalism is prone to impose limits on the fundamental right to freedom of expression. This fundamental right is not an absolute right however, which means that it can be limited, but only through the prescribed legal conditions and not through extrajudicial means by certain individuals and groups in society. Yet, since innumerable studies have been conducted on the extrajudicial menaces posed to the right to freedom of expression, the scope of our study has been confined to the developments concerning the *de jure* limitations to this right that have yet to gain the necessary scholarly attention. And it is in this context that we should not lose sight of the fact that the law confers rights on the human person as the sole bearer of rights, which the law simultaneously aims to protect. Nevertheless, the legal developments show that various attempts have been made to further confine this fundamental right in a way that would go beyond the contemporary legal limitations in force so that not only protection is provided to the human person but also to religion and all its venerated features. But despite these attempts, we have seen that, in recent years, a reverse development has taken place whereby, once again, more importance is attached to the fundamental right to freedom of expression by not accepting the limitations imposed upon it by the discourse on defamation of religion.

[645] UNHRC, 'Report of the Special Rapporteur on the Promotion and protection of the right to freedom of opinion and expression' (2012) UN Doc A/67/357

[646] UNGA, Second session 'World Conference Against Racism, Racial Discrimination, Xenophobia and Related Intolerance, Preparatory Committee' (22 March 2001) UN Doc A/CONF.189/PC.2/24

Thus, although an attempt had been made to protect religions as well as their venerated objects including religious dogmas and persons of veneration in general and Islam and its Prophet in particular, it is, nonetheless, tempting to cite Mill who contends that "the holiest of men, it appears, cannot be admitted to posthumous honors, until all that the devil could say against him is known and weighed. If even the Newtonian philosophy were not permitted to be questioned, mankind could not feel as complete assurance of its truth as they now do".[647] This is why, according to Mill, "there can be no fair discussion of the question of usefulness, when an argument so vital may be employed on one side, but not on the other. And in point of fact, when law or public feeling do not permit the truth of an opinion to be disputed, they are just as little tolerant of a denial of its usefulness. The utmost they allow is an extenuation of its absolute necessity, or of the positive guilt of rejecting it".[648] Thus, as Mill puts it, the price of intellectual pacification is the sacrifice of the entire moral courage of the human mind for it is on the disinterested bystander that the clash among opinions is salubrious: "Not the violent conflict between parts of the truth, but the quiet suppression of half of it, is the formidable evil; there is always hope when people are forced to listen to both sides".[649] Hence, it remains to be seen how this reversal tendency can be kept alive within the constantly changing landscape of world affairs with newly emerging powers and the changing compositions of international organizations. What is more, and as has been stated in the course of our inquiry, the rise of civilizational clashes and their tendency to pose limitations on the freedom of expression do not only occur at the international level but, as we will examine hereafter, also at the European and national level.

2.4. The Right to Freedom of Expression at the European Level

As touched upon in the preceding paragraph, besides the legal limitations in force, the contemporary civilizational collisions are deemed to have posed a delineating threat to the fundamental right to freedom of expression. It is pertinent to recall that the pivotal question of whether and to what extent this fundamental right is confined by the contemporary civilizational clashes is being examined at three strata in this study: international, European, and national. In the previous paragraph, we have enquired about the legal developments that have posed a limitation on this right at the international level. In the present section an attempt will be made to conduct the same survey but this time at the European level in order to determine what the impact has been of an accelerated multicivilizationalism on the fundamental right to freedom of expression in a legal sense. And in the final part of this research, the third stratum wherein civilizational collisions tend to affect this fundamental right will occupy our attention. Accordingly, in order to elaborate on the aforementioned central

---

647 Stefan Collini (ed), *J. S. Mill: On Liberty and Other Writings* (CUP, Cambridge 2010) 24
648 Ibid 26
649 Ibid 34-35, 53

question at the European level, it is, firstly, imperative to take a closer look at the fundamental right to freedom of expression as it is regulated in the laws in force in Europe. After expounding the legal framework, an attempt will be made to elaborate the effects of civilizational clashes on the freedom of expression, which is considered to be the cornerstone of democracy in Europe. Prior to conducting this survey, it is, however, ineluctable and a necessary prerequisite to clarify what is meant by the aforesaid 'European level', for Europe is not characterized by one unequivocal organization, but is composed of numerous organizations. For this research, the relevant European organizations that deal with the fundamental right to freedom of expression are, as elaborated hereafter, the Organization for Security and Co-operation in Europe (OSCE), the European Union (EU), and the Council of Europe (CoE), even if not all of them are equally important in addressing our central question – as we will see below.

2.4.1. The Organization for Security and Co-operation in Europe

Though concerned with the fundamental right to freedom of expression – albeit in a narrow sense – the Organization for Security and Co-operation in Europe, does not, however, have a judicial body that would supervise compliance with this fundamental right and could, accordingly, render judgments as regards to it.[650] Besides, it is intriguing to note that this organization deals merely with one of the many dimensions of this fundamental freedom, namely, the freedom of the media. Furthermore, this organization has, as elaborated hereafter, three main institutions: the High Commissioner on National Minorities, the Representative on Freedom of the Media, and the Office for Democratic Institutions and Human Rights. The mandate of the High Commissioner had been determined in the document named the "Challenges of Change" adopted at the Third CSCE[651] Summit of Heads of State or Government on the 9th and 10th of July 1992, in Helsinki, Finland. Also in this Helsinki Summit Declaration, reference is made to democracy as the foundation of all endeavors of this

[650] The Organization for Security and Co-operation in Europe (OSCE) is, however, not completely a European organization but reaches beyond the European borders, meaning that it is rather a trans-Atlantic organization with international cooperating partners. In the context of the OSCE, freedom of expression is monitored by the OSCE Representative on Freedom of the Media which was created in 1997 and functions, in the same spirit as the organization, on the basis of the early-warning mechanism as regards possible breaches of the freedom of expression and attempts to promote the compliance of the member states in conformity with the principles and commitments of this organization. It is, however, not a judicial organ but only one of the four mechanisms for the promotion of this fundamental right by operating on the basis of monitoring, consultation and reporting in which vein it also enacts guidance, recommendations and declarations

[651] Concerning the change of name of this organization from CSCE to OSCE, see Speech at the Conference "Twenty years of the Helsinki Final Act – Towards a New European Security Model" delivered on 17 July 1995 in Moscow <http://www.osce.org/secretariat/15666> accessed 6-10-2013

organization which, against the background of the historical occurrences and experiences with totalitarianism, is inevitably connected with the fundamental rights and freedoms that it aims to maintain and protect.[652] In light of the challenges that the countries involved had been facing, the commitment is made that this organization plays the central role of fostering and managing change in the region because the conviction is that "in this era of transition, the CSCE is crucial to our efforts to forestall aggression and violence by addressing the root causes of problems and to prevent, manage and settle conflicts peacefully by appropriate means".[653] As regards the High Commissioner, the 1992 Helsinki Decisions asserted that "(23) The Council will appoint a High Commissioner on National Minorities. The High Commissioner provides "early warning" and, as appropriate, "early action" at the earliest possible stage in regard to tensions involving national minority issues that have [not yet developed beyond an early warning stage, but, in the judgment of the High Commissioner have] the potential to develop into a conflict within the CSCE area, affecting peace, stability, or relations between participating States [requiring the attention of and action by the Council or the CSO]. The High Commissioner will draw upon the facilities of the Office for Democratic Institutions and Human Rights (ODIHR) in Warsaw". To this end, "(5a) The High Commissioner will consider national minority issues occurring in the State of which the High Commissioner is a national or a resident, or involving a national minority to which the High Commissioner belongs, only if all parties directly involved agree, including the State concerned. (5b) The High Commissioner will not consider national minority issues in situations involving organized acts of terrorism. (5c) Nor will the High Commissioner consider violations of CSCE commitments with regard to an individual person belonging to a national minority. (6) In considering a situation, the High Commissioner will take fully into account the availability of democratic means and international instruments to respond to it, and their utilization by the parties involved. (7) When a particular national minority issue has been brought to the attention of the CSO, the involvement of the High Commissioner will require a request and a specific mandate from the CSO".[654]

The second main institution concerns the Representative on Freedom of the Media which, as its name already indicates, is concerned with only one dimension of the freedom of expression, namely, freedom of the media. The mandate of this organ is elaborated in Decision No.193[655] whereby – based on an acknowledgment of the fact that "[...] freedom of expression is a fundamental and internationally recognized human right and a basic component of a

[652] Conference for Security and Co-operation in Europe (1992 Summit, Helsinki), 'CSCE Helsinki Document 1992, The Challenges of Change' (Helsinki Summit Declaration)
[653] Ibid
[654] OSCE, *National minority standards. A compilation of OSCE and Council of Europe texts* (Council of Europe Publishing, Strasbourg 2007)
[655] Organization for Security and Co-operation in Europe, 'Mandate of the OSCE Representation on Freedom of the Media' (5 November 1997) PC.DEC No.193, PC Journal No 137

democratic society and that free, independent and pluralistic media are essential to a free and open society and accountable systems of government" – it is asserted that this institution is entrusted with the task of assisting the states involved, in a spirit of co-operation, in their continuing commitment to the furthering of free, independent and pluralistic media. To this very end, the OSCE Representative on Freedom of the Media observes, among others, relevant media developments in the member states based on, for example, collected and received information on the situation of the media as well as requests, suggestions and comments from all bona fide sources, and, on this basis, advocates and promotes full compliance with OSCE principles and commitments regarding the freedom of expression and free media. In so doing, this Representative operates on the basis of an early-warning system in order to address serious problems caused by, *inter alia*, obstruction of media activities and unfavorable working conditions for journalists. Hence, this body, besides consultation and (annual) reporting, concentrates on a rapid response to serious non-compliance with OSCE principles and commitments by participating states with respect to freedom of expression and free media. And in case of allegation of serious non-compliance, an attempt is made to directly contact, in an appropriate manner, the participating state and other parties involved in order to assess the facts, to assist the state concerned, and to contribute to a resolution of the situation. It is pertinent to note that, as explicitly stated in the decision, "the OSCE Representative on Freedom of the Media does not exercise a juridical function, nor can his or her involvement in any way prejudge national or international legal proceedings concerning alleged human rights violations. Equally, national or international proceedings concerning alleged human rights violations will not necessarily preclude the performance of his or her tasks as outlined in this mandate".[656]

The third body of the OSCE is the Office for Democratic Institutions and Human Rights (ODIHR), which, as the main institution, deals with the so-called "Human Dimension" which is, according to the Helsinki Decisions, mainly concerned with the "respect for human rights and fundamental freedoms, to abide by the rule of law, to promote the principles of democracy and, in this regard, to build, strengthen and protect democratic institutions, as well as to promote tolerance throughout society". Furthermore, one of the pivotal realms with which this organ is concerned is the area of 'tolerance and non-discrimination'. In this regard, the Decision underlines that "the participating States: (30) Express their concern over recent and flagrant manifestations of intolerance, discrimination, aggressive nationalism, xenophobia, anti-Semitism and racism and stress the vital role of tolerance, understanding and co-operation in the achievement and preservation of stable democratic societies [...]".[657] Emphasis is also put on the adherence of member states to the International Convention on the Elimination of All Forms of Racial Discrimination which we have elaborated heretofore. For this purpose, the states are, firstly, summoned to take appropriate measures within their constitutional frameworks and in conformity with their international

[656] Ibid
[657] Ibid

obligations to provide everyone, including foreigners, within their territories the necessary protection against discrimination and acts of violence on racial, ethnic and religious grounds. Secondly, the state parties are tasked with developing programmes with which they can create the conditions for promoting non-discrimination and cross-cultural understanding. What is more, the essential notion within the realm of 'tolerance and non-discrimination', with which this institution is concerned, is the concept of 'hate crime'.[658]

According to this institution, hate crimes comprise two elements: (i) a criminal offense; (ii) offense is committed with a bias motive.[659] The first element entails that a committed act has to constitute an offense under ordinary criminal law. This criminal act is referred to in this guide as the "base offense". Because there are small variations in legal provisions from country to country, there are some divergences in the kind of conduct that amounts to a crime; but in general most countries criminalize the same type of violent acts. Hate crimes always require a base offense to have occurred. If there is no base offense, there is no hate crime. The second element of a hate crime is that the criminal act is committed with a particular motive, referred to in this guide as "bias". It is this element of bias motive that differentiates hate crimes from ordinary crimes. This means that the perpetrator intentionally chooses the target of the crime because of some protected characteristic. The target may be one or more people, or it may be property associated with a group that shares a particular characteristic. A protected characteristic is a characteristic shared by a group, such as race, language, religion, ethnicity, nationality, or any other similar common factor.[660] However, a distinction is made between this crime and the prohibition of

[658] The special features of hate crime are described as follows: "Hate crimes differ from ordinary crimes not only because of the motivation of the offender, but also because of the impact on the victim. The perpetrator selects the victim because of his or her membership of a group; this suggests that one member of such a group is interchangeable with any other. Unlike victims of many other criminal acts, hate crime victims are selected on the basis of what they represent rather than who they are. The message that is conveyed is intended to reach not just the immediate victim but also the larger community of which that victim is a member. Thus, they are sometimes described as symbolic crimes. Hate crimes are designed to intimidate the victim and the victim's community on the basis of their personal characteristics. Such crimes send a message to the victim that they are not welcome; they have the effect of denying the victim's right to full participation in society. They also send a message to members of the community sharing the characteristic that they also do not belong, and could equally be a target. Hate crimes, therefore, can damage the fabric of society and fragment communities"; in OSCE/ODIHR, *Hate Crime Laws: A Practical Guide* (OSCE Office for Democratic Institutions and Human Rights, Warsaw 2009) 172

[659] An act that involves prejudice and bias of the sort described above but which does not amount to a crime is denoted as a "hate-motivated incident". The term describes acts motivated by prejudice ranging from those that are merely offensive to those constituting criminal acts in which the crime has not been proven. Thus, they share the second but not the first element of a hate crime; in OSCE/ODIHR, *Preventing and responding to hate crimes: A resource guide for NGOs in the OSCE region* (OSCE Office for Democratic Institutions and Human Rights, Warsaw 2009) 16

[660] OSCE/ODIHR, *Hate Crime Laws: A Practical Guide* (OSCE Office for Democratic Institutions and Human Rights, Warsaw 2009) 15

discrimination[661] in that "acts of discrimination lack the essential element of an act constituting a crime".[662]

Interesting for this study is still the similarity of this crime with the prohibition of discrimination, for both are based on particular characteristics such as race, language, religion, ethnicity, nationality, or any other similar common factor, and both have a person or a group of persons as their target. It is, however, conspicuous that also 'property associated with a group' falls within the scope of the notion of 'hate crime' against which it ought to be protected. Furthermore, 'hate crime' is distinguished from 'hate speech' because speech is bound to content, and without a specific prohibited content the speech would, as such, not be a crime. Hence, the contention here is that "[...] hate speech lacks the first essential element of hate crimes. If the bias motive or content were removed there would be no criminal offence. For example, a rock concert featuring songs glorifying violent fascism or the Holocaust would be hate speech, and in some States would be a crime, but it is not a hate crime because there is no criminal base offense. The first essential element of a hate crime is missing".[663] As regards 'hate crime', it is ineluctable to note that the way in which the ODIHR aims to combat it is by means of the production of an annual report – Incidents and Responses – in order to underline the prevalence of this crime and the good practices that both the states and civil society have developed to counter this crime. It also aims to assist the states in drafting their laws wherein this crime gains attention. In addition, it attempts to provide training for the officials engaged in the criminal justice systems and law enforcements within the member states, but also to raise awareness of this crime, and to support civil society in dealing with it.

The elaboration above leads us to the conclusion that, even though relevant for the combat against hatred, this organization is, nonetheless, not felicitous for the present inquiry on hate speech for the reasons elaborated above, the main aspects of which were, in short, as follows. Firstly, this organization does not deal with hate speech as such. Secondly, the scope of action of this organization is, as far as it deals with freedom of expression, limited to one single dimension of this freedom which is not our point of concern. Thirdly, this organization is political in nature and neither has any judicial power or mechanism nor the power to prejudge national or international legal proceedings concerning alleged human rights violations. And since the present study is not concerned with the political dimension but mainly, if not only, with the legal angle of this fundamental right, a further discussion of this organization falls outside the scope of the current scrutiny.

---

[661] Ibid 25

[662] OSCE/ODIHR, *Preventing and responding to hate crimes: A resource guide for NGOs in the OSCE region* (OSCE Office for Democratic Institutions and Human Rights, Warsaw 2009) 17

[663] OSCE/ODIHR, *Hate Crime Laws: A Practical Guide* (OSCE Office for Democratic Institutions and Human Rights, Warsaw 2009) 25

2.4.2. The European Union

The second organization in our survey is the European Union. This Union started as an economic and political organization underpinned with its own judicial system, namely, the Court of Justice of the European Union comprising the Court of Justice, the General Court, and the Civil Service Tribunal.[664] Fundamental human rights had not been the explicit concern upon which this organization was founded. Still, they have always been the underlying essence of this organization since its establishment, as we can infer from the old Article 6 of the Treaty on European Union which reads as follows:

"*1. The Union is founded on the principles of liberty, democracy, respect for human rights and fundamental freedoms, and the rule of law, principles which are common to the Member States.*

2. The Union shall respect fundamental rights, as guaranteed by the European Convention for the Protection of Human Rights and Fundamental Freedoms signed in Rome on 4 November 1950 and as they result from the constitutional traditions common to the Member States, as general principles of Community law.

3. The Union shall respect the national identities of its Member States.

4. The Union shall provide itself with the means necessary to attain its objectives and carry through its policies".

The first attempt to explicitly make fundamental human rights part of the codified European law was with the Treaty establishing a Constitution for Europe in 2004 which had, in its Part II, incorporated the EU Charter of Fundamental Rights that was already adopted in 2000 but had, till then, not gained any legally binding force. This Charter was reinforced by the Lisbon Treaty that entered into force on 1 December 2009. The Lisbon Treaty is composed of two main parts: the Treaty on European Union, and the Treaty on the Functioning of the European Union. In Article 2 of the Treaty on European Union, it is stated that "*the Union is founded on the values of respect for human dignity, freedom, democracy, equality, the rule of law and respect for human rights, including the rights of persons belonging to minorities. These values are common to the Member States in a society in which pluralism, non-discrimination, tolerance, justice, solidarity and equality between women and men prevail*".

---

[664] This Court is entrusted with the task of ensuring that 'the law is observed' 'in the interpretation and application' of the Treaties. In so doing, as stated on the official website of this Court, it "reviews the legality of the acts of the institutions of the European Union, ensures that the Member States comply with obligations under the Treaties, and interprets European Union law at the request of the national courts and tribunals. The Court thus constitutes the judicial authority of the European Union and, in cooperation with the courts and tribunals of the Member States, it ensures the uniform application and interpretation of European Union law" <http://curia.europa.eu/jcms/jcms/Jo2_6999/> accessed 3-102013

And in Article 6 of the Treaty on European Union, we can, for the first time[665], find a reference to the Charter, due to which we need to take a closer look at the wording of this provision which states that:

"*1. The Union recognizes the rights, freedoms and principles set out in the Charter of Fundamental Rights of the European Union of 7 December 2000, as adapted at Strasbourg, on 12 December 2007, which shall have the same legal value as the Treaties.*

The provisions of the Charter shall not extend in any way the competences of the Union as defined in the Treaties.

The rights, freedoms and principles in the Charter shall be interpreted in accordance with the general provisions in Title VII of the Charter governing its interpretation and application and with due regard to the explanations referred to in the Charter, that set out the sources of those provisions.

2. The Union shall accede to the European Convention for the Protection of Human Rights and Fundamental Freedoms. Such accession shall not affect the Union's competences as defined in the Treaties.

3. Fundamental rights, as guaranteed by the European Convention for the Protection of Human Rights and Fundamental Freedoms and as they result from the constitutional traditions common to the Member States, shall constitute the general principles of the Union's law".

Although perceived as having the same legal status as the Treaties – against the background of the foundational aims of this organization and in the light of political considerations and objections during the process concerning the Treaty establishing a Constitution for Europe – it was finally decided to not explicitly incorporate the Charter, in its entirety, into the Lisbon Treaty and the concession was, at the end, reached to make, as we can see in this provision, only a mere reference to this document within the legal canon of the organization. It is, however, worth reminding that "it was not until 1969 that the Court of Justice established a body of case-law [starting with the *Stauder v City of Ulm* judgment[666]] to serve as a framework of fundamental rights. This was because in the early years the Court had rejected all actions relating to basic rights on the grounds that it need not concern itself with matters falling within the scope of national constitutional law. The European Court of Justice (ECJ) had to alter its position not least because it was itself the embodiment of the primacy of Union law and its precedence over national law; this primacy can only be firmly established if Union law is sufficient in itself to guarantee the protection of basic rights with the same legal force as under the national constitutions".[667] The new approach adopted since the *Stauder v City of Ulm* judgment was further extended in the *Internationale Handelsgesellschaft* case[668] wherein it was asserted that "3. Recourse to the legal rules or concepts of national law in order to judge the

[665] It is noteworthy that the ECJ has also referred to this Charter in its case-law, the first example of which is the Case C-540/03 *European Parliament v Council* [2006] ECR I-5769

[666] Case 29/69 *Stauder v City of Ulm* [1969] ECR 419

[667] <http://eur-lex.europa.eu/en/editorial/abc_c02_r1.htm#h7> accessed 3 October 2013

[668] Case 11/70 *Internationale Handelsgesellschaft* [1970] ECR 1125

validity of measures adopted by the institutions of the Community would have an adverse effect on the uniformity and efficacy of Community law. The validity of such measures can only be judged in the light of Community law. In fact, the law stemming from the Treaty, an independent source of law, cannot because of its very nature be overridden by rules of national law, however framed, without being deprived of its character as Community law and without the legal basis of the Community itself being called in question. Therefore the validity of a Community measure or its effect within a Member State cannot be affected by allegations that it runs counter to either fundamental rights as formulated by the constitution of that State or the principles of a national constitutional structure. 4. However, an examination should be made as to whether or not any analogous guarantee inherent in Community law has been disregarded. In fact, respect for fundamental rights forms an integral part of the general principles of law protected by the Court of Justice. The protection of such rights, whilst inspired by the constitutional traditions common to the Member States, must be ensured within the framework of the structure and objectives of the Community. It must therefore be ascertained, in the light of the doubts expressed by the Verwaltungsgericht, whether the system of deposits has infringed rights of a fundamental nature, respect for which must be ensured in the Community legal system".

Notwithstanding this extension and other efforts in this context[669], the ECJ lacked thus an effective legal basis for rendering judgments beyond the generally developed principles[670], which had caused legal uncertainty for EU institutions, member states, and EU citizens. Dissatisfaction with this undesirable situation can be illustrated by the reasoning of the German judiciary who did not want to leave German citizens, despite the supremacy of European law[671], to the grace of the ECJ when it concerned their fundamental rights. Thus, while the ECJ had said that "[...] the validity of a Community measure or its effect within a Member State cannot be affected by allegations that it runs counter to either fundamental rights as formulated by the constitution of that State or the principles of a national constitutional structure"[672], the German Court contended that "the part of the Constitution dealing with fundamental rights is an inalienable essential feature of the valid Constitution of the Federal Republic of Germany and one which forms part of the constitutional structure of the

[669] For instance, the ECJ has argued that the Member States, in their conduct with regard to the EC law, have to comply with the fundamental rights elucidated in the ECHR; see, e.g., Cases C-465/00, 138 & 139/01 *Rechnungshof v Österreichischer Rundfunk* [2003] ECR I-12489

[670] In its jurisprudence, the ECJ has recognized two foundations of the general principles of law: the common national constitutional traditions and cultures, and the international human rights instruments, which we can find in the Case 4/73 *Nold v Commission* [1974] ECR 491. It is also interesting to remind that, even though not binding, the commitment to the general principles of law was also, for the first time, recognized by the joint declaration [1977] OJ C103/1 by the European Parliament, the Commission, and the Council

[671] The supremacy of the EC law over the national law was determined in the famous judgment: Case 6/64 *Flaminio Costa v ENEL* [1964] ECR 585, 593

[672] Case 11/70 *Internationale Handelsgesellschaft* [1970] ECR 1125

Constitution. [...] The Community still lacks a democratically legitimated Parliament directly elected by general suffrage which possesses legislative powers and to which the Community organs empowered to legislate are fully responsible on a political level. It still lacks in particular a codified catalogue of fundamental rights, the substance of which is reliably and unambiguously fixed for the future in the same way as the substance of the Constitution [...]. Provisions, therefore, in the hypothetical case of a conflict between Community law and [...] the guarantees of fundamental rights in the Constitution [...] the guarantee of fundamental rights in the Constitution prevails as long as the competent organs of the Community have not removed the conflict of norms in accordance with the Treaty mechanism".[673]

Against the aforesaid background, one of the proposed solutions for this vital deficit was to accede to the Convention for the Protection of Human Rights and Fundamental Freedoms (ECHR). Yet, back in the days, this was impossible since, with the laws in force, the EU lacked the competence to do it. Thus, the competence to accede to the aforementioned Human Rights Convention had to be made explicit. This was realized with the aforementioned Article 6 which provides for this possibility by asserting in its second paragraph that "the Union shall accede to the European Convention for the Protection of Human Rights and Fundamental Freedoms".[674] However, it emphasizes that "such accession shall not affect the Union's competences as defined in the Treaties", and when this is read in the same breath with the sequent paragraph, which states that the "fundamental rights, as guaranteed by the European Convention for the Protection of Human Rights and Fundamental Freedoms [...] shall constitute general principles of the Union's law", it is questionable how far fundamental rights can reach in terms of their fundamentality and whether this goes far enough to be more than just 'general principles'.[675] And even though strengthened *de jure*, it remains to be seen whether this codification will also strengthen *de facto* the value of fundamental rights and freedoms beyond the mere general principles of law which had already been developed by the Court through its case-law.

[673] *Internationale Handelsgesellschaft mbH v Einfuhr- und Vorratsstelle für Getreide und Futtermittel* [1974] 2 CMLR 540. The translation of this case is taken from Paul Craig and Gráinne de Búrca, *EU Law. Text, Cases, and Materials* (4th edn, Oxford, OUP 2008) 358

[674] Notwithstanding the legal developments, the process of accession has been hampered by the Court in its Opinion 2/13 EU Accession to the ECHR [2014] in which it states that "The agreement on the accession of the European Union to the European Convention for the Protection of Human Rights and Fundamental Freedoms is not compatible with Article 6(2) TEU or with Protocol (No 8) relating to Article 6(2) of the Treaty on European Union on the accession of the Union to the European Convention on the Protection of Human Rights and Fundamental Freedoms"

[675] Interesting in this regard is the following judgment: Case C-617/10 *Åklagaren v Hans Åkerberg Fransson*, 26 February 2013, ECLI:EU:C:2013:105

Yet, the mere accession[676] of the European Union to the European Convention on Human Rights will presumptively contribute to this strengthening and, thence, to the legal certainty and protection of human rights, since, among others, the conduct of the European Union will fall within the jurisdiction of the European Court of Human Rights. It is also worth noting that the aforementioned Charter is limited in scope and, hence, in efficiency due to the subsidiarity principle which comes to the fore in Article 51 of this Charter: "*1. The provisions of this Charter are addressed to the institutions and bodies of the Union with due regard for the principle of subsidiarity and to the Member States only when they are implementing Union law. They shall therefore respect the rights, observe the principles and promote the application thereof in accordance with their respective powers. 2. This Charter does not establish any new power or task for the Community or the Union, or modify powers and tasks defined by the Treaties*". Firstly, unlike the ECHR, this Charter is mainly, if not merely, applicable to the institutions, bodies and agencies of the Union, and with due regard for the principle of subsidiarity, and to the Member States in a limited field of operation as it has been determined in the jurisprudence of the ECJ.[677] Secondly, it remains to be seen how the two courts will compete or concede as regards their competence in legal matters concerning fundamental human rights. But until then, these fundamental rights and freedoms – although legally binding – remain vague and uncertain if not legally unenforceable within the ambit of the European Union. Henceforth, based on the preceding points, a further discussion of this organization is for all intents and purposes inconsequential to our study due to which we need to inquire farther into the next entity, as elaborated hereinafter, the Council of Europe.

2.4.3. The Council of Europe

The third organization in our inquiry at this European level which has sporadically been mentioned above is the Council of Europe (CoE). This Council was established on 5 May 1949 with the Treaty of London. In the assay conducted hereinafter, the scope of reference to human rights at the European level is narrowed to the framework of this organization, since this is the only institution that deals exclusively with fundamental human rights and freedoms through a judicial organ, the European Court of Human Rights (ECtHR), and a legally binding instrument, the Convention for the Protection of Human Rights and Fundamental Freedoms (ECHR) – supervised by this Court that has rendered judgments which are pivotal for our present inquiry – to which even the aforementioned Charter makes direct reference in its Article 52, paragraph 3: "*In*

---

[676] For further information see Johan Callewaert, *The accession of the European Union to the European Convention on Human Rights* (Council of Europe Publishing, Strasbourg 2014)

[677] Case 5/88 *Wachauf v Bundesamt Für Ernährung und Forstwirtschaft* [1989] ECR 2609; Case C-309/96 *Daniele Annibaldi v Sindaco del Comune di Guidonia and Presidente Regione Lazio* [1997] ECR I-7493

so far as this Charter contains rights which correspond to rights guaranteed by the Convention for the Protection of Human Rights and Fundamental Freedoms, the meaning and scope of those rights shall be the same as those laid down by the said Convention. This provision shall not prevent Union law providing more extensive protection". Applied to the freedom of expression, which is contained in Article 11 of the EU Charter of Fundamental Rights[678], it means thus that for the utilization and application of this right we primarily need to consult the Convention for the Protection of Human Rights and Fundamental Freedoms. Especially when Article 53 of this Charter states that "*nothing in this Charter shall be interpreted as restricting or adversely affecting human rights and fundamental freedoms as recognized, in their respective fields of application, by Union law and international law and by international agreements to which the Union, the Community or all the Member States are party, including the European Convention for the Protection of Human Rights and Fundamental Freedoms, and by the Member States' constitutions*". Hence, the Charter ought to be conceived as being subsidiary to the Human Rights Convention when considering the 'European level' meaning that precedence has, thus, to be given to the Convention. Accordingly, in our scrutiny hereafter of the question as to what extent the fundamental right to freedom of expression is confined by the accelerated multicivilizationalism at the European level, this Convention will form our focal point of departure as regards the content, scope, and limitations of this fundamental right.

2.4.4. Limitations of Freedom of Expression at the European Level

The right to freedom of expression at the European level is contained in Article 10 of the Convention for the Protection of Human Rights and Fundamental Freedoms (ECHR) which reads as follows:

"*1. Everyone has the right to freedom of expression. This right shall include freedom to hold opinions and to receive and impart information and ideas without interference by public authority and regardless of frontiers. This article shall not prevent States from requiring the licensing of broadcasting, television or cinema enterprises.*

2. The exercise of these freedoms, since it carries with it duties and responsibilities, may be subject to such formalities, conditions, restrictions or penalties as are prescribed by law and are necessary in a democratic society, in the interests of national security, territorial integrity or public safety, for the prevention of disorder or crime, for the protection of health or morals, for the protection of the reputation or the rights of others, for preventing the disclosure

[678] This article reads as follows: "*1. Everyone has the right to freedom of expression. This right shall include freedom to hold opinions and to receive and impart information and ideas without interference by public authority and regardless of frontiers. 2. The freedom and pluralism of the media shall be respected*"

of information received in confidence, or for maintaining the authority and impartiality of the judiciary".

As is evident from the *travaux préparatoires* as well as the Preamble of this Convention, this fundamental freedom is created in the spirit of the international legal tools we had elaborated in the preceding section. As we can read in this provision, freedom itself is formulated in absolute terms, and only the exercise of it is subjected to limitation that has a tripartite structure: a limitation imposed must be prescribed by law; it must meet one of the legitimate aims mentioned in this provision; and it must be necessary in a democratic society. And it is actually this last condition which is at stake in contemporary Western democracies that are characterized by an accelerated pluralism of civilizations which have, oftentimes, resulted in collisions. Accordingly, the question that arises is: to what extent this colliding pluralism has confined *de jure* the freedom of expression?

This question is concerned with the exigency in democratic societies of making the coexistence of various civilizations possible. In other words, this is a question about the pressing social needs within a democratic society for making peaceful cohabitation feasible. As regards the prerequisite of 'necessary in a democratic society' in this provision, it is also worth noting that since the very beginning of the codification of this fundamental right at the European level, both this right and its necessity have inevitably been connected with 'democracy'.[679] This is also plainly mirrored in the established case-law of the European Court of Human Rights, according to which "[...] some compromise between the requirements of defending democratic society and individual rights is inherent in the system of the Convention".[680] It also emphasized that, as we will discuss below, "democracy is without doubt a fundamental feature of the European public order [...]. That is apparent, firstly, from the Preamble to the Convention, which establishes a very clear connection between the Convention and democracy by stating that the maintenance and further realization of human rights and fundamental freedoms are best ensured on the one hand by an effective political democracy and on the other by a common understanding and observance of human rights [...]. The Preamble goes on to affirm that European countries have a common heritage of political tradition, ideals, freedom and the rule of law. The Court has observed that in that common heritage are to be found the underlying values of the Convention [...]; it has pointed out several times that the Convention was designed to maintain and promote the ideals and values of a democratic society [...]. The only type of necessity capable of justifying an interference with any of those rights is, therefore, one which may claim to spring from 'democratic society'. Democracy thus appears to be the only political model contemplated by the Convention and, accordingly, the only one compatible with it".[681]

679 For instance, in the case of *The United Communist Party of Turkey and Others v Turkey* (App no 19392/92) ECHR 1998-I, the Court states that "democracy is without doubt a fundamental feature of the European public order"
680 Ibid
681 Ibid

Also at the beginning, it was argued by Congress, which was entrusted with codification, that this organ "(9) Considers that the resultant Union or Federation should be open to all European Nations democratically governed and which undertake to respect a Charter of Human Rights. (10) Resolves that a Commission should be set to undertake immediately the double task of drafting such a Charter and of laying down standards to which a State must conform if it is to deserve the name of a democracy. (11) Declares that in no circumstances shall a State be entitled to be called a democracy unless it does, in fact as well as in law, guarantee to its citizens liberty of thought, assembly and expression, as well as the right to form a political opposition".[682] Hence, it is apparent that the aim had been to create an organization that could serve as the statue for the triumph of democracy to which only those who are diligent enough would be allowed. This can be best apprehended against the epoch and background wherein this event took place, upon which the heralding theories concerning the ultimate triumph of democracy, such as the one of Francis Fukuyama in the first section of this study, are built.

It is dexterous to remark that the impact of the epoch had also been profoundly present in the consciousness of those involved in the drafting of this legal instrument in general and this provision in particular, as it is, for instance, evident from the comment of the British representative, Mr. Foster, who asserted that "[...] we have had totalitarian dictatorships only too recently in Europe which have ground down their people and disregarded the rights, to which the ordinary man must be able to look forward, of free speech, [...], freedom to express himself [...]".[683] Due to the horrifying experiences of Europe with totalitarianism, the interrelationship between democracy and human rights was, from the very beginning, considered to be ineluctable and self-evident as it finally came to be engraved in the Preamble of this Convention which states that the signatory governments are, by means of this Convention, "*reaffirming their profound belief in those fundamental freedoms which are the foundation of justice and peace in the world and are best maintained on the one hand by an effective political democracy and on the other by a common understanding and observance of the human rights upon which they depend*". As stated above, the Human Rights Court also rehearses in its established case-law this ineluctable interwovenness of democracy and human rights[684], but goes even so far as to

[682] Council of Europe, European Court of Human Rights, 'Preparatory Work on Article 10 of the European Convention on Human Rights' (5 March 1975) Confidential CDH (75) 6, 2

[683] Ibid 4

[684] For instance, the Court says in *The United Communist Party of Turkey and Others v Turkey* (App no 19392/92) ECHR 1998-I that "democracy is without doubt a fundamental feature of the 'European public order'[...]. That is apparent, firstly, from the Preamble to the Convention, which establishes a very clear connection between the Convention and democracy by stating that the maintenance and further realisation of human rights and fundamental freedoms are best ensured on the one hand by an effective political democracy and on the other by a common understanding and observance of human rights[...]. The Preamble goes on to affirm that European countries have a common heritage of political tradition, ideals, freedom and the rule of law. The Court has observed that in that common heritage are to be found the

acknowledge democracy's right to defend itself against anti-democratic forces.[685] What is more, an attempt had been made to narrow even the scope of these rights to the mere functioning and preservation of democracy. For example, Lord Layton from the United Kingdom argued: "I urge that the list of rights should be limited to the absolute minimum necessary to constitute the cardinal principles for the functioning of political democracy".[686] In this same vein, it is interesting to recall the observation made by the Swedish representative, Mr. Edberg, during the preparatory work on Article 10 in the Plenary sitting on 19 August 1949: "[...] Fundamental to every true democracy is the right of all citizens, not only to have different opinions upon political matters, but to join with other citizens in order to promote the realization of those opinions. Another fundamental right is that no individual should be persecuted or discriminated against on account of his opinions".[687] In this, he is, in principle, advocating for not only the freedom of expression but also the freedom of assembly, and the pivotal notion that he adds is the *prohibition of discrimination* on the basis of (political) opinions.

This principle of non-discrimination, as also elaborated at the international level heretofore, is what we will touch upon hereinafter within the context of the limitations of this freedom at the European level. Before doing so, it is, however, important to understand that, at the European level, more than at the international level, democracy and fundamental rights are conceived to be interdependent and inextricable. Especially when limitations of this fundamental right must be convincingly established[688] in order to be conceived as necessary in a *democratic*

underlying values of the Convention [...]; it has pointed out several times that the Convention was designed to maintain and promote the ideals and values of a democratic society[...]. In addition, Articles 8, 9, 10 and 11 of the Convention require that interference with the exercise of the rights they enshrine must be assessed by the yardstick of what is 'necessary in a democratic society'. The only type of necessity capable of justifying an interference with any of those rights is, therefore, one which may claim to spring from 'democratic society'. Democracy thus appears to be the only political model contemplated by the Convention and, accordingly, the only one compatible with it." It is even stated in numerous judgments – such as *Kjeldsen, Busk Madsen and Pedersen v Denmark* (App nos 5095/71, 5920/72, 5926/72) (1976) Series A no 23, and *Soering v the United Kingdom* (App no 14038/88) (1989) Series A no 161 – that the "Convention was designed to maintain and promote the ideals and values of a democratic society". It is worth mentioning that as regards this interrelationship, the Parliamentary Assembly of the Council of Europe "[...] reaffirms that there cannot be a democratic society without the fundamental right to freedom of expression'. [But also] 'Freedom of thought, conscience and religion constitutes a necessary requirement for a democratic society and one of the essential freedoms of individuals for determining their perception of human life and society"; in Parliamentary Assembly of the Council of Europe Res 1510 'Freedom of expression and respect for religious beliefs' (24 June 2006) CoE Report Doc 10970, Parliamentary Assembly of the Council of Europe Rec 1396 'Religion and democracy' (27 January 1999) CoE Report Doc 8270

685 *Vogt v Germany* (App no 17851/91) (1995) Series A no 323

686 Council of Europe, European Court of Human Rights, 'Preparatory Work on Article 10 of the European Convention on Human Rights' (5 March 1975) Confidential CDH (75) 6, 7

687 Ibid 6, 3

688 *Barthold v Germany* (App no 8734/79) (1985) Series A no 90, *Autronic AG v Switzerland* (App no 12726/87) (1990) Series A no 178

society, as Article 10 of the ECHR requires. This is because, as the French delegate, Mr. Teitgen, asserted on 16 August 1950 during the Consultative Assembly, "[…] it is impossible to reach an understanding upon the meaning and positive content of any freedom which it is desired to guarantee, if you do not first make it perfectly clear that you are speaking of a freedom that is being exercised in a democratic regime. It is therefore quite clearly from democracy that the freedoms we wish to guarantee derive their practical content".[689] As regards this mode of governance which underpins the Convention, it is imperative to note that it is itself underpinned by the prerequisite of pluralism. Thus, "as the Court has said many times, there can be no democracy without pluralism. It is for that reason that freedom of expression as enshrined in Article 10 is applicable, subject to paragraph 2, not only to 'information' or 'ideas' that are favorably received or regarded as inoffensive or as a matter of indifference, but also to those that offend, shock or disturb […]"[690], since "such are the demands of that pluralism, tolerance and broadmindedness without which there is no 'democratic society' ".[691]

Hence, for a proper functioning of a pluralist democracy, even offending, shocking or disturbing expressions are ineluctable. Therefore, the freedom of expression is subject to a number of exceptions which must be *narrowly* interpreted and the necessity for any restrictions must be *convincingly* established.[692] But such restrictions are inevitable, especially when one takes into account the collisions that have occurred in pluralistic European societies due to which appeal is, oftentimes, made to each citizen's duties and responsibilities.[693] However, interference in the exercise of these rights, and particularly this fundamental right, has to be, as the Court states, "[…] assessed by the yardstick of what is "necessary in a democratic society". The only type of necessity capable of justifying an interference with any of those rights is, therefore, one which may claim to spring from "democratic society". Democracy thus appears to be the only political model contemplated by the Convention and, accordingly, the only one compatible with it. The Court has identified certain provisions of the Convention as being characteristic of democratic society. […] [In this regard] the Court has on many occasions stated […] that freedom of expression constitutes one of the essential foundations of a democratic society and one of the basic conditions for its progress and each individual's [development[694] and] self-

[689] Council of Europe, European Court of Human Rights, 'Preparatory Work on Article 10 of the European Convention on Human Rights' (5 March 1975) Confidential CDH (75) 6, 22

[690] *The United Communist Party of Turkey and Others v Turkey* (App no 19392/92) ECHR 1998-I, *Handyside v the United Kingdom* (App no 5493/72) (1976) Series A no 24

[691] This formula can be found, among others, in *Vogt v Germany* (App no 17851/91) (1995) Series A no 323, *Handyside v the United Kingdom* (App no 5493/72) (1976) Series A no 24

[692] See for instance *Vogt v Germany* (App no 17851/91) (1995) Series A no 323, *Handyside v the United Kingdom* (App no 5493/72) (1976) Series A no 24, *Axel Springer AG v Germany* (App no 39954/08) ECHR 7 February 2012

[693] *Handyside v the United Kingdom* (App no 5493/72) (1976) Series A no 24

[694] Ibid

fulfillment [...]".[695] Henceforth, democracy is not only linked with human rights in general but inevitably with freedom of expression in particular. This is a confinement that renders the right to freedom of expression no longer as an absolute right but subject to possible restrictions as deemed necessary in a democratic society. In other words, although "freedom of expression constitutes one of the essential foundations of a democratic society and one of the basic conditions for its progress and each individual's self-fulfillment" [696] it, nonetheless, needs to be subjected to limitations that are necessary for making, among others, peaceful coexistence in a pluralistic society possible.

As regards the adjective 'necessary' within the scope of Article 10(2) of the ECHR, the Court states that this notion is neither synonymous with being 'indispensable' nor does it have the flexibility of such expressions as 'admissible', 'ordinary', 'reasonable', or 'desirable'.[697] This adjective implies rather the existence of a 'pressing social need'[698] which has to be initially assessed by the national authorities who are perceived to be better placed for doing this than an international judge who thus plays a subsidiary role. For this assessment a certain 'margin of appreciation' is left to the states. But this margin is not unlimited, for the Court is empowered to give the final ruling on whether a 'restriction' is reconcilable with the freedom of expression. This means that the supervisory role of this Court concerns both the aim of the measure being challenged and its necessity in a democratic society.[699] Henceforth, the main principles relevant for the assessment of what tends to be 'necessary' in a democratic society, as it comes to the fore in the jurisprudence of the Court, can be summed up as follows: "Firstly, 'necessary' in this context does not have the flexibility of such expressions as 'useful' or 'desirable'. [...] Secondly, pluralism, tolerance and broadmindedness are hallmarks of a 'democratic society'. Although individual interests must on occasion be subordinated to those of a group, democracy does not simply mean that the views of a majority must always prevail: a balance must be achieved which ensures the fair and proper

---

[695] *The United Communist Party of Turkey and Others v Turkey* (App no 19392/92) ECHR 1998-I

[696] *Vogt v Germany* (App no 17851/91) (1995) Series A no 323

[697] *Handyside v the United Kingdom* (App no 5493/72) (1976) Series A no 24, *The Sunday Times v The United Kingdom* (App no 6538/74) (1979) Series A no 30

[698] *Observer and Guardian v the United Kingdom* (App no 13585/88) (1991) Series A no 216, *Vogt v Germany* (App no 17851/91) (1995) Series A no 323

[699] Ibid. In this same case, the Court asserts with regard to the margin of appreciation that it is not its task to replace the national authorities: "This does not mean that the supervision is limited to ascertaining whether the respondent State exercised its discretion reasonably, carefully and in good faith; what the Court has to do is to look at the interference complained of in the light of the case as a whole and determine whether it was "proportionate to the legitimate aim pursued" and whether the reasons adduced by the national authorities to justify it are "relevant and sufficient" [...]. In so doing, the Court has to satisfy itself that the national authorities applied standards which were in conformity with the principles embodied in Article 10 (art. 10) and, moreover, that they based their decisions on an acceptable assessment of the relevant facts [...]." *Handyside v the United Kingdom* (App no 5493/72) (1976) Series A no 24

treatment of minorities and avoids any abuse of a dominant position.[700] [...] Thirdly, any restriction imposed on a Convention right must be proportionate to the legitimate aim pursued [...]".[701]

This brings us to the aforementioned principle of non-discrimination which has gained more assiduity in the last decade with the acceleration of cultural pluralism whereby, due to the tensions and clashes, more attention is being paid to the rights of minorities within Western democracies by authorities who are, simultaneously, forced to strike the right balance among the rights and interests involved. This is why it is pertinent to bestow some thoughts on this fundamental principle which underpins the Convention in its entirety and forms, particularly, a confinement of the fundamental freedom at hand.

The principle of non-discrimination is contained in Article 14 of the ECHR which reads as follows: "*The enjoyment of the rights and freedoms set forth in this Convention shall be secured without discrimination on any ground such as sex, race, color, language, religion, political or other opinion, national or social origin, association with a national minority, property, birth or other status*".[702] In addition, it is worthwhile noting that the Court provides in this regard a complementary remark regarding this provision by stating that "discrimination for the purposes of Article 14 of the Convention means treating differently, without an objective and reasonable justification, persons in relevantly similar situations. There will be no objective and reasonable justification if the difference in treatment does not pursue a 'legitimate aim' or if there is not a reasonable relationship of proportionality between the means employed and the aim sought to be realized".[703] Notwithstanding, there is also Protocol No.12 which determines in a broader sense the scope of this principle that goes beyond the provided grounds and description, and makes this principle of non-discrimination, unlike Article 14, a free-standing principle. However, since this protocol is not ratified by all the member states, a further discussion of it falls outside the scope of the present discourse. It suffices to note that, besides the case-law of the Human Rights Court, this Protocol makes evident that the list of

[700] Although the Court contends that the view of the majority need not prevail, nonetheless, we see in all the discussed cases that, in the context of the assessment of what is 'necessary in a democratic society', the Court is attentive to the view of the majority of the people in any given society

[701] *Young, James and Webster v The United Kingdom* (App nos 7601/76, 7806/77) (1981) Series A no 55

[702] As regards the grounds mentioned in this provision, it is worth noting that they are considered to be inseparable from each other as we can, for instance, see in *Timishev v Russia* (App nos 55762/00, 55974/00) ECHR 13 December 2005 whereby it is stated that "ethnicity and race are related and overlapping concepts. Whereas the notion of race is rooted in the idea of biological classification of human beings into subspecies according to morphological features such as skin color or facial characteristics, ethnicity has its origin in the idea of societal groups marked by common nationality, tribal affiliation, religious faith, shared language, or cultural and traditional origins and backgrounds"

[703] *Aksu v Turkey* (App nos 4149/04, 41029/04) ECHR 15 March 2012. But see also, among others, *D.H. and Others v the Czech Republic* (App no 57325/00) ECHR 2007-IV, and *Burden v the United Kingdom* (App no 13378/05) ECHR 29 April 2008

the grounds provided for in the aforementioned provision is not exhaustive, as it is also evident from the formulation of this provision itself which leaves the door open for other grounds as indicated by the phrase 'other status'. What is more, the principle of non-discrimination, as contained in Article 14, is not only an underpinning principle for the enjoyment of the rights and freedoms that are encompassed in the Convention but it denotes, at the same time, that this principle is confined and applicable only to the rights and freedoms as set forth in this same document. Moreover, it can be applied merely when it is conjugationally considered with one of the substantive rights or freedoms contained in this Convention, as, for example, an application of it in conjunction with Article 10 of the ECHR. In other words, as the Court states, "[...] according to the established case-law of the Convention institutions, Article 14 only complements the other substantive provisions of the Convention and the Protocols. It has no independent existence since it has effect solely in relation to 'the enjoyment of the rights and freedoms' safeguarded by those provisions".[704]

The application of this principle together with the freedom of expression becomes intriguing, especially when we take serious note of the fact that the pursued aim is to ensure a proper functioning of democracy wherein not only freedom of expression forms a guarantee of this mode of governance but also the confinement of this fundamental freedom by means of the prohibition of discrimination. This becomes pertinent when we take note of the accelerated pluralism that characterizes the Western democratic societies, in which context the Court says that "[...] no difference in treatment which is based exclusively or to a decisive extent on a person's ethnic origin is capable of being objectively justified in a contemporary democratic society built on the principles of pluralism and respect for different cultures".[705] An example of a case wherein expressions were considered to be discriminatory due to which they were prohibited in order to protect the rights and reputation of others was the *Vejdeland and Others v Sweden* judgment wherein the Court asserted that "[...] although these statements did not directly recommend individuals to commit hateful acts, they are serious and prejudicial allegations [and it stressed, in addition, that] '[...] discrimination based on sexual orientation is as serious as discrimination based on 'race, origin or color' ".[706]

Henceforth, mere faith in the responsibilities and duties of which each human being is a bearer is not enough for guaranteeing the protection of fundamental rights and freedoms, due to which we still need more safeguards to guarantee these rights and freedoms. It is also to this very end that the prohibition of discrimination has to be comprehended which can form a restricting ground for the freedom of expression. Especially when a balance needs to be struck among the rights and interests involved in a pluralistic society wherein the protection of

---

[704] *Chaare Shalom Ve Tsedek v France* (App no 27417/95) ECHR 2000-VII

[705] *Sejdić and Finci v Bosnia and Herzegovina* (App nos 27996/06, 34836/06) ECHR 22 December 2009, *Timishev v Russia* (App nos 55762/00, 55974/00) ECHR 13 December 2005

[706] *Vejdeland and Others v Sweden* (App no 1813/07) ECHR 9 February 2012. See also *Smith and Grady v the United Kingdom* (App nos 33985/96, 33986/96) ECHR 1999-VI

the reputation or rights of others can make limitations justifiable and necessary.[707] The principle of non-discrimination is not only embedded in this European Convention to which an appeal can be made for limiting the freedom of expression, but it can also be found in, as elaborated in the preceding section, the international legal instruments, the most important of which is the 1965 International Convention on the Elimination of All Forms of Racial Discrimination, which can also be invoked at the European level, as one can see in the case of *Jersild v Denmark*.[708] As we can read in this judgment, Article 10 of the ECHR ought not to be interpreted in a way that would limit, derogate from or destroy the right to the protection against racial discrimination as it is contained in the aforementioned UN Convention. The Court underlines from the very outset the vital importance of combating racial discrimination in all its forms and manifestations, in which context it asserts that the object and purpose pursued by the UN Convention are, thence, of great weight in determining whether the condition of 'necessary' within the meaning of paragraph 2 of Article 10 is met. Still, it is, nonetheless, not for the Court to interpret [the "due regard" clause in Article 4 of] the UN Convention.[709]

As stated already, the scope of the requisite 'necessary' has, in the first place, to be assessed by the national authorities within the margin of appreciation left to them, for they are considered to be in a better position to consider the 'pressing social needs' at the appropriate time in their societies. This becomes more pertinent once we take note of the plurality of civilizations present in the Western democratic societies which can be a detrimental and decisive factor in this assessment.[710] The question that arises is, then, to what extent is the freedom of expression *de jure* confined by this pluralism of civilizations within the Western democratic societies. In order to assess this, it is at first imperative to continue our discussion about the scope of the requisite 'necessity' in its generality within a democratic society as expounded by the Court. Subsequently, we will elucidate, in this context, the development of the legitimate aims of 'morals' and the 'reputation or rights of others'.

One of the landmark cases in this regard is the *Lingens v Austria* judgment wherein the reputation and rights of others were at stake and for which the perpetrator was convicted for defamation since the criminal law at hand provided for the protection of the reputation and rights of others against defamation. The central question was whether interference with the applicant's right to freedom of expression was 'necessary in a democratic society'. In this regard, he had invoked his role as a political journalist in a pluralist society due to which he considered it, just like the Human Rights Commission, justified to criticize politicians especially when it concerned a politician who used to attack his opponents, and because of which he had also to expect fiercer criticisms than

[707] *Jersild v Denmark* (App no 15890/89) (1994) Series A no 298
[708] Ibid
[709] Ibid
[710] As regards the content of expressions that ought to be limited for the protection of the rights and reputations of others, Article 10(2) has to be read together with Article 17 of the ECHR

other people.[711] However, the government did not agree with this and argued that the national courts did have the discretion to ensure that political debate did not degenerate into personal insult. The Court refers, firstly, to its earlier jurisprudence and asserts that the adjective 'necessary' within the boundaries of this provision implies the existence of a 'pressing social need' which can be assessed by national authorities within their margin of appreciation but that the Court retains its supervisory jurisdiction when it concerns limitations imposed on this fundamental right. In this quality, the Court recalls that the freedom of expression constitutes one of the fundamental foundations of a democratic society and one of the basic conditions for its progress and for each individual's development. Subject to paragraph 2 of Article 10 are not only 'information' or 'ideas' that are favorably received or regarded as inoffensive or as a matter of indifference, but also those that offend, shock or disturb. In addition, it is worth noting that Article 10 protects not only the *substance* of the ideas and information expressed but also the *form* in which they are conveyed.[712]

Expressions have this wide scope for such are the demands of pluralism, tolerance and broadmindedness without which there is no 'democratic society' as had already been established in the *Handyside v the United Kingdom* case[713], and which has ever since become the standard formula in the case-law of the Court. Against this background, the Court states that although the press must not overstep[714] the bounds set, *inter alia*, for the "protection of the reputation of others", it is nevertheless incumbent on it to impart information and ideas on political issues just as on those in other areas of public interest. Not only does the *press* have, as purveyor of information and public watchdog[715], the task of imparting such information and ideas but, as it had already been elaborated in the *Sunday Times* case, also the *public* has a right to receive them.[716] Thence, the importance of this fundamental freedom for the press is evident when one takes one of its vital roles into consideration which is to afford "[...] the public one of the best means of discovering and forming an opinion of the ideas and attitudes of political leaders. More generally, freedom of political debate is at the very core of the concept of a democratic society which prevails throughout the

[711] *Lingens v Austria* (App no 9815/82) (1986) Series A no 103, *Lindon, Otchakovsky-Laurens and July v France* (App nos 21279/02, 36448/02) ECHR 22 October 2007

[712] *De Haes and Gijsels v Belgium* (App no 19983/92) ECHR 1997-I

[713] *Handyside v the United Kingdom* (App no 5493/72) (1976) Series A no 24

[714] In light of the criterion 'duties and responsibilities' in Article 10, the Court states that journalists enjoy the protection of this provision provided that they act in good faith in order to provide accurate and reliable information in accordance with the ethics of journalism; see for instance: *Fressoz and Roire v France* (App no 29183/95) ECHR 1999-I, *Bergens Tidende and Others v Norway* (App no 26132/95) ECHR 2000-IV

[715] *Barthold v Germany* (App no 8734/79) (1985) Series A no 90. The Court even states that "the national margin of appreciation is circumscribed by the interest of democratic society in enabling the press to exercise its vital role of "public watchdog" ". *Chauvy and Others v France* (App no 64915/01) ECHR 29 June 2004, *Bladet Tromsø and Stensaas* (App no 21980/93) ECHR 1999-III

[716] *Lingens v Austria* (App no 9815/82) (1986) Series A no 103

Convention".[717] The prevalence of freedom concerning political debate is also evident from the instant case wherein the applicant's critique, as a value-judgment, had two dimensions that are essential for this freedom. On the one hand, it concerned political issues of public interest which gave rise to heated discussions. In this, the tone and content of the critique were – given the particular context and circumstances – considered to be fairly balanced and in no way unusual in 'the bitter tussles of politics'. On the other hand, this critique came from a person in his capacity as politician which is also a decisive factor. Against this background, the Court concluded in this case that there had been an infringement on the freedom of expression of the applicant ex Article 10 of the ECHR.

Accordingly, what comes to the fore from the case-law of the Human Rights Court is the importance attached to 'public debate' [718] which can allow expressions to go so far as to offend, shock or disturb, since such are considered to be the demands of pluralism, tolerance and broadmindedness without which no democratic society can exist. This conveys the impression that pluralism does not confine the freedom of expression but, to the very opposite, it even demands a broader scope for this freedom. This impression may even be confirmed when we take into consideration the role of the press[719] that, although not explicitly mentioned in Article 10, it is, nevertheless, one of the vital actors in the public debate within democracy, that not only "impart[s] information and ideas on political questions and on other matters of public interest"[720] but also affords, on the one hand, "the public one of the best means of discovering and forming an opinion of the ideas and attitudes of their political leaders", while and on the other, "it gives politicians the opportunity to reflect and comment on the preoccupations of public opinion; it thus enables everyone to participate in the free political debate which is at the very core of the concept of a democratic society". [721] This brings us to the other crucial actor within the democratic process that could further strengthen our presumption about the broadness of the scope of the freedom of expression. This pivotal actor that we have on the other side of the spectrum of the democratic process is the 'politician', and by extension the 'political parties', after all the freedom to freely choose is considered to be "[...] inconceivable without the participation of a plurality of political parties representing the different shades of opinion to be found within a country's population. By relaying this range of opinion, not only within political

[717] Ibid

[718] However, the freedom of political debate is not absolute in nature; *Observer and Guardian v the United Kingdom* (App no 13585/88) (1991) Series A no 216

[719] The unequivocal role of the press as purveyor of information and public watchdog has been emphasized in numerous case-laws. In this light, reference can be made to the following exemplary cases: *Schwabe v Austria* (App no 13704/88) Series A no 242-B, *Krone Verlag GmbH and Co. KG v Austria* (App no 34315/96) ECHR 26 February 2002, *Dalban v Romania* (App no 28114/95) ECHR 1999-VI

[720] *Handyside v the United Kingdom* (App no 5493/72) (1976) Series A no 24

[721] *Lingens v Austria* (App no 9815/82) (1986) Series A no 103, *Castells v Spain* (App no 11798/85) (1992) Series A no 236

institutions but also – with the help of the media – at all levels of social life, political parties make an irreplaceable contribution to political debate, which is at the very core of the concept of a democratic society".[722]

It is, thus, worthwhile to emphasize the ineluctability and necessity of the broadness of this fundamental freedom within democracy, and for the main players within it, as confirmed in the Court's established case-law, an example of which is the *Castells v Spain* judgment wherein the applicant had been accused of having overstepped the normal limits of political debate by insulting a democratic government in order to destabilize it during a very sensitive and critical period for Spain. After reiterating the general importance of freedom of expression for democracy, and "the pre-eminent role of the press in a State governed by the rule of law", the Court asserts that "while freedom of expression is important for everybody, it is especially so for an elected representative of the people. He represents his electorate, draws attention to their preoccupations and defends their interests. Accordingly, interferences with the freedom of expression of an opposition member of parliament, like the applicant, call for the closest scrutiny on the part of the Court".[723] Although on the basis of the *Castells v Spain* judgment the freedom of expression is considered to be of an unprecedented value, Tom Zwart argues that since 2008 [724] the Court is reiterating from this line of thought whereby the emphasis has shifted towards more tolerance and respect for the equal dignity within the democratic and pluralistic society, as evident from the two landmark cases of *Feret v Belgium* and *Le Pen v France*.[725] However, other scholars, like Rick Lawson, reject such a separation between such two lines of reasoning of the Court by arguing that the roots of this development have always been present in the jurisprudence of the Court which encumbers a personal responsibility on whomever aims to exercise his right to freedom of expression.[726]

Yet, whether these two lines of reasoning are separable or not, it goes without saying that, in recent years, as both scholars acknowledge, a modification of approach towards more tolerance has taken place. What is more, the enjoyment of a higher protection of the right to freedom of expression is not only dependent on the capacity of the person involved, as an elected representative, but also on the expressions as such when they are of an extreme importance to the general

---

[722] *The United Communist Party of Turkey and Others v Turkey* (App no 19392/92) ECHR 1998-I. It is also in this context that parliamentary immunity has to be apprehended.

[723] *Castells v Spain* (App no 11798/85) (1992) Series A no 236, *Malisiewicz-Gasior v Poland* (App no 43797/98) ECHR 6 April 2006

[724] This development is held to be set in motion in *Soulas and Others v France* (App no 15948/03) ECHR 10 July 2008, and continued with other cases such as *Balsyte-Lideikiene v Lithuania* (App no 72596/01) ECHR 4 November 2008, *Feret v Belgium* (App no 15615/07) ECHR 16 July 2009, *Le Pen v France* (App no 18788/09) ECHR 12 May 2010

[725] Afshin Ellian, Gelijn Molier and Tom Zwart (eds), *Mag ik dit zeggen? Beschouwingen over de vrijheid van meningsuiting* (Boom Juridische Uitgevers, Den Haag 2011) 333

[726] Ibid 197

concern within the public debate.[727] Thence, conviction for defamation cannot be considered proportionate and therefore 'necessary in a democratic society' within the meaning of Article 10 when the expressions are of extreme importance for the debate on a matter of general concern in the context of which the impugned comments were uttered.[728] In such instances, "the margin of appreciation available to the authorities in establishing the "need" for the impugned measure [is] particularly narrow"[729] except when the expressions concerned "[...] incite violence against an individual or a public official or a sector of the population, [only then] the State authorities enjoy a wider margin of appreciation when examining the need for an interference with freedom of expression [...]. The Court also acknowledges that in situations of conflict and tension particular caution is called for on the part of the national authorities when consideration is being given to the publication of opinions which advocate recourse to violence against the State lest the media become a vehicle for the dissemination of hate speech and the promotion of violence' [...] [But] 'where a publication cannot be categorized as inciting to violence, Contracting States cannot with reference to the prevention of disorder or crime restrict the right of the public to be informed by bringing the weight of the criminal law to bear on the media".[730] As can be observed, the freedom of expression has thus a broad scope that can go so far as to offend, shock and disturb, all of which has to be tolerated in the name of tolerance and broadmindedness in a pluralist democratic society unless violence is advocated.[731] Although the threshold is put on the incitement of violence for limiting the freedom of expression, as we can observe, the Court brings the dissemination of 'hate speech' into the ambit of prohibited speech, but without defining it.[732] However, before elucidating this notion, it is ineluctable to recall briefly one more crucial aspect of the utmost boundaries of the freedom of expression.

---

[727] *Mamere v France* (App no 12697/03) ECHR 2006-XIII, *Bladet Tromsø and Stensaas* (App no 21980/93) ECHR 1999-III, *VgT Verein gegen Tierfabriken v Switzerland*, (App no 24699/94) ECHR 2001-VI, *Vides Aizsardzības Klubs v Latvia* (App no 57829/00) ECHR 27 May 2004, *Steel and Morris v the United Kingdom* (App no 68416/01) ECHR 2005-II

[728] *Mamere v France* (App no 12697/03) ECHR 2006-XIII

[729] Ibid. *Ceylan v Turkey* (App no 23556/94) ECHR 1999-IV, *Verein gegen Tierfabriken Schweiz (VgT) v Switzerland* (no. 2) (App no 32772/02) ECHR 30 June 2009, *Mouvement raëlien Suisse v Switzerland* (App no 16354/06) ECHR 13 July 2012

[730] *Erdogdu v Turkey* (App no 25723/94) ECHR 2000-VI

[731] It is worthwhile to note that the Court has stated that, as in the case of "racially motivated attacks, when investigating violent incidents, State authorities have the additional duty to take all reasonable steps to unmask any religious motive and to establish whether or not religious hatred or prejudice may have played a role in the events"; *Milanović v Serbia* (App no 44614/07) ECHR 14 December 2010

[732] It is worth noting that the notion of 'hate speech' is, although used, nowhere (explicitly) defined by the Court. Still, a description of this notion can be found in the recommendations enacted by the Committee of Ministers of the Council of Europe. Committee of Ministers of the Council of Europe, 607th meeting of the Ministers' Deputies 'Of The Committee of Ministers to Member States on "Hate Speech" ' (30 October 1997) Rec No R (97) 20

In addition to the aforementioned discriminatory speech which is not protected and covered by Article 10 of the ECHR, for protecting the rights of others, the Court makes also a careful distinction between speeches that are either 'facts' or 'value-judgments'. The difference between the two, simply asserted, is that existence of facts can be demonstrated, whereas the truth of value-judgments is not susceptible to proof.[733] In this regard, the Court has, time and again, underlined that "[...] people prosecuted as a result of comments they make about a topic of general interest must have an opportunity to absolve themselves of liability by establishing that they acted in good faith and, in the case of factual allegations, by proving they are true [...]".[734] But in this, the Court also stresses that "[...] any individual who takes part in a public debate of general concern [...] must not overstep certain limits, particularly with regard to respect for the reputation and the rights of others, a degree of exaggeration, or even provocation, is permitted".[735] Yet, what is remarkable about the demeanor of the Court concerning *facts* is that while clearly established historical facts, e.g. the Holocaust, the negation or revision of which do not fall within the protection of Article 10, the Court states that it is, nonetheless, not its task to settle issues about which an ongoing debate is still taking place among historians concerning the events and their interpretation.[736]

This demeanor conveys the impression that the Court implicitly relativizes the indisputability of horrific historical facts when it, later on, states that "even though remarks [like those the applicants made] are always likely to reopen the controversy and bring back memories of past sufferings, the lapse of time makes it inappropriate to deal with such remarks, forty years on, with the same severity as ten or twenty years previously. That forms part of the efforts that every country must make to debate its own history openly and dispassionately".[737] Especially, one ought to bear in mind that the Court also adds that expressions that offend, shock or disturb are protected since such are the demands of pluralism, tolerance and broadmindedness without which there is no 'democratic society'.[738] Although the Court[739] has upheld the threshold of indisputableness of clearly established historical facts such as the Holocaust one can notice that

[733] *Lingens v Austria* (App no 9815/82) (1986) Series A no 103. The relevance of the distinction between truth and value-judgment is evident from, for instance, the case of *Castells v Spain* (App no 11798/85) (1992) Series A no 236, *Pedersen and Baadsgaard v Denmark* (App no 49017/99) ECHR 2004-XI, *Otegi Mondragon v Spain* (App no 2034/07) ECHR 15 March 2011

[734] *Mamere v France* (App no 12697/03) ECHR 2006-XIII, *Castells v Spain* (App no 11798/85) (1992) Series A no 236, *Colombani and Others v France* (App no 51279/99) ECHR 2002-V

[735] *Mamere v France* (App no 12697/03) ECHR 2006-XIII, *Steel and Morris v the United Kingdom* (App no 68416/01) ECHR 2005-II

[736] *Lehideux and Isorni v France* (App no 24662/94) ECHR 1998-VII

[737] Ibid

[738] Furthermore, reference can be made to *Open Door and Dublin Well Woman v Ireland* (App no 14235/88) (1992) Series A no 246, and *Vogt v Germany* (App no 17851/91) (1995) Series A no 323

[739] *Lehideux and Isorni v France* (App no 24662/94) ECHR 1998-VII, *Garaudy v France* (App no 65831/01) ECHR 2003-IX

nonetheless – besides the time relativization – the Court also asserts in its later jurisprudence that, in general, "[...] where historical or scientific events are concerned, new facts may emerge over the years that enrich the debate and improve people's understanding of what actually happened".[740] This has to be understood in the context of the fact that the Court argues that "[...] it is an integral part of freedom of expression to seek historical truth and it is not the Court's role to arbitrate the underlying historical issues, which are part of a continuing debate between historians that shapes opinion as to the events which took place and their interpretation".[741] Hence, based on the overall reasoning of the Court, it can be argued that this Court upholds the indisputableness of well-established historical facts which are beyond any reasonable doubt, but it does this with a lot of reticence which is perilous since it leaves a lot of doors open to developments in the future that can undermine the fundamental rights of others, just as it is stressed in the Concurring Opinion of Judge Thomassen who asserts that "just like anyone else, historians are entitled to freedom of expression" whereby not 'the fundamental rules of historical method' should form the point of departure but the 'importance of other interests' has to be 'the most decisive factor in determining the scope of freedom of expression for justifying any restrictions'.[742]

In this light, he agrees that certain expressions – like the book concerned – can constitute a direct assault on the integrity and identity of the human person which should also be fostered and respected by historical works. One interpretation of this opinion can be that indisputableness of facts is not what has to be decisive but the 'importance of other interests', that is, 'the protection of the reputation or the rights of others' has to be critical. Further, this view is perilous for it likewise relativizes facts that are actually independent from how the interests of others are valued, not to mention who has the authority for doing this, besides the fact that such dependency puts facts into perspective.[743] In the context of the Holocaust, it remains to be seen how the Court will assess the necessity and the need to protect the reputation or the rights of others in the future based on, among others, its time-relativization criterion. But fortunately, for the time being, the Court upholds the indisputableness of well-established historical facts and the imperativeness of the rights and reputation of others as a legitimate aim within the historical and social context in which the expressions are uttered.[744]

---

[740] *Mamere v France* (App no 12697/03) ECHR 2006-XIII

[741] *Chauvy and Others v France* (App no 64915/01) ECHR 29 June 2004

[742] Ibid; Concurring Opinion of Judge Thomassen

[743] A positive legal development whereby the indisputability of well-established historical facts, such as the Holocaust, is acknowledged concerns the limitation of internet, and Holocaust-denying sites, one of the limiting criteria of which is the proportionality of such measures that provide for a balance to be struck between freedom of expression and the competing interests

[744] *Hoffer and Annen* (App nos 397/07, 2322/07) ECHR 13 January 2011, *Rekvényi v Hungary* (App no 25390/94) ECHR 1999-III, *ETA Deutschland v Germany* (App no 43481/09) ECHR 18 March 2013

The inference that can be drawn, thus far, is that public debate, wherein the freedom of expression – which is the basic foundation of a democratic society and the condition for each individual's development and self-fulfillment – can come to its full realization in a democracy, requires pluralism, tolerance and broadmindedness in so far as to allow expressions to be offending, shocking or disturbing, especially when they concern the main players that can contribute to this debate in the public interest. This broad interpretation and scope given to this fundamental freedom entails that, on the one hand, the press must, however, not overstep the bounds provided for the exercise of this right, and on the other, although politicians have within the aforementioned boundaries a broader freedom of expression[745] at their disposal, they can, simultaneously, expect more critique in return.[746] And more than with politicians, "the limits of permissible criticism are wider with regard to the Government' [which entails that] 'in a democratic system the actions or omissions of the Government must be subject to the close scrutiny not only of the legislative and judicial authorities but also of the press and public opinion"[747] even if the remarks are perceived to be insulting or provocative [748] lest they incite violence or disseminate hate speech. Henceforth, although the demands of pluralism, tolerance and broadmindedness – which are considered to be the hallmarks of a democratic society – require that offending, shocking or disturbing expressions (when they are not discriminatory in nature[749], do not undermine well-established historical facts, or incite to violence or hatred) ought to be allowed even if they are insulting or provocative, yet, when it comes down to the rights or reputation of others, insulting

---

[745] *Feret v Belgium* (App no 15615/07) ECHR 16 July 2009

[746] The fact that politicians enjoy more freedom of speech is evident from the fact that states have a narrow and limited margin of appreciation in confining the fundamental freedom of expression of politicians, as it is, for instance, apparent from the case of *Incal v Turkey* (App no 22678/93) ECHR 1998-IV, and the case of *Erbakan v Turkey* (App no 59405/00) ECHR 6 July 2006. An exception to this concerns the category of civil servants about whom the Court states that "civil servants must enjoy public confidence in conditions free of undue perturbation if they are to be successful in performing their tasks and it may prove necessary to protect them from offensive verbal attacks when on duty; this also applies to defamatory allegations concerning acts performed in the exercise of their duties. [...] [However] As the Court also pointed out in *Janowski*, while it cannot be said that civil servants knowingly lay themselves open to close scrutiny of their every word and deed to the extent to which politicians do, in certain cases civil servants acting in an official capacity are subject to wider limits of acceptable criticism than ordinary citizens."; *Mamere v France* (App no 12697/03) ECHR 2006-XIII; see for example *Busuioc v Moldova* (App no 61513/00) ECHR 21 December 2004

[747] *Castells v Spain* (App no 11798/85) (1992) Series A no 236, *Erdogdu v Turkey* (App no 25723/94) ECHR 2000-VI

[748] *Özgür Gündem v Turkey* (App no 23144/93) ECHR 2000-III

[749] Interesting in this regard are the Committee of Ministers of the Council of Europe, 607th meeting of the Ministers' Deputies 'Of The Committee of Ministers to Member States on The Media and The Promotion of a Culture of Tolerance' (30 October 1997) Rec No R (97) 21 and Committee of Ministers of the Council of Europe, 872nd meeting of the Ministers' Deputies 'Declaration on freedom of political debate in the media' (12 February 2004)

utterances, as seen in the *Jersild v Denmark* judgment[750], can, nonetheless, result in the delineation of this fundamental freedom. In other words, the necessity of limiting this fundamental freedom in a democratic society has a narrow scope but when it comes down to the morals, rights or reputation of others who have made their presence felt in Western pluralistic societies it seems that the scope of protection is widened so far as to cover also insulting, offending and provocative expressions. This modification of approach is also evident from other cases as regards to which different commentators have argued that the broad scope of this fundamental freedom, which we could not explicitly discern until the *Castells v Spain* judgment, has, since 2008, changed[751] with more importance being attached to tolerance and respect for equal dignity within a democratic and pluralistic society.[752] Thus, the acceleration of pluralism is deemed to have a detrimental effect on the balance that, in the context of pressing social needs, has to be struck for what is considered to be necessary in a democratic society. It is, then, also in this regard that the notion of 'hate speech' comes, more than ever, into the picture.

The notion of 'hate speech' has never been (explicitly) defined by the Human Rights Court, despite the frequent occurrence. In addition, it is congruous to note that to date there is also no universally accepted definition of the notion. Notwithstanding such a lack, for the sake of argument, an attempt will be made to provide a description of this notion. In so doing, we will take two distinct documents into consideration. On the one hand, we have the documents delivered by the Council of Europe and, on the other, the jurisprudence of the Human Rights Court which will provide us with insights into a better understanding of the concept. The first relevant document delivered by this Council's Committee of Ministers is the Recommendation 97(20). This Recommendation asserts that "[...] 'hate speech' shall be understood as covering all forms of expression which spread, incite, promote or justify racial hatred, xenophobia, anti-Semitism or other forms of hatred based on intolerance, including: intolerance expressed by aggressive nationalism and ethnocentrism,

---

[750] *Jersild v Denmark* (App no 15890/89) (1994) Series A no 298; the Court says in this case that "there can be no doubt that the remarks in respect of which the Greenjackets were convicted [...] were more than insulting to members of the targeted groups and did not enjoy the protection of Article 10 [...] However, even having regard to the manner in which the applicant prepared the Greenjackets item [...], it has not been shown that, considered as a whole, the feature was such as to justify also his conviction of, and punishment for, a criminal offence under the Penal Code. [...] Having regard to the foregoing, the reasons adduced in support of the applicant's conviction and sentence were not sufficient to establish convincingly that the interference thereby occasioned with the enjoyment of his right to freedom of expression was 'necessary in a democratic society'; in particular the means employed were disproportionate to the aim of protecting 'the reputation or rights of others'. Accordingly the measures gave rise to a breach of Article 10 (art. 10) of the Convention"

[751] *Soulas and Others v France* (App no 15948/03) ECHR 10 July 2008, *Balsyte-Lideikiene v Lithuania* (App no 72596/01) ECHR 4 November 2008, *Feret v Belgium* (App no 15615/07) ECHR 16 July 2009, *Le Pen v France* (App no 18788/09) ECHR 12 May 2010

[752] Afshin Ellian, Gelijn Molier and Tom Zwart (eds), *Mag ik dit zeggen? Beschouwingen over de vrijheid van meningsuiting* (Boom Juridische Uitgevers, Den Haag 2011) 197, 333

discrimination and hostility against minorities, migrants and people of immigrant origin".[753]

Although this definition is not enough to comprehend this notion, it, nonetheless, provides us with its main characteristics which are as follows. In the first place, it has to be about 'hatred' – few examples of which are given in this definition – which is based on 'intolerance'.[754] Hereafter, in Principle 4, this Recommendation asserts that "national law and practice should allow the courts to bear in mind that specific instances of hate speech may be so insulting to individuals or groups as not to enjoy the level of protection afforded by Article 10 of the European Convention on Human Rights to other forms of expression. This is the case where hate speech is aimed at the destruction of the rights and freedoms laid down in the Convention or at their limitation to a greater extent than provided therein". Interesting in this elucidation is that 'hatred', expressed through speech aimed at individuals or groups, contains insult which needs to be of such a severe nature, i.e. destruction or unprecedented limitation of the rights and freedoms, that it would fall outside the ambit of the protection of the Convention which is, in fact, in line with Article 17 of the ECHR.[755] This Article forbids the abuse of rights by asserting that "*nothing in this Convention may be interpreted as implying for any State, group or person any right to engage in any activity or perform any act aimed at the destruction of any of the rights and freedoms set forth herein or at their limitation to a greater extent than is provided for in the Convention*".[756] Crucial in this regard is the understanding of the notion of 'hate speech' by the Human Rights Court. This Court states, for instance, in the *Gündüz v Turkey* case "[...] that tolerance and respect for the equal dignity of all human beings constitute the foundations of a democratic,

---

[753] Appendix to Committee of Ministers of the Council of Europe, 607th meeting of the Ministers' Deputies 'Of The Committee of Ministers to Member States on "Hate Speech"' (30 October 1997) Rec No R (97) 20. Reference can also be made to, e.g., Parliamentary Assembly of the Council of Europe Rec 1805 'Blasphemy, religious insults and hate speech against persons on grounds of their religion' (29 June 2007) CoE Report Doc 11296 wherein it is asserted that "for speech to qualify as hate speech in this sense, it is necessary that it be directed against a person or a specific group of persons. National law should penalize statements that call for a person or a group of persons to be subjected to hatred, discrimination or violence on grounds of their religion"

[754] The notion of intolerance is not defined, but when we consult the ECRI General Policy Rec No 7 'On National Legislation to Combat Racism and Racial Discrimination' (13 December 2002), it becomes evident that this concept is brought within the ambit of the term racism which is defined in the broadest sense of the word. It is, for instance, stated that "in the Recommendation, the term "racism" should be understood in a broad sense, including phenomena such as xenophobia, anti-Semitism and intolerance" yet without defining these concepts

[755] In the case of *Lawless v Ireland* the Court says that "this provision which is negative in scope cannot be construed a contrario as depriving a physical person of the fundamental individual rights guaranteed by [Articles 5 and 6 (art. 5, art. 6) of] the Convention"; *Lawless v Ireland* (No 3) (App no 332/57) (1961) Series A no 3

[756] Reference can be made to the case of *Hizb Ut-Tahrir and Others v Germany* (App no 31098/08) ECHR 12 June 2012

pluralistic society. That being so, as a matter of principle it may be considered necessary in certain democratic societies to sanction or even prevent all forms of expression which spread, incite, promote or justify hatred based on intolerance (including religious intolerance), provided that any 'formalities', 'conditions' or 'penalties' imposed are proportionate to the legitimate aim pursued".[757]

If we put this next to the preceding formula concerning pluralism and democracy, then, interesting developments come to the fore, for as we had discussed heretofore, the Court had asserted that there can be no democracy without pluralism and for that reason freedom of expression as enshrined in Article 10 of the ECHR is applicable not only to information and ideas that are favorably received or regarded as inoffensive or as a matter of indifference, but also to those that offend, shock or disturb[758], again, because such are considered to be the demands of pluralism, tolerance and broadmindedness without which there is no democratic society. Thenceforth, freedom of expression, as enshrined in Article 10, can be subject to restrictions that ought to be *narrowly* interpreted and whose necessity must be *convincingly* established.[759] Yet, in comparing these two descriptions, it is conspicuous that even though pluralism and tolerance, as prerequisites of democracy, demand openness to expressions that could go as far as to offend, shock and disturb, with the introduction of the notion of hate speech, however, the demand of (religious) tolerance within a democratic pluralist society requires curtailment of such offending utterances. And although formerly the imposition of limitations had to be narrowly interpreted and could take place only when their necessity was convincingly established due to which a narrow margin of appreciation was at the disposal of the states, with the notion of hate speech the proportionality of the limitations for pursuing a legitimate aim is deemed to suffice without any high thresholds and with a wider margin of appreciation at the avail of the states.

The reason for this shift in demeanor as required by pluralism is, according to the Court, that "[...] whoever exercises the rights and freedoms enshrined in the first paragraph of that Article [10] undertakes 'duties and responsibilities'. Among them – in the context of religious opinions and beliefs – may legitimately be included an obligation to avoid as far as possible expressions that are *gratuitously offensive* to others and thus an infringement of their rights, and which therefore do not contribute to any form of public debate capable of furthering progress in human affairs".[760] This is why, according to the Court, "[...] a certain margin of appreciation is generally available to the Contracting States when regulating freedom of expression in relation to matters liable to

---

[757] *Gündüz v Turkey* (App no 35071/97) ECHR 2003-XI. This same formula is reiterated by the Court in other judgments like in the case of *Erbakan v Turkey* (App no 59405/00) ECHR 6 July 2006

[758] *The United Communist Party of Turkey and Others v Turkey* (App no 19392/92) ECHR 1998-I, *Handyside v the United Kingdom* (App no 5493/72) (1976) Series A no 24

[759] *Vogt v Germany* (App no 17851/91) (1995) Series A no 323, *Handyside v the United Kingdom* (App no 5493/72) (1976) Series A no 24, *Axel Springer AG v Germany* (App no 39954/08) ECHR 7 February 2012

[760] *Gündüz v Turkey* (App no 35071/97) ECHR 2003-XI [emphasis added]

offend intimate personal convictions within the sphere of morals or, especially, religion".[761] The reason that the Court provides for this reasoning in its judgments is that, "[...] as at the time of the *Handyside* judgment [...], it is not possible to find in the legal and social orders of the Contracting States a uniform European conception of morals. The view taken of the requirements of morals varies from time to time and from place to place, especially in our era, characterized as it is by a far-reaching evolution of opinions on the subject. By reason of their direct and continuous contact with the vital forces of their countries, State authorities are in principle in a better position than the international judge to give an opinion on the exact content of these requirements as well as on the 'necessity' of a 'restriction' or 'penalty' intended to meet them".[762] Thus, generally speaking, as regards the adjustment of rights and freedoms, a certain margin of appreciation is left to the states[763], but when it concerns the sphere of morals or religion, as said above, this margin tends to be wider in scope.[764]

The *raison d'être* behind the lowering of this threshold and the extension of the freedom of expression is that, according to the Court, "[...] in democratic societies, in which several religions coexist within one and the same population, it may be necessary to place restrictions on this freedom in order to reconcile the interests of the various groups and ensure that everyone's beliefs are respected. [...] The Court has frequently emphasized the State's role as the neutral and impartial organizer of the exercise of various religions, faiths, and beliefs, and stated that this role is conductive to public order, religious harmony and tolerance in a democratic society. It also considers that the State's duty of neutrality and impartiality is incompatible with any power on the State's part to assess the legitimacy of religious beliefs [...] and that it requires the State to ensure mutual tolerance between opposing groups [...]".[765] Furthermore, it is notable that the margin of appreciation left to the states for assessing the necessity of limitations, and thus the pressing social needs within a democratic society to pursue in a proportionate manner a legitimate aim concerns the aims that are encompassed in Article 10 of the ECHR among which 'religion' is not (explicitly) mentioned. And whereas, previously, one was allowed to utter expressions that could be, among others, offending, now, in the context of religious opinions and beliefs, expressions that gratuitously offend intimate personal convictions within the sphere of morals and especially religion have to

---

[761] Ibid

[762] *Müller and Others v Switzerland* (App no 10737/84) (1988) Series A no 133. See, for instance, also *Wingrove v The United Kingdom* (App no 17419/90) ECHR 1996-V

[763] *Gündüz v Turkey* (App no 35071/97) ECHR 2003-XI

[764] Parliamentary Assembly of the Council of Europe Rec 1805 'Blasphemy, religious insults and hate speech against persons on grounds of their religion' (29 June 2007) CoE Report Doc 11296

[765] *Refah Partisi and Others v Turkey* (App nos 41340/98, 41342/98, 41343/98, 41344/98) ECHR 31 July 2001, *Chaare Shalom Ve Tsedek v France* (App no 27417/95) ECHR 2000-VII, *Metropolitan Church of Bessarabia and Others v Moldova* (App no 45701/99) ECHR 2001-XII

be confined for they do not enjoy the protection afforded by Article 10 of the Convention.

Interesting, in this regard, is the balance sought between the aforementioned broad scope of freedom of expression and the narrow scope given to it in the case of religious and moral matters as we can read in '*a preliminary report on the national legislation in Europe concerning blasphemy, religious insults and inciting religious hatred*' wherein the European Commission for Democracy through Law, oftentimes indicated as the Venice Commission, asserts that "in its Resolution 1510(2006) on freedom of expression and respect for religious beliefs, the Parliamentary Assembly of the Council of Europe addressed the question of whether and to what extent respect for religious beliefs should limit freedom of expression. It expressed the view that freedom of expression should not be further restricted to meet increasing sensitivities of certain religious groups, but underlined that hate speech against any religious group was incompatible with the European Convention on Human Rights".[766]

It is, however, remarkable for the Commission to state that "in a democratic society, religious groups must tolerate, as other groups must, critical public statements and debate about their activities, teachings and beliefs, provided that such criticism does not amount to *intentional and gratuitous insult* and does not constitute incitement to disturb the public peace or to discriminate against adherents of a particular religion".[767] Hence, what seems notable is that, although the Commission acknowledges (in line with the Court) the illicitness of intentional and gratuitous insult, it, nevertheless, attempts to prevent any privilege or additional protection that would be given to religious matters just as it also asserts that "far more controversial is the extent to which it is necessary to restrict freedom of expression in order to protect the religious beliefs and practices of certain individuals and groups of persons".[768] It interprets "the concepts of pluralism, tolerance and broadmindedness on which any democratic society is based, [in a way that it] mean[s] that the right to freedom of expression does not, as such, envisage that an individual is to be protected from exposure to a religious view simply because it is not his or her own".[769] This is a view stemming from the jurisprudence to which the Court adds that it is not to be excluded that an expression, which is not on its face offensive, could have an offensive impact in certain circumstances. In assessing this, the Court takes

---

[766] European Commission for Democracy through Law (Venice Commission), *Preliminary Report: On the national legislation in Europe concerning blasphemy, religious insults and inciting religious hatred* (adopted by the Commission at its 70th plenary session, Venice, 16-17 March 2007)

[767] Ibid. Parliamentary Assembly of the Council of Europe Rec 1805 'Blasphemy, religious insults and hate speech against persons on grounds of their religion' (29 June 2007) CoE Report Doc 11296

[768] European Commission for Democracy through Law (Venice Commission), *Preliminary Report: On the national legislation in Europe concerning blasphemy, religious insults and inciting religious hatred* (adopted by the Commission at its 70th plenary session, Venice, 16-17 March 2007)

[769] Ibid

various factors into consideration, e.g. the type of expression, the particular manner through which it is expressed, and the particularity of the circumstances of the case such as country-specific religious sensitivities.[770]

Nonetheless, the Court maintains the modified approach, encompassing the lowering of the threshold, which it applies to religious and moral matters as is evident from the established case-law of the Court. Notable in this regard is the case of *Otto-Preminger-Institut v Austria.*[771] This judgment was about the forfeiture and seizure of a film with the aim to protect the rights of others, particularly the right to respect religious feelings and, subsequently, to prevent disorder.[772] Firstly, besides the freedom of expression, the Court also emphasizes that the right to freedom of thought, conscience and religion which is safeguarded in Article 9 of the ECHR is one of the foundations of the democratic society: "It is, in its religious dimension, one of the most vital elements that go to make up the identity of believers and their conception of life [as we had also discussed in the first section of this research within the context of the formation of civilizations]. Those who choose to exercise the freedom to manifest their religion, irrespective of whether they do so as members of a religious majority or a minority, cannot reasonably expect to be exempt from all criticism. They must tolerate and accept the denial by others of their religious beliefs and even the propagation by others of doctrines hostile to their faith.[773] However, the manner in which religious beliefs and doctrines are opposed or denied is a matter which may engage the responsibility of the State, notably its responsibility to ensure the peaceful enjoyment of the right guaranteed under Article 9 (art.9) to the holders of those beliefs and doctrines. Indeed, in extreme cases the effect of particular methods of opposing or denying religious beliefs can be such as to inhibit those who hold such beliefs from exercising their freedom to hold and express them".[774]

At the outset, the first impression being conveyed is that the standard formula concerning freedom of expression whereby utterances may go so far as to shock, offend, or disturb is also applicable to religious beliefs and doctrines since the Court states that adherents of religions cannot expect to be exempted from critique and must tolerate and accept denial of their beliefs even if they are hostile in nature. However, in sequence, the Court puts, in the case of religious and moral matters, the emphasis on the 'duties and responsibilities' that Article 10 brings along, and reiterates its standard formula that "[...] whoever exercises the rights and freedoms enshrined in the first paragraph of that Article (art.10-1)

---

[770] *Murphy v Ireland* (App no 44179/98) ECHR 2003-IX

[771] *Otto-Preminger-Institut v Austria* (App no 13470/87) (1994) Series A no 295-A

[772] It is worth noting that the Parliamentary Assembly of the Council of Europe has argued in its Parliamentary Assembly of the Council of Europe Rec 1805 'Blasphemy, religious insults and hate speech against persons on grounds of their religion' (29 June 2007) CoE Report Doc 11296 that "[...] national law should only penalize expressions about religious matters which intentionally and severely disturb public order and call for public violence"

[773] This reasoning can also be found in other cases of the Court. Reference can be made, for instance, to *I.A. v Turkey* (App no 42571/98) ECHR 2005-VIII

[774] *Otto-Preminger-Institut v Austria* (App no 13470/87) (1994) Series A no 295-A

undertakes 'duties and responsibilities'. Among them – in the context of religious opinions and beliefs – may legitimately be included an obligation to avoid as far as possible expressions that are [as regards issues of veneration[775]] gratuitously offensive to others [and profane[776]] and thus an infringement of their rights, and which therefore do not contribute to any form of public debate capable of furthering progress in human affairs. This being so, as a matter of principle it may be considered necessary in certain democratic societies to sanction or even prevent improper attacks on objects of religious veneration, provided always that any 'formality', 'condition', 'restriction' or 'penalty' imposed be proportionate to the legitimate aim pursued [...]".[777]

Two important aspects, which are striking in this reasoning, should be highlighted. The notion of *gratuitously offensive expressions* seems to be introduced by the Court to mean improper attack that can be directed against *objects of religious veneration*. How this ought to be understood is that protection tends to be provided for religious subjects that are exposed to such a manner of treatment "[...] as to be calculated (that is, bound, not intended) to outrage those who have an understanding of, sympathy towards and support for the Christian [– or any other religious[778] –] story and ethic, because of the contemptuous, reviling, insulting, scurrilous or ludicrous tone, style and spirit in which the subject is presented [...]. This is an aim which undoubtedly corresponds to that of the protection of 'the rights of others' within the meaning of paragraph 2 of Article 10 (art.10-2). It is also fully consonant with the aim of the protections afforded by Article 9 (art.9) to religious freedom".[779] As regards this latter, the Court emphasizes that "the respect for the religious feelings of believers as guaranteed in Article 9 (art.9) can legitimately be thought to have been violated by provocative portrayals of objects of religious veneration; [or unwarranted and offensive attacks on religious principles and dogmas[780] that are held to be sacred[781], such as, e.g., abusive attacks on the Prophet of Islam[782]]; and

---

[775] *Murphy v Ireland* (App no 44179/98) ECHR 2003-IX

[776] Ibid. *I.A. v Turkey* (App no 42571/98) ECHR 2005-VIII. However, based on this latter case, it is argued in the literature that the Court is moving towards a more protective approach in relation to extreme speech; see Ivan Hare and James Weinstein (eds), *Extreme Speech and Democracy* (OUP, Oxford 2009) 305

[777] *Otto-Preminger-Institut v Austria* (App no 13470/87) (1994) Series A no 295-A

[778] Abusive attacks can concern any religion and can be offending and insulting to feelings about any religion as we can see in the Court's application of this reasoning to Islam in *I.A. v Turkey* (App no 42571/98) ECHR 2005-VIII

[779] *Wingrove v The United Kingdom* (App no 17419/90) ECHR 1996-V. The Court states that such cases concern actually a weighing of the conflicting interests involved within the exercise of two fundamental freedoms as we can see, among others, in *I.A. v Turkey* (App no 42571/98) ECHR 2005-VIII and *Otto-Preminger-Institut v Austria* (App no 13470/87) (1994) Series A no 295-A

[780] The European Commission for Democracy through Law (Venice Commission), *Preliminary Report: On the national legislation in Europe concerning blasphemy, religious insults and inciting religious hatred* (adopted by the Commission at its 70th plenary session, Venice, 16-17 March 2007)

[781] *Wingrove v The United Kingdom* (App no 17419/90) ECHR 1996-V

such portrayals can be regarded as malicious violation of the spirit of tolerance, which must also be a feature of democratic society. The Convention is to be read as a whole and therefore the interpretation and application of Article 10 (art.10) in the present case must be in harmony with the logic of the Convention [...]".[783]

Hence, provocative portrayals of objects, figures and doctrines of religious veneration are considered to be *gratuitously offensive* for they do not respect religious feelings in their manner of expression and are, therefore, considered to be malicious violation of the spirit of tolerance. The inference that we can draw here is that religious feelings are, although not explicitly mentioned, yet read into the spirit of Article 9 which are subsequently protected through the notion of 'morals' and the clause of 'rights and reputation of others' in Article 10 of the ECHR.[784] For protecting these feelings, objects of religious veneration as well as principles and dogmas need to be protected against provocative portrayals and manners that are perceived to be gratuitously offensive. In this way, protection is not only provided for religious feelings but also, in an indirect manner, for objects of religious veneration, principles and dogmas. In other words, not only individuals are protected against offensive speech but also object and dogmas of veneration. And in assessing and determining when such protection has to be provided through a prohibition of offensive expressions, the states have a wider margin of appreciation[785] because, in the Court's point of view, as previously stated, "as in the case of 'morals' it is not possible to discern throughout Europe a uniform conception of the significance of religion in society [...]; even within a single country such conceptions may vary. [Nor is there "sufficient common ground in the legal and social orders of the member States of the Council of Europe to conclude that a system whereby a State can impose restrictions on the propagation of material on the basis that it is blasphemous is, in itself, unnecessary in a democratic society and thus incompatible with the Convention".[786]] For that reason it is not possible to arrive at a comprehensive definition of what constitutes a permissible interference with the exercise of the right to freedom of expression where such expression is directed against the religious feelings of others".[787]

---

[782] *I.A. v Turkey* (App no 42571/98) ECHR 2005-VIII

[783] *Otto-Preminger-Institut v Austria* (App no 13470/87) (1994) Series A no 295-A

[784] It is interesting to note that as regards this issue, it is argued that "*Otto Preminger Institut* seems to suggest that 'the rights of others' in Article 10(2) can only be understood by reference to Article 9 (right to religious freedom). In contrast, Judge Pettiti, one of the majority in *Wingrove*, declares without further elaboration that Article 9 cannot be 'in issue' in cases of offence to religious feelings and that the 'rights of others' restriction in Article 10(2) is capable of serving as a self-standing ground of restraint"; in Ivan Hare and James Weinstein (eds), *Extreme Speech and Democracy* (OUP, Oxford 2009) 319

[785] This can also be found in other cases, an example of which is *I.A. v Turkey* (App no 42571/98) ECHR 2005-VIII

[786] *Wingrove v The United Kingdom* (App no 17419/90) ECHR 1996-V

[787] *Otto-Preminger-Institut v Austria* (App no 13470/87) (1994) Series A no 295-A

To this lack of uniformity, the argument is added that, as noted above[788], "what is likely to cause substantial offence to persons of a particular religious persuasion will vary significantly from time to time and from place to place, especially in an era characterized by an ever growing array of faiths and denominations" [789], which is particularly relevant in the contemporary multicultural societies in Europe. Especially when the Parliamentary Assembly of the Council of Europe insists that it "underlines the importance of respect for, and understanding of, cultural and religious diversity in Europe and throughout the world and recognizes the need for ongoing dialogue. Respect and understanding can help avoid frictions within society and between individuals. Every human being must be respected, independently of religious beliefs. [Particularly] in multicultural societies it is often necessary to reconcile freedom of expression and freedom of thought, conscience and religion".[790]

Furthermore, as regards the aforementioned judgment, a comparable reasoning can also be found in other cases wherein the Court reiterates its formula. A prime example of such a landmark case is the *Giniewski v France* judgment which was concerned with the protection of the rights and reputation of others against defamation on the basis of their membership in a particular religion[791] – Christianity. In this case, the biblical doctrine of the 'fulfillment' of the Old Covenant in the New was disputed, and it was argued that this doctrine contains the fundament of anti-Semitism which fostered the idea and implementation of the Holocaust. In its assessment, the Court argues that "[...] although the applicant's article criticizes a papal encyclical and hence the Pope's position, the analysis it contains cannot be extended to Christianity as a whole, which, as pointed out by the applicant, is made up of various strands, several of which reject papal authority. The Court considers, in particular, that the applicant sought primarily to develop an argument about the scope of a specific doctrine and its possible links with the origins of the Holocaust. In so doing he had made a contribution, which by definition was open to discussion, to a wide-ranging and ongoing debate [...], without sparking off any controversy that was gratuitous or detached from the reality of contemporary thought." [792] And when such

[788] *Müller and Others v Switzerland* (App no 10737/84) (1988) Series A no 133

[789] *Murphy v Ireland* (App no 44179/98) ECHR 2003-IX

[790] Parliamentary Assembly of the Council of Europe Rec 1805 'Blasphemy, religious insults and hate speech against persons on grounds of their religion' (29 June 2007) CoE Report Doc 11296

[791] However, in one case we can see that the Court applies its standard formula and states that although the expressions might be offensive and shocking, yet they should not be confined as long as they do not incite to violence and hatred; see *Nur Radyo Ve Televizyon Yayinciligi A.S. v Turkey* (App no 6587/03) ECHR 27 November 2007. Yet in other cases, we see that the Court provides a higher protection to religious groups, an example of which is the judgment *Norwood v the United Kingdom* (App no 23131/03) ECHR 16 November 2004 wherein the Court states that "[...] vehement attack against a religious group, linking the group as a whole with a grave act of terrorism, is incompatible with the values proclaimed and guaranteed by the Convention, notably tolerance, social peace and non-discrimination"

[792] *Giniewski v France* (App no 64016/00) ECHR 2006-I

contributions have an added value to discourses that are of great interest in a democratic society, limitations on the fundamental freedom of expression are to be strictly construed, especially when the contribution does not contain attacks on religious beliefs *par excellence* [793] but aims to seek historical truth – without casting doubt on clearly established historical facts – which is considered to be an integral part of the freedom of expression. Thus, a decisive factor that we have to be cognizant of in this regard is the public debate and the contribution that is made to it by the utterances. In such cases, "[...] the Court considers it essential in a democratic society that a debate on the causes of acts of particular gravity amounting to crimes against humanity should be able to take place freely"[794] even if the discourses at hand would offend, shock or disturb some people.[795] Henceforth, it was confirmed that the aim of the interference indeed corresponded to that of the protection of the reputation or rights of others. It was then reiterated that the exercise of the freedom of expression carries with it duties and responsibilities, "amongst them – in the context of religious opinions and beliefs – may legitimately be included an obligation to avoid as far as possible expressions that are gratuitously offensive to others and thus an infringement of their rights, and which therefore do not contribute to any form of public debate capable of furthering progress in human affairs".[796] And as a standard formula, also in this case, it is reiterated that there is no "[...] uniform European conception of the requirements of the protection of the rights of others in relation to attacks on their religious convictions [which thus] broadens the Contracting States' margin of appreciation when regulating freedom of expression in relation to matters liable to offend intimate personal convictions within the sphere of morals or religion".[797] The difference in scope when it comes to the margin of appreciation is, again, plainly elucidated in *Wingrove v The United Kingdom*. Herein, the Court states that "whereas there is little scope under Article 10 para.2 of the Convention (art.10-2) for restrictions on political speech or on debate of questions of public interest [...] a wider margin of appreciation is generally available to the Contracting States when regulating freedom of expression in relation to matters liable to offend intimate personal convictions within the sphere of morals or, especially, religion".[798]

---

[793] The same can be seen with regard to the utterances that concerned an archbishop and not a part of the population on the basis of their Catholic belief; see *Klein v Slovakia* (App no 72208/01) ECHR 31 October 2006

[794] *Giniewski v France* (App no 64016/00) ECHR 2006-I

[795] See also *De Haes and Gijsels v Belgium* (App no 19983/92) ECHR 1997-I

[796] *Giniewski v France* (App no 64016/00) ECHR 2006-I, *Otto-Preminger-Institut v Austria* (App no 13470/87) (1994) Series A no 295-A, *Wingrove v The United Kingdom* (App no 17419/90) ECHR 1996-V, and *Gündüz v Turkey* (App no 35071/97) ECHR 2003-XI

[797] *Giniewski v France* (App no 64016/00) ECHR 2006-I, *Otto-Preminger-Institut v Austria* (App no 13470/87) (1994) Series A no 295-A, *Wingrove v The United Kingdom* (App no 17419/90) ECHR 1996-V, and *Murphy v Ireland* (App no 44179/98) ECHR 2003-IX, *Aydin Tatlav v Turkey* (App no 50692/99) ECHR 2 May 2006

[798] *Wingrove v The United Kingdom* (App no 17419/90) ECHR 1996-V

Thus, expressions that attack intimate personal convictions – encompassing objects of religious veneration and religious principles and dogmas that are held to be sacred – are considered to be gratuitously offensive and subject to limitations, regarding which a wider margin of appreciation is made available to the states. But, as the Court insists, "the extent of insult to religious feelings must be significant, as is clear [for instance] from the use of the [national] courts of the adjectives 'contemptuous', 'reviling', 'scurrilous', 'ludicrous' to depict material of a sufficient degree of offensiveness".[799] Still, it is in the literature that since the *I.A. v Turkey* case and despite the verdict in this judgment, we can observe an inversion in the Court's attitude whereby it is moving towards a more protective demeanor towards freedom of expression. An argument on the basis of the dissenting opinions attached to this verdict contends "[...] that a democratic society is not a theocratic one and that the time had come to revisit the *Otto-Preminger* and *Wingrove* judgments which, in their view, placed too much emphasis on conformism or uniformity of thought and reflected an overcautious and timid conception of freedom of the press. Furthermore, [it is argued that] the Court has shown itself less willing to protect religious sensibilities in recent cases concerning criticism of secularism and calls for the introduction of Sharia in Turkey and suggestions that aspects of Catholic doctrine may have contributed towards the causes of the Holocaust".[800] Although a change in maneuver is admittedly noticeable, as this dissenting opinion also suggests, yet, it is premature to draw far-reaching conclusions from the mere opinions of dissenters that are contrary to our findings in the study above. Nonetheless, it remains, indeed, to be seen what the sequence of this maneuver will be in the future against the background of an accelerated pluralism. In addition and for the sake of argument, one vital point regarding irreligious and religious utterances needs to be elucidated, and for which the sharia law is taken as our point of departure.

What has become evident in the foregoing is the variable demeanor of the Court towards irreligious and religious speeches. Whereas the Court confines irreligious expressions by lowering the threshold for them, it, nonetheless, allows religious utterances that are *par excellence* incompatible with human rights and democracy as is evident from the example of sharia law which, by definition, is considered to be irreconcilable with the fundamental principles of democracy and human rights as envisaged in the Convention. For as the Court argues, "[...] sharia, which faithfully reflects the dogmas and divine rules laid down by religion, is [conceived to be] stable and invariable [whereby] principles such as pluralism in the political sphere or the constant evolution of public freedoms have no place in it [and thus] [...] it is difficult to declare one's respect for democracy and human rights while at the same time supporting a regime based on sharia, which clearly diverges from Convention values, particularly with regard to its criminal law and criminal procedure, its rules on the legal status of women and the way it intervenes in all spheres of private and public life in

---

[799] Ibid

[800] Ivan Hare and James Weinstein (eds), *Extreme Speech and Democracy* (OUP, Oxford 2009) 305

accordance with religious precepts [due to which] [...] a political party whose actions seem to be aimed at introducing sharia in a State party to the Convention can hardly be regarded as an association complying with the democratic ideal that underlies the whole of the Convention".[801]

Subsequently, the Court states that "in view of the very clear link between the Convention and democracy [...] no one must be authorized to rely on the Convention's provisions in order to weaken or destroy the ideals and values of a democratic society. [And therefore] pluralism and democracy are based on a compromise that requires various concessions by individuals or groups of individuals, who must sometimes agree to limit some of the freedoms they enjoy in order to guarantee greater stability of the country as a whole".[802] This conveys the impression that, in accordance with this indisputable intertwining of democracy and human rights, an advocated ideology that is inherently incompatible with these fundamental notions has to be subdued to limitations. Still, it is remarkable for the Court to assert that – provided that one does not incite to violence or hate speech based on (religious) intolerance[803] – "[...] a political party animated by the moral values imposed by a religion cannot be regarded as intrinsically inimical to the fundamental principles of democracy, as set forth in the Convention".[804] Accordingly, a political party has the right to propose, for example, constitutional changes but on the basis of two conditions: "firstly, the means used to that end must be legal and democratic; secondly, the change proposed must itself be compatible with fundamental democratic principles. It necessarily follows that a political party whose leaders incite to violence or put forward a policy which fails to respect democracy or which is aimed at the destruction of democracy[805], and the flouting of the rights and freedoms recognized in a democracy cannot lay claims to the Convention's protection against penalties imposed on those grounds".[806] This also means that "the mere fact of defending sharia, without calling for violence to establish it, cannot [in the Court's view] be regarded as 'hate speech' "[807], even if sharia is inherently incompatible with the fundamental principles of democracy and the rights and freedoms enshrined in the Convention. Advocacy of this is thus

---

[801] *Refah Partisi and Others v Turkey* (App nos 41340/98, 41342/98, 41343/98, 41344/98) ECHR 31 July 2001

[802] Ibid

[803] *Gündüz v Turkey* (App no 35071/97) ECHR 2003-XI

[804] *Refah Partisi and Others v Turkey* (App nos 41340/98, 41342/98, 41343/98, 41344/98) ECHR 31 July 2001

[805] Thus, democracy is conceived to be vigilant, i.e. militant in defending itself as we have seen in the case of *Vogt v Germany* (App no 17851/91) (1995) Series A no 323

[806] *Refah Partisi and Others v Turkey* (App nos 41340/98, 41342/98, 41343/98, 41344/98) ECHR 31 July 2001, *Yazar and Others v Turkey* (App nos 22723/93, 22724/93 and 22725/93) ECHR 2002-II, and, *mutatis mutandis*, the following judgments: *Stankov and the United Macedonian Organisation Ilinden v Bulgaria* (App nos 29221/95 and 29225/95) ECHR 2001-IX, and *Socialist Party and Others v Turkey* (App no 21237/93) ECHR 1998-III

[807] *Gündüz v Turkey* (App no 35071/97) ECHR 2003-XI. The combination of hate speech and glorification of violence can be found in, for instance, *Sürek v Turkey* (no. 1) (App no 26682/95) ECHR 1999-IV

protected by Article 10 even though it runs counter to the fundamental values of the Convention, whereas irreligious expressions do not enjoy the same level of protection as it is, for instance, apparent from the judgment of *Norwood v the United Kingdom* whereby a "[...] vehement attack against a religious group, linking the group as a whole with a grave act of terrorism, is [considered to be] incompatible with the values proclaimed and guaranteed by the Convention, notably tolerance, social peace and non-discrimination".[808] Thus, the discussion of these exemplary cases and the developments therein – such as the employed standards – convey the impression that the protection given to irreligious expressions also differs from that related to religious utterances. However, this is also dependent on factors such as national circumstances which are left to the judgment of national authorities. This is also apparent from the reasoning of the Court in, for example, *Gündüz v Turkey* case whereby it states that "[...] as a matter of principle it may be considered necessary *in certain democratic societies* to sanction or even prevent all forms of expression which spread, incite, promote or justify hatred based on intolerance (including religious intolerance) [...]".[809]

In conclusion, although the Court itself is a majoritarian thinker in its verdicts[810], as we have seen, for example, in the *Otto-Preminger Institut*[811] and the *I. A. v Turkey*[812] judgments, the majority position in democracy is not considered to be decisive, and thus the views of the majority do not always prevail. Instead, a balance must be struck that would ensure a fair and proper treatment of minorities and would thus avoid any abuse of a dominant position.[813] It is, perhaps, due to this that the Court lowers the threshold of allowable expressions and gives the states a wider margin of appreciation in order to also protect the religious feelings and convictions of the minorities. However, the lowering of this threshold does not mean that religious expressions are equally protected among the European states, for this margin also provides national authorities with the freedom to decide how to deal with religious

---

[808] *Norwood v the United Kingdom* (App no 23131/03) ECHR 16 November 2004. The same bearing can be observed in other cases such as that of *Gündüz v Turkey* (App no 35071/97) ECHR 2003-XI

[809] *Gündüz v Turkey* (App no 35071/97) ECHR 2003-XI [emphasis added]

[810] It is important to bear in mind that the Court, as a majoritarian thinker, tends to take the feelings and beliefs of the majority in a society into consideration in striking a balance among the interests and rights involved which can be detrimental to the scope of freedom of expression. In this light, one can also imagine the effect of the change in this composition whereby the minority of today – as calculated and predicted by some – would become the majority of tomorrow

[811] *Otto-Preminger-Institut v Austria* (App no 13470/87) (1994) Series A no 295-A

[812] *I.A. v Turkey* (App no 42571/98) ECHR 2005-VIII

[813] Although the Court contends that the view of the majority need not prevail, nonetheless, we see in all the discussed cases that in the context of the assessment of what is 'necessary in a democratic society' the Court is attentive to the view of the majority of the people in any given society

expressions within the public sphere.[814] Yet, the lowering of the threshold concerns not only the protection of individuals as bearers of certain fundamental rights, but it seems that the objects and doctrines of veneration in which the individuals believe are, with the aforementioned modification of approach, also gaining protection. Thence, the Court seems to provide additional protection to religion in the broadest sense of the term – that it is even added as an additional 'legitimate aim' to the positive law in force – which, accordingly, tends to underpin the preeminence of social needs in a democratic society. And the more religious feelings are voiced and made to be felt within the acceleration of pluralism, the more the Court seems to be willing to accept the necessity of interference by national authorities on the basis of their wider margin of appreciation for limiting the right to freedom of expression.

2.5. The Right to Freedom of Expression at the National Level

The tensions and collisions among cultures in the broadest sense of the word have been most tangible at the national level where numerous civilizations are in direct contact with each other. At this same level, these direct clashes have put the right to freedom of expression into perspective. One of the key countries where these collisions have been and are most tangible is the Netherlands, on account of which this country is chosen for our case study at the national level. The menace posed to this fundamental freedom, as already touched upon in this inquiry, has manifested itself both in extrajudicial and judicial forms. In this regard, two exemplary cases of this manifestation can be provided which highlight the aptness of this country to this discourse on the fundamental right to freedom of expression.[815] Yet, for the sake of argument, a brief *de facto* discussion of these two cases should suffice, for the scope of this research is narrowed to the mere *de jure* impact of the assaults on this fundamental freedom.

The first case concerns the assassination of the Dutch politician Wilhelmus Simon Petrus (Pim) Fortuyn on 6 May 2002. Fortuyn was a fierce critic of Islam as well as multiculturalism[816], and was assassinated by Volkert van der Graaf who happened to be an environmentalist. He killed Fortuyn because of the

[814] M.L.P. (Titia) Loenen, 'Mensenrechten en diversiteit in Europa: gelijke monniken, ongelijke kappen?' (Oratie (in verkorte vorm) uitgesproken door Prof.dr. M.L.P. (Titia) Loenen bij de aanvaarding van het ambt van hoogleraar op het gebied van Mensenrechten en Diversiteit aan de Universiteit Leiden op vrijdag 15 november 2013)

[815] Afshin Ellian, 'Volkert van der G., Mohammed B. en Mohammed A.' in *Hoe nu verder? 42 visies op de toekomst van Nederland na de moord op Theo van Gogh* (Spectrum, Utrecht 2005) 86-98

[816] Pim Fortuyn, *Tegen de islamisering van onze cultuur: Nederlandse identiteit als fundament* (A.W. Bruna Uitgevers, Utrecht 1997). For a perspicuous analysis of Fortuyn's arguments as regards multiculturalism, see, for instance, Paul Cliteur, 'Pim Fortuyn en de multiculturele samenleving' (2004) Civis Mundi 80-84

victim's critical views.[817] Van der Graaf, who saw Fortuyn as "a threat to the society", was convicted by the court and sentenced to eighteen years' imprisonment on 15 April 2003[818], a decision that was also upheld by the Court of Appeal on 18 July 2003.[819] Noteworthy in this case is the reasoning of the Public Prosecutor who argued that through the manslaughter of a politician, the "[...] suspect has pierced the heart of the democratic process in an irreversible and criminal way. The assassination has unprecedentedly disrupted society: the political climate has been severely altered because [the personal] security of politicians and their families has become inevitable and, for a long period of time, many citizens have had an anxious feeling that standing up for a more outspoken opinion can trigger violence".[820] The second exemplary case of such an extrajudicial confinement of the fundamental right to freedom of expression is the manslaughter of the Dutch columnist and film producer, Theo Van Gogh, by Mohammed Bouyeri.[821] Van Gogh had produced the movie '*Submission*'[822], together with the former politician, Ayaan Hirsi Ali[823], which contained a fierce critique of Islam and its treatment of women.[824]

The assassin, Mohammed Bouyeri, has never shown regret or remorse for the brutal assassination and has always been convinced that his conduct had been nothing but his religious duty to wage Holy War or *Jihad*.[825] This had also been mirrored in the indictment of the Public Persecutor wherein the enmity of the perpetrator towards, among others, 'democracy' had been exposed, which he, *inter alia*, had aimed to destroy by waging *Jihad* against it.[826] What is more, "in a ruling by a Dutch court of January 23, 2008, after the murder, the murderer of Van Gogh gave some new insights into his motives. He declared: the reason for the murder of Van Gogh is that he offended the Prophet. According to the law,

[817] Johan Faber, *Wat bezielde Volkert van der G.* (Nijgh & Van Ditmar Uitgeverij, Amsterdam 2008)
[818] Rb. Amsterdam 15 April 2003, *LJN* AF7291
[819] Hof Amsterdam18 July 2003, *NJ* 2003, 580
[820] Rb. Amsterdam 15 April 2003, *LJN* AF7291 [own translation]
[821] Rb. Amsterdam 26 July 2005, *JIN* 2005, 360. For a documentation and discussion of this case, see Ron Eyerman, *The Assassination of Theo van Gogh: From Social Drama to Cultural Trauma* (DUP, Duke 2008)
[822] Van Gogh's ideas can also be found in the following book: Theo van Gogh, *Allah weet het beter* (Xtra Producties, Amsterdam 2003)
[823] Mohammed Bouyeri had pierced a letter to the body of van Gogh wherein Ayaan Hirsi Ali was announced to be the next on the death list
[824] Iveta Jusová, 'Hirsi Ali and Van Gogh's *Submission:* Reinforcing the Islam v. women binary' (2008) 31 Women Stud Int Forum148-155
[825] Paul Cliteur, 'De eigen-schuld theorie' in *Hoe nu verder? 42 visies op de toekomst van Nederland na de moord op Theo van Gogh* (Spectrum, Utrecht 2005) 14-20
[826] A further elaboration of the religious context wherein the perpetrator had conducted his deed can be found in the report of Ruud Peters to which also the public prosecutor had made reference in his indictment. Ruud Peters (Mei 2005) "De Ideologische en Religieuze Ontwikkeling van Mohammed B.: Deskundigenrapport in de strafzaak tegen Mohammed B. in opdracht van het Openbaar Ministerie opgesteld voor de arrondissementrechtbank Amsterdam"

he deserved the death penalty which I have executed... Theo van Gogh considered himself to be a soldier. He fought against Islam. On November 2, Allah sent a soldier to cut his throat... This is Jihad in the most literal sense. Van Gogh saw himself as a soldier and he had to be slaughtered. Van Gogh knew what he was doing. He stepped into the arena".[827]

These two cases illustrate why it is imperative to take a closer look at the impact of pluralism on the fundamental right to freedom of expression in the Netherlands, for the extrajudicial menace posed to this fundamental freedom is most tangible in this country, and it even goes so far as to form a clear and present danger to the Dutch society, the extent and magnitude of which are not fully determined and mapped out yet, but keeps, nonetheless, everyone hostage in its terror. This raises the question over what impact, if not limitation, the collisions between cultures will have on the fundamental right to freedom of expression with the acceleration of pluralism within Western societies, and especially in the Netherlands where this impact has been most tangible. However, since the literature on the documentation and analyses of the *extrajudicial* curtailment is in abundance, as previously observed, the scope of this inquiry is limited to the mere judicial, viz. *de jure* curtailment of the fundamental right to freedom of expression. Thus, besides the extrajudicial restraints imposed on the fundamental right to freedom of expression, we have the option of the judicial confinement of this fundamental freedom at the national level, which has become more pronounced in terms of the intensified collisions among civilizations that seem most tense at this level due to multiculturalism that underpins Western democracies whereby various cultures come into direct contact with one another.

Furthermore, an inquiry at the national level becomes even more pertinent when we take into consideration the fact that, before one can file a complaint with the Human Rights Court, all domestic remedies must have been exhausted as we can read in Article 35 of the ECHR, on account of which the Court has, time and again, stated that it merely fulfills a subsidiary role. This brings us then to the national level in the context of our chosen country especially with regard to the limitations that can be imposed on the fundamental right to freedom of expression. For as we could observe in the previous section, the Court provides national authorities with a wider margin of appreciation for assessing the necessity of imposing limitations in the context of European pluralistic societies. Hence, before elaborating on the impact of multiculturalism on the freedom of expression in order to determine whether (and to what extent) the accelerated presence of numerous civilizations has confined the freedom of expression at the national level, it is, first of all, important to assess and apprehend this fundamental right at this level. The fundamental right to freedom of expression is also acknowledged within the Dutch legal system itself, as it can be seen in Article 7 of the Constitution of the Kingdom of the Netherlands which we will discuss hereinafter.

---

[827] Paul Cliteur, 'State and religion against the backdrop of religious radicalism' (2012) 10 Int Jnl of Constitutional Law 127, 139

Article 7 of the Dutch Constitution reads as follows:

"*Article 7. (1) No-one requires prior permission in order to publish thoughts or feelings via the press, save for everybody's responsibility according to law.*[828]

(2) Statute provides for regulations regarding radio and television. There is no supervision in advance of the content of a radio or television broadcast.

(3) For the publication of thoughts or feelings via means other than the ones stipulated in the preceding paragraph,[829] *no-one requires prior permission regarding the content thereof, save for everybody's responsibility according to the law. Statute may regulate the rendering of displays accessible to persons younger than sixteen years of age for protection of good morals.*

(4) The preceding paragraphs do not apply to commercial advertisement".[830]

Before continuing, it is important to bear in mind that due to the (moderate) monism that underpins the Dutch legal system, (the provisions of) the European Convention on Human Rights – and thus also Article 10 of this Convention – can be directly invoked before the national courts without any further need for domestic legal transformation. This is unequivocal because the Dutch system is characterized by the 'prohibition of constitutional review'[831] which, briefly said, entails that the formal laws[832] may not be assayed against the (Dutch) Constitution but only against the international treaties that are binding upon everyone.[833] Thus, within the Dutch legal system, there are two constructions for

[828] Although the prohibition of censorship is regulated in this provision – except in the case of children younger than sixteen years old – it does not mean that every expression can be uttered without any limitation, since there are limitations being provided for, as, for instance, in the Dutch Penal Code

[829] The ways of publication are not limited to those provided for in this provision, since the case-law makes evident that the means are assessed on a case-by-case basis due to which a variety of forms of publication of feelings and thoughts are recognized and can be recognized. See for instance HR 27 February 1951, *NJ* 472, HR 27 February 1951, *NJ* 473, HR 30 May 1967, *NJ* 1968, HR 24 January 1967, *NJ* 270

[830] The translation of the Dutch Constitution as used here and in the course of our study is taken from the following source: Philipp Kiiver (ed), *Sources of Constitutional Law: Constitutions and Fundamental Legal Provisions from the United States, France, Germany, the Netherlands, the United Kingdom, the ECHR and the EU* (2nd edn European Law Publishing, Groningen 2010)

[831] Article 120 of the Dutch Constitution

[832] A formal law is, in the Dutch legal terminology, a regulation which is enacted by the government in close cooperation with the States General according to the legislative procedure as it is prescribed within the constitution ex Article 81 of the Dutch Constitution. It is worth noting that the concept of 'law' employed in the Constitution has a more stringent meaning than the usage of the same term in the ECHR which only requires that the Act concerned is foreseeable and accessible

[833] In this regard, the following two provisions of the Dutch Constitution have to be taken into account. Article 93 which states that "*Provisions of treaties and of decisions of international organizations, which by virtue of their content can be binding upon everyone, become binding after they have been published*"; and Article 94 which states that "*Statutory regulations in force within the Kingdom are not applicable if such application is incompatible with*

limiting fundamental rights and freedoms which tend to operate side by side: the system embedded in the Constitution which is underpinned by the formal legality principle, and the human rights system that is mainly anchored in the ECHR which is, as we have seen in the preceding section, underpinned by the necessity and proportionality requirements.[834] As regards the formal legality principle, it is important to note that, as this provision indicates with regard to the clause '*save for everybody's responsibility according to law*', the limitation of the freedom of expression, as a matter of principle, stems from a formal law.[835] The main example of such a formal law – that imposes legal limitations on the fundamental freedom of expression – which also underpins our present study, is the Dutch Penal Code. The limitation of the fundamental right to freedom of expression can take place, just as we saw at both the international and European level, through the principle of non-discrimination whose main legal tool is the International Convention on the Elimination of All Forms of Racial Discrimination.

Against the background of this Convention, wherein the principle of non-discrimination is anchored, many Western democracies, including the Netherlands, have enacted laws against group defamation on the basis of race, ethnicity, religion, and more recently sexual orientation.[836] In the Netherlands, the protection of persons against defamation on the basis of what is characteristic for them can be found in Title V of the Dutch Penal Code. The main relevant provisions, in this regard, are Articles 137c and 137d of this Penal Code[837] which are characterized by the fact that they prohibit publicly uttered expressions aimed at a group of persons who are, as we will see below, identifiable on the basis of their distinct characteristics. And as pointed out already, this makes good sense if and when we recall that these provisions are created in the light of the aforementioned Convention. In other words, as we will elaborate hereinafter, "[...] the Netherlands Criminal Code penalizes insults expressed publicly for the purpose of discriminating on a variety of grounds (Article 137c): incitement to hatred, discrimination, and violence on ground of, inter alia, race (Article 137d); [...]".[838] Before elaborating on these provisions[839], it would be helpful to present them here in full.

---

provisions of treaties and decisions of international organizations that are binding on everyone"

[834] *Parliamentary Papers II* 2007/08, 31570, nr. 3, p 27

[835] JCA de Poorter and HJThM van Roosmalen, *Rol en betekenis van de Grondwet: Constitutionele toetsing in relatie tot de Raad van State,* (Raad van State, Den Haag 2010). However, only in the case of the second paragraph is delegation of legislative power allowed for the prescribed situations

[836] Ivan Hare and James Weinstein (eds), *Extreme Speech and Democracy* (OUP, Oxford 2009) 58

[837] Article 137e of the Penal Code is also part of this set, but the reason for not mentioning it is that this provision is a supplementary article which is only concerned with the manners in which offensive utterances of the preceding provisions can be made public

[838] Ivan Hare and James Weinstein (eds), *Extreme Speech and Democracy* (OUP, Oxford 2009) 379

[839] The translation used for the provisions of the Penal Code is from Lisanne Groen and Martijn Stronks, *Entangled Rights of Freedom. Freedom of speech, freedom of religion and the non-*

"*Article 137c of the Penal Code reads:*

1. *The person who in public, orally or in writing or by means of images, is deliberately offensive about a group of persons on account of their racial origin, religion or ideological beliefs, their heterosexual or homosexual orientation or their physical, psychological or mental disability, shall be liable to imprisonment for up to one year or a third category fine.*
2. *Where the offence is committed by a person for whom it has become a profession or custom or by two or more united persons, a prison sentence of up to two years or a fourth category fine shall be imposed*".

"*Article 137d of the Penal Code reads:*

1. *A person who in public, orally or in writing or images is guilty of incitement of hatred of or discrimination against people or violent acts against people or the property of people on account of their racial origin, religion or ideological beliefs, their gender, their heterosexual or homosexual orientation or their physical, psychological or mental disability, shall be liable to a term of imprisonment of up to one year or a third category fine.*
2. *Where the offence is committed by a person for whom it has become a profession or custom or by two or more united persons, a prison sentence of up to two years or a fourth category fine shall be imposed*".

According to the legal history of Article 137c, "the mere harming of self-confidence of a group of persons or bringing the group into discredit because it is of a certain racial origin, practices a certain religion, or has certain ideological beliefs is punishable by law. However, criticism of views or conduct, in whatever form, falls outside the scope of the drafted penal provision".[840] Although it is still not clear what is meant by 'mere harming' or 'discredit' and how such notions determine the scope of this provision, it is obvious that no human beings as such are allowed to be the subject of utterances but, *per contra*, their *conduct* and *views* may be targeted by such expressions. The recent jurisprudence of the Dutch judiciary has also confirmed this reasoning, for example, in the *Wilders* judgment.[841] As we will see below, the Dutch court asserts that targeting a group of persons is punishable whereas targeting their views and conduct, such as religious doctrines and practices, is permissible and thus not liable to punishment. As elaborated hereafter, this tends to contrast recent developments at the international level but also with the evolution of the jurisprudence of the European Human Rights Court, as seen in the preceding sections of this study. For as clarified in the discussion of the UN defamation discourse, and particularly in the case law of the Human Rights Court, objects and ideologies of veneration have of recent gained protection against offensive expressions.

---

discrimination principle in the Dutch Wilders case (Forum Institute for Multicultural Affairs, Eleven international publishing, The Hague 2010)

[840] *Parliamentary Papers II* 1969/70, 9724, nr. 6, p 4. Lisanne Groen and Martijn Stronks, *Entangled Rights of Freedom. Freedom of speech, freedom of religion and the non-discrimination principle in the Dutch Wilders case* (Forum Institute for Multicultural Affairs, Eleven international publishing, The Hague 2010) 36

[841] Rb. Amsterdam 23 June 2011, *NJ* 2012, 370

Prior to discussing this at the national level, it is important to grasp the notion of 'offense' as contained in the first provision. Although this notion is not explicitly defined in these articles, a further study of the law as well as jurisprudence should bring relief. As adjudged in the vast jurisprudence, what constitutes an *offense* against a group of persons in the sense of the former provision is, after assessing the expression independently, determined by the *context* wherein the expressions have been uttered, to which we will return instantly. Offense in terms of the second provision is easier to determine since two forms of it are mentioned in this Article: 'hatred' and 'discrimination'. What is meant by the term 'hatred' has been described in the case-law as an utterance that poses an 'intrinsically discordant dichotomy' between groups of people.[842] And a definition of the concept of 'discrimination' can be found in the Penal Code itself. Article 90quarter of this Code defines discrimination as follows: "*discrimination or discriminating shall be understood to include any distinction, exclusion, restriction or preference which has the purpose or could have the effect of nullifying or impairing the recognition, enjoyment or exercise, on an equal footing, of human rights and fundamental freedoms in a political, economic, social or cultural or any other field of life in society*".[843]

As regards the notion of 'offense' in Article 137c, to which we had promised to return, an elaboration of the case-law is ineluctable for, as mentioned, this notion is context-bound.[844] The context of expressions is, *mutatis mutandis*, decisive for Article 137d of the Penal Code. For instance, as regards the notion of 'discrimination', the Dutch Supreme Court argued in the *Janmaat* judgment that although utterances concerning multicultural society and its abolition were, as such, not discriminatory, nonetheless, once considered within the *context* wherein such expressions were uttered, they had to be conceived as discriminatory remarks.[845] This is perhaps on account of the fact that, as asserted in the legal history, "for the formulation of a fundamental right and the limiting clauses added to it [...] a satisfactory delineation has to be sought between, on the one hand, the major achievement that each person has to be free to express himself and, on the other, the rights of others and the community interests, which

---

842 HR 2 April 2002, *NJ* 2002, 421

843 Lisanne Groen and Martijn Stronks, *Entangled Rights of Freedom. Freedom of speech, freedom of religion and the non-discrimination principle in the Dutch Wilders case* (Forum Institute for Multicultural Affairs, Eleven international publishing, The Hague 2010) 40. Besides the description of the notion of discrimination in the Penal Code, we can also find the provision on discrimination in the Dutch Constitution, the first Article of which states: "*All persons in the Netherlands shall be treated equally in equal circumstances. Discrimination on the grounds of religion, belief, political opinion, race or sex or on any other grounds whatsoever shall not be permitted*". The translation of this Article is taken from: <http://legislationline.org/> accessed 5 November 2013

844 The scope of the notion of offence, which is the central point of this inquiry, is not the same as the definition of this notion. Thus, these two ought not to be confused with each other

845 HR 18 May 1999, *NJ* 1999, 634

have to be of such importance that the individual right has to recede".[846] This burdens the judiciary with the task of striking a fair balance between the two interests involved.[847] Yet, the inherent menace of this is that the judiciary can easily find itself on the edge of politically sensitive circumstances, if not judgments, just as it was in the aforementioned *Janmaat* judgment wherein the Court defined multiculturalism as multiracialism[848] based on which the person concerned was incriminated for discrimination. This menace is also evident from the criticism that was voiced against this judgment which argued that "[...] by taking into consideration the meaning that is assigned, in the literature, to the term multiculturalism, an indication of (incitement of) discrimination does not ensue, *ipso facto*, from the actual description within the indictment but rather from the name and reputation of the person who is conceived to be the suspect".[849]

However, besides this judicial solecism, it remains doubtful whether a mere personal profile had been decisive, for we should not forget that 'context' remains crucial in this, as we also saw at the European level. This is, for instance, apparent from the reasoning of the Dutch judiciary in the case of Wilders which is elaborated hereinafter. In this, the judiciary asserted that during the period wherein Wilders uttered his views, multiculturalism had a prominent place within the public discourse. And as this discourse intensifies, the scope of the fundamental right to freedom of expression is broadened.[850] Thus, 'context' is one of the decisive factors for the scope of this fundamental right. This decisiveness is also evident from other cases wherein, due to the context, the defamatory nature of expressions is taken away when such utterances are in themselves offensive or discriminatory, but lose the aggrieving or discriminatory character when they are considered within their *context*. The significance of context is thus apparent from the judgments that will be discussed momentarily.[851]

The first case is the *Van Dijke* judgment[852] wherein the Dutch Supreme Court states: "The opinion of the Court of Appeal that the comparison of practicing homosexuality with other conduct which, in the religious views of the accused are equally sinful, even if they appear as criminal offenses in the Dutch Penal Code, remained within the bounds of what is acceptable and were not therefore of a defamatory nature, does not evidence an inaccurate interpretation of the law. The Court of Appeal was justified in taking into account, in that opinion, the fact that freedom of religion and freedom of expression can also be deciding factors

---

[846] *Parliamentary Papers II* 1975-1976, 13872, *Parliamentary Papers II* 1980-1981, 16905, came into force on 28 January 1983 (*Stb.* 1983, 19)

[847] The balance that ought to be struck involves also the weighing up of the two fundamental rights concerning the freedom of expression and the freedom of religion

[848] HR 18 May 1999, *NJ* 1999, 634

[849] Ibid, note 't Hart [own translation]

[850] Afshin Ellian, Gelijn Molier and Tom Zwart (eds), *Mag ik dit zeggen? Beschouwingen over de vrijheid van meningsuiting* (Boom Juridische Uitgevers, Den Haag 2011) 335

[851] ALJ Janssens and AJ Nieuwenhuis, *uitingsdelicten* (2nd edn Kluwer, Deventer 2008) 155

[852] HR 9 January 2001, *NJ* 2001, 203

in determining whether or not the remarks (in themselves injurious or hurtful) should be deemed to be of a defamatory nature. The Supreme Court takes into account in this that the Court of Appeal's considerations imply that these remarks ostensibly bore a direct relationship to the expression of the religious views of the accused and are significant as such to him in the social debate".[853] Thus, the context can take the offensive nature of an expression away provided that it is not unnecessarily aggrieving and that it contributes to the public debate. What is more, it seems that religious persuasions can underpin the justifiability of the context, but, as stated heretofore, the context can also make a permissible expression become prohibited when it is unnecessarily aggrieving and does not contribute to the social discourse.[854]

Another case concerning expressions uttered in the context of religious convictions is the *Van der Wende* case.[855] This case also concerned expressions regarding homosexuality which deemed to be based on religious convictions, for the defendant said that the fact that homosexuality is equated with heterosexuality is comparable to the equation of larceny with benefaction or battery with nursing. In this case, the Court of Appeal was of the view that expressions as such were offending for homophiles for, in this comparison, the dignity of the group of persons in question was repudiated. Yet, this Court argued, by considering the expressions in their context, that this context removes the offensive nature of the expressions in question, since, from this context, it can be deduced that the defendant has expressed himself, on the one hand, within the ongoing public debate regarding the question of whether a place has to be provided to homosexuality within the law, and, on the other, on the basis of his religious (biblical) convictions regarding homosexuality. In the Court's view, whoever, like the accused, denounces homosexual praxis on the basis of his Christian conviction [extendable to religion in general], which he does by choosing analogy as the style of his expression, has no choice but to explicitly mention and name in his comparison the evil concerned.

Thence, for the assessment of the context, a special importance seems to be attached to the religious convictions of the person concerned. This is considered to be permissible because the Court contends that in a democratic society there has to be room for such a debate, provided that it takes places within the acceptable proportions which would then render a limitation to the freedom of expression redundant. Be that as it may, it has to be borne in mind that the relevance of the context within a public debate is not only limited to religious utterances but, as we will see hereinafter, it also applies to non-religious

[853] This translation is taken from Lisanne Groen and Martijn Stronks, *Entangled Rights of Freedom. Freedom of speech, freedom of religion and the non-discrimination principle in the Dutch Wilders case* (Forum Institute for Multicultural Affairs, Eleven international publishing, The Hague 2010)

[854] ALJ Janssens and AJ Nieuwenhuis, *uitingsdelicten* (2nd edn Kluwer, Deventer 2008) 155, HR 9 November 2001, *NJ* 2002, 76, HR 22 September 1987, *NJ* 1988, 300

[855] HR 9 January 2001, *NJ* 2001, 204

expressions provided that they are not unnecessarily aggrieving.[856] The present judgment has resulted in the fact that the expression in question, considered within its context, is not perceived as unnecessarily aggrieving and, thus, not necessarily an offense in the sense of Article 137c of the Penal Code. Thenceforth, the Supreme Court also agrees with this overall assessment of the Court of Appeal and asserts that this latter Court has not given an incorrect interpretation of the term 'insult' in the provision at hand.

The last judgment wherein expressions were uttered on the basis of religious convictions is the *Herbig* judgment.[857] Again, in this case, the accused had expressed defamatory opinions concerning homosexuality, arguing that it is a filthy and obscene sin. The Court of Appeal considered the remarks to be of themselves independent from the context, and thus offensive towards homosexuals in denying them their dignity. Still, these remarks, which were considered *par excellence* to be offensive and aggrieving for homosexuals, had lost their defamatory character since they were uttered as expressing a religious view which entails that homosexuality is a sin. Thus, the accused repudiated homosexuality in his capacity as preacher on the basis of his Christian conviction. Therefore, he attempted to warn humanity against homosexuality. Based on this, the expressions were conceived to be relevant for the accused as his contribution to the public debate. This had led to the inference that expressions can lose their defamatory nature because of the context wherein religious views are conveyed. Accordingly, in the case at hand, the remarks – although offensive in nature – had lost their defamatory character due to the context which was underpinned by religious convictions. In following the Court of Appeal in its reasoning and agreeing with it, the Supreme Court had also asserted that this Court had not departed from an erroneous interpretation of the notion of 'offense' as contained in Article 137c of the Penal Code.

Based on the foregoing, we can thus infer that, in principle, the expression in question can either be offensive or discriminatory, but its offensive or discriminatory nature can be eradicated, and thus justified, by the context within the public debate wherein the expressions are uttered. Hence, the context is detrimental to the assessment of Article 137c and 137d of the Penal Code. But *how* this context is determined is, according to some commentators, based on the aforementioned exemplary judgments[858], bias in that it seems that religious expressions gain more protection than non-religious ones, since the subjective religious convictions in the former form of utterance – i.e. as long as the expression stands in direct connection with religious persuasions and so long as it

[856] ALJ Janssens and AJ Nieuwenhuis, *uitingsdelicten* (2nd edn Kluwer, Deventer 2008) 155

[857] HR 14 January 2003, *NJ* 2003, 261. See also Hof 's-Gravenhage 18 November 2002, *NJ* 2003, 24

[858] The commentators compare these cases with the case of Janmaat (HR 18 May 1999, *NJ* 1999, 634), wherein the accused had expressed himself against a multicultural society based on his political persuasions for which he was convicted. From this comparison the conclusion is, subsequently, drawn that religious expressions gain more protection than their non-religious counterparts

is in itself relevant for the accused within the public debate – decide the complexion of the context[859], whereas the same cannot be said of non-religious expressions.[860] In other words, the conclusion is, oftentimes, drawn that religious expressions tend to enjoy more protection than non-religious ones.[861] This distinction which can be observed at the national level is, *inter alia*, similar to our survey conducted at the European level whereby the threshold of freedom of expression is deemed to be lowered for religious expressions compared to non-religious ones. If this would be the case, then, the consequence would unavoidably be that with the acceleration of pluralism within democratic societies, religious expression, even if it is offensive, can be (more) freely uttered due to the mere fact that it is based on religion, whereas non-religious expression can be confined because of its offending nature as it lacks any justifiable religious basis. In other words, religion can have an exculpatory effect on defamatory expressions that are based on it, while non-religious expressions are punishable since they lack any religious foundation. Thus, "[...] such an approach could lead indirectly to defamatory remarks with a religious background receiving more protection than other defamatory remarks".[862] The peril of the arbitrariness of 'context', due to its vagueness, can also be observed in legal history whereby "it is evident that the situations wherein these forms of expression function differ enormously. It is also clear that the regulatory competences that the government needs, have to fit the situation concerned. This has the effect that the limiting possibilities can vary per situation, i.e., from one form of expression to the other".[863]

However, contrary to the hypothesis that unlike non-religious expressions, religious ones tend to enjoy more protection due to the mere fact that they are built upon *religious* persuasions which have, within the public debate, subjective relevance[864] for the person in question, we see that the same subjectivity formula

---

[859] Afshin Ellian, Gelijn Molier and Tom Zwart (eds), *Mag ik dit zeggen? Beschouwingen over de vrijheid van meningsuiting* (Boom Juridische Uitgevers, Den Haag 2011) 214, 215, 221; ALJ Janssens and AJ Nieuwenhuis, *uitingsdelicten* (2nd edn Kluwer, Deventer 2008) 37

[860] HR 18 May 1999, *NJ* 1999, 634, Rb. Amsterdam 13 June 1995, *NJ* 1995, 664, HR 15 April 2003, *NJ* 2003, 334

[861] It is worth noting that in the supplementary note of Mevis annexed to HR 14 January 2003, *NJ* 2003, 261, it is assumed that this presumption is void for it cannot be assumed that the Supreme Court can ever have such an intention. The denial of such an intention can also be observed in ALJ Janssens and AJ Nieuwenhuis, *uitingsdelicten* (2nd edn Kluwer, Deventer 2008) 160-161

[862] Lisanne Groen and Martijn Stronks, *Entangled Rights of Freedom. Freedom of speech, freedom of religion and the non-discrimination principle in the Dutch Wilders case* (Forum Institute for Multicultural Affairs, Eleven international publishing, The Hague 2010) 50

[863] *Parliamentary Papers II* 1975-1976, 13872, *Parliamentary Papers II* 1980-1981, 16905, came into force on 28 January 1983 (*Stb*. 1983, 19)

[864] Yet, it should be taken into account that both the provisions and the case-law explicitly narrow the scope of subjectivity by asserting that persuasions have to be *directly* reducible to religion. Nonetheless, the phenomenon of religion is comprehended in a broad sense and is, thus, not limited to conventional religions in practice (See for instance HR 9 January 2007, *LJN* AZ 2497)

is, *mutatis mutandis*, applied to the person who expresses himself on the basis of *political* convictions that have subjective relevance for him. This is, for instance, evident from a judgment of the Dutch Court of First Instance rendered on 7 April 2008.[865] In this case, the accused had expressed his opinion in public about Islam and the Koran by making a comparison with fascism and by calling the Prophet Mohammed a 'barbarian' and the Koran 'the Islamic Mein Kampf'. The question was whether a conviction, i.e. a limitation to freedom of expression, was necessary for the protection of the rights of Muslims in the Netherlands and not to aggrieve their religious feelings. The Court, firstly, notes that the answer to this question depends, as we saw heretofore, on the weighing of the relevant circumstances at hand, and states that a total limitation of this fundamental freedom beforehand is against Article 10 of the ECHR and Article 7 of the Constitution, since such a limitation constitutes (preventive) censorship. With this in mind, the Court assesses the case on hand and argues, in line with the European Court of Human Rights, that although certain expressions can be experienced as shocking and offending or that religion can be subjected to severe critique, these are not decisive grounds for limiting the freedom of expression. The expressions uttered by the accused, despite their defamatory nature, were considered permissible since they were perceived within their context which stood *in direct connection with his political convictions*.

Thence, the freedom of expression prevailed, for the utterances were *as such* relevant for the accused within the public debate concerning the position of Islam in the Netherlands, the causes of Muslim extremism, and integration problems. This reasoning is deemed thus to have clarified that the subjectivity assessment as regards the context is not merely applicable in cases of religious persuasions but also in cases of political convictions that are in themselves relevant for the person concerned. In this regard, it can be adduced that both forms of expression – religious and non-religious – enjoy the same level of protection provided that, as stated hitherto, they contribute to the public discourse and are not unnecessarily aggrieving. In other words, although on the basis of the aforementioned cases the impression had been conveyed that religious expressions had gained more protection than their non-religious counterparts, since this judgment, we can witness the start of an inversion towards the same amount of protection being provided to non-religious utterances. This reversal makes apparent that, although pluralism poses a confining menace to the freedom of expression, the judiciary at the national level, in striking a balance between the interests involved, has chosen to attach more weight to this fundamental right than protecting the feelings of groups of people within pluralist societies.

Yet, this reversal resuscitates the question as to what the course will be that the judiciary would steer in the future in its task of striking a balance, particularly with the acceleration of multiculturalism within an unprecedentedly pluralist society, and, of course, the rise of political populism. Especially when we take into account that the Supreme Court – albeit with some delay – seems to follow

[865] Rb. 's-Gravenhage 7 April 2008, *LJN* BC8732

the European Court when it asserts in its judgment of 16 December 2014 that 'in assessing the impermissibility of an expression for being defamatory in nature towards a group of persons and/or inciting to discrimination within the meaning of the provisions of the (Dutch) Penal Code, due regard has to be paid to the wording of an expression as well as the context in which it is uttered. Therewith, it has to be taken into account whether the offensive expression can contribute to the public debate or whether it is artistic in nature. It has also to be taken into account whether the expression concerned is not unnecessarily aggrieving. In the assessment of the question whether an expression is unnecessarily aggrieving – if the person concerned is a politician who expresses himself within the context of the public debate (which also encompasses the political debate) – on the one hand, special attention has to be paid to the importance of the fact that a politician has to be able to raise matters of public interest even if his expressions can offend, shock, or disturb, but on the other hand, due regard has also to be paid to the responsibility that a politician has within the public debate in preventing the dissemination of expressions that tend to be inconsistent with the (rule of) law and the basic principles of democracy. This does not only concern expressions that incite to hatred, violence, or discrimination but also expressions that incite to intolerance'.[866] It is thus this new development that conveys the impression that the freedom of expression could be narrowed under the multicultural pressure.

However, based on the foregoing judgment, it is imperative to consider the reverse whereby expressions are uttered *about* doctrines and objects of veneration. As we can read in the two provisions at hand, defamation must be about a 'group of persons' and not about the doctrines and objects of veneration. At the surface, it seems thus that defamation of objects and doctrines is not covered by these provisions and if they are the subject of defamatory expressions, then, the court still attempts to see whether they are deducible to groups of people that can, as the only legal subjects, gain protection by means of these provisions. This is, for instance, apparent in the judgment of the Dutch Court of Appeal rendered on 21 January 2009 concerning the expressions of the Dutch politician Geert Wilders about Islam. In this case, the Public Persecutor had arrived at the conclusion that the expressions of Wilders, although defamatory and aggrieving, were exculpated once they were considered in their context and their relevance for the public debate. What is more, according to the Public Persecutor, the remarks were not defamatory for Muslims as such, but they were an expression of his political convictions that were merely aimed at the *religion* of Islam.[867] The Court agreed that the context is decisive but argued that the context must be rightly comprehended. Firstly, a few isolated expressions

---

[866] HR 16 December 2014, ECLI: NL:HR:2014:3583

[867] However, when Wilders targeted a *group of people* during an election campaign, the Dutch Public Prosecutor decided to prosecute him; Sam de Voogt 'Openbaar Ministerie vervolgt Wilders voor discriminatie' *nrc.nl* (Amsterdam 18 December 2014) <http://www.nrc.nl/nieuws/2014/12/18/openbaar-ministerie-vervolgt-wilders-voor-discriminatie/> accessed 18 December 2014

need not be considered within the political context, whereupon the political context would be put forward as exculpation; however, in the Court's view, the coherence of Wilder's expressions must also be taken into account. Subsequently, from this coherence in his expressions, the Court drew the conclusion that Wilder's expressions were not only aimed at Muslim adherents (and not merely Islam as a religion) but that his remarks had also – willingly or not – an aggrieving effect on Muslims as a societal and religious group for, as such, they were brought into discredit.

The context of his utterances made evident that he continuously made a link between Islam and adherents of the Islamic faith, and even if he did not explicitly make this link, still the defamation of the group could be deduced from his disqualification and contempt of certain characteristics, traditions and symbols (e.g. Allah, Mohammed, and the Koran). It was contended that it is artificial to argue that offending or ridiculing religious personalities or symbols cannot at the same time entail the 'defamation *for* a group' or 'defamation *about* a group'. This so-called 'indirect' defamation, i.e. offending a group through the infringement of its symbols of veneration, is in line with the European Court of Human Rights[868] and accepted by the Dutch Supreme Court.[869] Thus, like the European Court, the Supreme Court argued that hate speech based on intolerance, including religious intolerance, is not protected by law. It had also been on this basis that the Court of Appeal had ordered the Public Persecutor to persecute the politician for the crimes entrapped in Articles 137c and 137d of the Penal Code. Accordingly, the politician had been persecuted whereupon the verdict was rendered on 23 June 2011.[870] Before conducting a survey of this latter judgment, it is pertinent to recall that the aforementioned 'indirect defamation', as we will elucidate farther hereinafter, still concerns the defamation of persons and not of symbols and doctrines. However, with the recognition of *in*direct defamation the threshold is admittedly lowered and tends to cover, perhaps in the future with the acceleration of multicivilizationalism, also symbols and doctrines.

Nevertheless, in the latter judgment of 23 June 2011, we can observe that the Dutch Court of First Instance, for the time being, reneges on this hinted development. This Court argues that based on the Parliamentary Papers regarding the enactment of the provisions, it is apparent that only the infringement of dignity or discrediting of the *group* due to its race, religion, or other convictions about life is liable for punishment. Criticism as regards convictions, even if it is severe, is not covered by the protection of the Penal Code and, hence, the scope of the provision(s) ought to be narrowly comprehended. The ground for this had already been laid by the Supreme Court in the *Gezwel* judgment[871] handed down in 2009. In this case, the Supreme Court stated that, unlike the Court of Appeal which made a link between Islam and

---

[868] *I.A. v Turkey* (App no 42571/98) ECHR 2005-VIII
[869] HR 14 January 2003, *NJ* 2003, 261
[870] Rb. Amsterdam 23 June 2011, *NJ* 2012, 370
[871] HR 10 March 2009, *NJ* 2010, 19

Muslims and gave thus – in the view of the Supreme Court an erroneous – interpretation to the phraseology 'a group of persons on account of their religion' in Article 137c of the Penal Code, the scope of this provision has to be narrowly construed. According to the Supreme Court, this provision criminalizes mere defamatory expressions aimed at a group of persons on account of their religion and not the defamation of a religion as such even if the adherents of that religion are hurt in their religious feelings. Hence, liable for punishment is any unnecessary aggrieving expression regarding a group of persons for the simple reason that they belong to a certain religion which is, thus, characteristic for them. In other words, expressions concerning a religion ought not to be equated with expressions regarding the adherents of that religion. With this reasoning, the Supreme Court distances itself from the relationship theory as regards a religion and its adherents.[872] This narrowly construed scope of Article 137c had been rehearsed by the Court of First Instance in the present case, whereupon it argued that the expressions of the politician had to be, *ipso facto*, aimed at a group of persons that are characterized by their religion. The mere fact that the aggrieving utterances about a religion offend also the adherents of it is thus not sufficient for equating them with expressions regarding the believers as such, that is, a group of persons on account of their religion.

Accordingly, in assessing the expressions of Wilders, the Court stated that his utterances were not directed at the group of persons on account of their religion but merely at Islam and the Koran. What is more, the Court recalled that, during the codification process, the legislator had seen no reason for enacting a general criminal provision for protecting the performance of institutions or organizations grounded on religion or any other ideological belief. To the very opposite, the opportunity must be provided to criticize, within the legally prescribed boundaries, precisely that performance even if it would offend the deepest convictions whereupon such institutions or organizations are built. Against this background, the Court drew the conclusion that the intention of the legislator had been nothing but the protection of persons belonging to a certain religion and not the religion itself. Furthermore, the Court agreed that there is hate speech when – considered within the context and circumstances wherein the expressions can convey the intended 'possible associations' as it had been circumscribed in the *Combat 18* case[873] – the expressions create an 'intrinsically discordant dichotomy', and that in order to foster and exhort hate speech, that is, an extreme emotion of deep aversion and animosity, it is required that the expression contains a reinforcing element. However, it underlined that an intrinsically

[872] Afshin Ellian, Gelijn Molier and Tom Zwart (eds), *Mag ik dit zeggen? Beschouwingen over de vrijheid van meningsuiting* (Boom Juridische Uitgevers, The Hague 2011) 222

[873] HR 23 November 2010, *NJ* 2011, 115; in this judgment, the Court states that "for the assessment of the question as to whether the text at hand contains hate speech or discrimination against people on the basis of their race, in terms of Article 137e of the (Dutch) Penal Code, the utterances should not be assayed independently, but have to be considered also in the light of the given circumstances and the possible associations they can generate" [own translation]

discordant dichotomy is not a prerequisite since mere reinforcement suffices. And even this latter element is not required when it concerns discrimination.

Based on the foregoing, the Court examined the expressions of the politician and inferred on the basis of his alleged statements that the accused, in his capacity as politician, had merely expressed his views about the evil aspects of Islam and the Koran. And since in these remarks the suspect addressed the religion and not the persons (Muslims), the Court did not consider it legally and convincingly proven that he, indeed, had incited hatred and/or discriminated against Muslims, as charged. And concerning those expressions that *were* directed against a group of persons, the Court said that the terminology of those expressions did not contain the reinforcing element for they had to be conceived as political proposals within the context of public debate as well as a critique uttered regarding the policy of the government or other policy makers in the field in which any politician, like the accused, has in principle a broader freedom for bringing his point of view to public attention. Conceived from the point of view of the suspect, these expressions were to be considered necessary in a democratic society for, in his point of view, he was critiquing societal problems. Especially, when, in the Court's view, one takes note of the period wherein multiculturalism and immigration happened to be the central themes of the public debate, the intensification of which required also a broader freedom of expression to the extent that expressions may be allowed to offend, shock, and disturb. Against this background, the Court considered the politician's expressions to be not of such a nature that they would be liable for punishment and exclusion from the public debate. Yet, what is conspicuous about this reasoning is that, as emphasized above, the Court takes the subjectivity of the person concerned as the point of departure which was also the case with the person who expressed himself on the basis of his religious convictions. This leads us to the inevitable conclusion that, as elaborated heretofore, religious expressions do not necessarily enjoy more protection than their irreligious counterparts. Furthermore, it is evident that, for the time being, religious symbols or doctrines are by no means protected. They can be relevant solely when they are employed as means to insult persons who, as the only recognized subjects of the law, enjoy protection.

Based on the foregoing survey, it can be inferred that at the national level, unlike the international and European level, multiculturalism has, at least *de jure*, had no confining effect on the right to freedom of expression which, despite the actual delineating menaces, has, thus far, been safeguarded by the Dutch judiciary system. However, this seems to change with the new developments whereby special attention is drawn to the incitement of intolerance and the prohibition thereof. Nonetheless, where, for instance, the Human Rights Court seems to have lowered the threshold in order to cover also religious feelings through the notion of *gratuitously offensive*, we observe, at the national level a reverse development that, with the abolition of the blasphemy law[874], religious feelings are no longer protected, or, rather, the adherents of any religion have to

[874] *Parliamentary Papers I* 2009/13, 32203, nr. 11

endure expressions that are offensive in nature.[875] Thus, with this development at the national level, the scope of the freedom of expression in terms of non-religious opinions is broadened, and the extent of tolerance of such utterances stretched[876], whereby it seems unlikely that issues of veneration would ever (again) gain protection. Yet again, the fact that no *de jure* limitation of this fundamental right can be observed and detected is not to say that no *de facto* confinement has taken place.

To the contrary, as we had touched upon in the course of this research, the acceleration of multiculturalism has had extrajudicial, if not judicial, effects on the fundamental right to freedom of expression. Unlike the majority of politicians at all three levels – international, European, and national – the judiciary seem to have opted for the protection of the fundamental right to freedom of expression and have attempted to safeguard it, albeit within a slow evolution towards more protection for minority groups and the issues that are dear to them. Thence, it remains to be seen what exactly the effects of the acceleration of pluralism will be on the fundamental rights and freedoms in general and the fundamental right to freedom of expression in particular.

[875] Ambrogino G Awesta, 'Alle ruimte om gelovigen te kwetsen' *Nederlands Dagblad* (Barneveld 9 December 2013)
[876] Ambrogino G Awesta, 'De afschaffing van het verbod op godslastering staat niet op zichzelf, maar heeft verdergaande consequenties' *Reformatorische Dagblad* (Apeldoorn 7 december 2013)

Concluding Remarks

Our contemporary era is underpinned by the process of globalization. This process has had an unprecedented impact on human life, leading to unforeseeable consequences that have allowed this era to be characterized as capricious. The level of uncertainty has increased the quest for certitude. Thus, globalization as a multidimensional process has had, despite the lack of a universally accepted definition, not only positive dimensions but also negative and disruptive sides as far as society is concerned. In this regard, it is worthwhile mentioning that despite the lack of a universal consensus concerning a definition of the globalization paradigm, for the purpose of this study we have tried to conceive this process, on the basis of the features that we have discussed in this research, as a precipitating set of continuous processes involving miscellaneous flows that encompass an ever-increasing number of global spaces in a compressed timescale, which result in deterritorialization and lead to an aggrandized integration, as well as an intensified and deepened interconnectedness albeit with the inevitable antagonisms. The accelerated interconnectedness among worldviews has been designated using the terms 'multicivilizationalism' and 'multiculturalism' – two notions that, as we have elaborated, are used interchangeably in this research.

However, for a considerable period of time, the globalization process has been approached from numerous angles such as the economic and technological dimensions, but hardly from the cultural angle, which has been marginally, if at all, touched upon. Hereby, the flow of people in terms of global migration has gained attention as only one of the many flows within this process, whereas their modes of life – in terms of 'culture' in the broadest sense of the word – have largely been neglected. In this context, globalism, as one of the three waves of globalization, has been defined this process solely in terms of 'modernization', which tends to homogenize cultures, i.e. as a global consumer culture. Consequently, this has been perceived as a new form of Western capitalist expansionism and imperialism. This narrow understanding of globalization only in terms of modernization is thus partial and relative, for it neglects features of human life such as '*politics*' and '*culture*' that do not always homogenize but even collide and foster antagonism. In this regard, the contingencies and challenges that are brought about by a plurality of cultures have resulted in the second wave of globalization called transformationalism. This wave has paid more attention to the features of human society within the globalization process by stressing that the flow of cultural products has taken place but not without its consequences for these products have been differently conceived by people around the world. Thus, the intensification of interactions among civilizations, which is fostered by globalization, does not necessarily entail homogenization, but rather evolution, transformation and hybridization. However, one shortcoming of this wave is that the possibility of tensions between cultures is not taken into account, which is actually the main aftereffect we are currently facing. It is, then, the third wave of globalization, i.e. skepticism, that takes this neglected dimension into account by focusing on the differentiating, polarizing, fragmentizing and colliding effects of globalization for which the West is oftentimes accused for imposing such a modernity project, viz. Western values. Thus, globalization in the broadest sense of the term is not only positive and innovative for human society, for it does not only homogenize and hybridize cultures but, as one can notice from the current conflicts at the different strata, it also has rather disruptive, disintegrative, and marginalizing consequences for our contemporary world that are held to be reconfigured along cultural lines. Thence, the pluralism being fostered, if not brought about, by the globalization process, and yet downplayed in this discourse, has had notably negative consequences for the fundamental rights and freedoms in general and the fundamental right to freedom of expression in particular.

And so, in order to determine whether the invocation or negligence of the notion of culture in the broadest sense of the term underpins the currently accelerated antagonism, an attempt has been made to elucidate the scope and nature of this antagonism, which is often designated by the notions of 'Orientalism' and 'Occidentalism'. In this discussion, the seminal study of Edward Said is employed, which we have approached from its essentially political dimension. In this, Said describes the notion of Orientalism as a discursive mechanism that underpins the demeanor of the West towards 'the rest' which is, in essence, a dichotomy between 'East' and 'West'. He contends that the roots of this can be traced back to the colonial and imperial times, which have, nonetheless, found their way into the modern versions. In other words, in his view, it is not so much the character of Orientalism but its source which has changed, whereby a mere shift in attitude from academic to instrumental has taken place. The core aspect of the notion of Orientalism is the interrelationship between 'knowledge' and 'power' that, simultaneously, underpins the aforementioned dichotomy and the contemporary clashes, for it has been the 'otherness' of the Orient against which the identity and, subsequently, the dominance of the Occident is formed. This is why he rejects this and considers Orientalism to be a Western cultural enterprise, i.e. a tradition that has a reality and presence in and for the West through the configuration and institutionalization of power to ensure its durability. Thence, the survey of the notion of Orientalism has revealed that the underlying fundament of this reciprocal antagonism is the concept of culture in the broadest sense of the term.

In this regard, and against the background of the foregoing discussion on this mutual antagonism, an attempt has been made to expound the underpinning concept of this reciprocal animosity, that is, the concept of culture in the broadest sense of the word. In so doing, the description of this concept by Said indicates that it encompasses not only practices that have relative autonomy from the economic, social, and political realms, but that it is also a source of identity, whereby various political and ideological causes reciprocally interact. This is evident from the notion of Orientalism, which Said attempts to elucidate by means of the 'novel', as the pivotal cultural institution, in order to clarify that while the interest of imperialism has been political, it has been the culture that created that interest. Said antagonizes this by conceiving it as ethnocentric, antihuman, hegemonic, and anthropocentric. It is worthwhile noting that other commentators apply this same line of reasoning to Occidentalism. In a word, as our study has shown, the concept of culture in the broadest sense of the term inherently underpins the current reciprocal antagonisms and clashes. More specifically, this has become a pressing issue in the globalization process, whereby freedom, peace, and security are imperiled by mutual animosities that are based on the concept of culture and are, simultaneously, aggravated and exacerbated by the acceleration of this same process, for which Said blames and antagonizes the Western world. However, he applies the concept of culture, as the underlying notion of the current clashes, only to the West and denies the ineluctability of it when it comes down to 'others'. This paradox makes his opposition to the 'Clash of Civilizations' of Samuel Huntington, which he calls the clash of ignorance, spurious for Said's own thesis is inevitably grounded on this civilizational interaction.

However, like Said but in a different guise, Huntington is also skeptical about the so-called Western universalization mission, that is, bringing Western civilization to 'others', which is often defined in terms of modernization. For while previously 'others' seemed to be in need of culture in order to become civilized, currently they seem to be in need of modernization to become civilized. Therefore, modernization, in terms of a missional tendency to *modernize* 'others', is conceived to be the same core feature of modern Orientalism, just as civilization had been the underpinning trait of classic Orientalism. Thus, as regards the connection between the two notions of modernization and civilization, it has been argued that the former concept is equated with the latter, which is, subsequently, conceived as the inextricable crux of Western civilization that contemporarily underpins the colliding reality. This tends to be further fostered by the decline in the globalist claims and, at the same time, the increase in the relative power of other civilizations, which has made them resistant to Western pressure regarding human rights and democracy at the international, regional, and national level. In this, the West itself is considered to be the culprit of the current antagonism. Even while antagonism is not only caused by the West itself, it is undeniable that it *is* fostered by it as we can discern from globalism's neglect and misinterpretation of the concept of civilization. The prime example of such a globalist theory is the one provided by Francis Fukuyama, that heralds the triumph of liberal democracy as the final stage of mankind's ideological evolution in which the realm of politics is considered to be autonomous from that of culture. This is rejected by Said who argues that this globalist thesis is a radical falsification of culture that strips it of its affiliations, pries it away from the terrain it contests, and denies it real influence.

Thus, the concept that currently underscores antagonism is undeniably the notion of culture, i.e. civilization and the plurality thereof. For making the inextricability of this concept from contemporary world affairs tangible, Fukuyama's thesis is further expounded in this research. In so doing, Jowitt's contention is adopted, according to which liberal capitalist democracy will always generate opposing challengers, since the dissolution of existing boundaries and identities can generate a corresponding potential for genuinely new ways of life that are antagonistic, if not militant, in nature. In this context, some have attempted to differentiate religion from the current clashes. Still, it would be an analytical error to downplay or neglect the role of religion within the current civilizational tensions, especially when it is accommodated by the states. Such an error blurs the perilous reality of the contemporary antagonism and can have unprecedented and unforeseeable consequences for the dignity and integrity of the human person. Despite the alluring theorizations, it is undeniable that the contemporary clashes emerge precisely when traditional cultural identities are made obscure, and a disjuncture between one's inner self and external social practice takes place. However, in the globalization process, little attention is paid, if any, to religion as the core social capital for understanding human interactions, whereas a consideration of this would reveal that the concepts of religion and culture are two indispensable components for the formation of civilization which underpins the current antagonism. Accordingly, for a better understanding, the two main dimensions of this disruption are elucidated: the historical and psychological. As regards the former, it has been argued that the contemporary clash is believed to have commenced in the aftermath of decolonization whereby, in abandoning traditional beliefs, newly independent countries recognized the inherent relativism that underpins all societies, systems of belief, and cultural practices. Consequently, this has ineluctably affected the psychological angle, whereby civilization is invoked to palliate the effects of modernity that have undermined the traditional systems and created a vacuum in the human psyche. Based on this, it has been inferred that the current global clashes can only be grasped when the concept of civilization is neither neglected nor overlooked.

The indispensable and critical role of civilization for comprehending the contemporary global clashes has also become evident through our discussion of the mechanism that underlies Fukuyama's globalist thesis. More concretely, Fukuyama fails to explain why liberal democracy has no appeal within the Islamic world, so was Jowitt who could not explicate why the dissolution of existing boundaries and identities generates new ways of life that are antagonistic and hostile in nature. As discussed in this study, the most fundamental mechanism is the Platonic notion of *thymos*, existing out of *isothymia* and *megalothymia*. *Thymos* is defined as the side of man that deliberately seeks out struggle and sacrifice, which goes beyond his materialistic and physical needs. Fukuyama considers this concept to be inextricable for the existence of the body politic, even if it must not only be cultivated but also tamed. He believes that this balance can be struck in the '*universal and homogenous state*', that is, liberal democracy which is grounded on economics and recognition. In other words, the universality of democracy is upheld, because one is convinced that this is the only mode of governance that is completely satisfactory to man. *Megalothymia* is considered to be the downside of *thymos* which, however, has not disappeared with this mode of governance, not even with the satisfaction of human desire through materialism and rational recognition. This suggests that the quest for ideals will continue, particularly when we take note of the resurgence of traditional *megalothymian* horizons, i.e. civilizations. Hence, it is questionable whether liberal democracy is vigorous enough to compete with the traditional value systems, since the unleashing of *megalothymia* by means of satisfying desire through material abundance and mere rational recognition has actually resulted in a greater reappearance and resurgence of *megalothymian* horizons. This is thus the shortcoming of this theory for, as Huntington contends, people are not likely to find in political principles the deep emotional content and meaning which is provided by traditional systems. We have designated such traditional systems with the notion of civilization, by means of which man is able to bridge the spiritual gap between the aforementioned objective material and subjective aesthetic harmony.

Fukuyama is aware of this deficit, but does not consider the contemporary challenges and clashes serious enough to pose a threat to his theory. Yet, he admits that *megalothymia* must continue to have a place in a vibrant liberal democracy, and also defends this latter against civilizations with an excess of *megalothymia.* To accommodate this, he states that a liberal democracy that could fight a short and decisive war every generation would be far healthier and more satisfied than having a continuous state of peace. Also Huntington, like many other commentators, attempts to incorporate the *megalothymian* factor into his theory in order to defend the uniqueness of Western civilization. This shows that neglect and underestimation of the concept of *megalothymia* and, by that, ignoring the concept of civilization may be detrimental as witnessed in the relativization of universalistic theories in recent years. Yet, both the aforementioned deficit and neglect have fueled antagonism, which has endangered international peace and security in general and the fundamental human rights and freedoms in particular. The perilous forbearance of the concept of civilization has thus fostered, if not brought about, the severe antagonism we discussed in our elaboration of Said's theory, that goes so far as to condone illegitimate resistance and blame the West for everything. Henceforth, this discussion has rendered beyond doubt the existence of civilizational antagonism that particularly endangers fundamental human rights and freedoms.

Among all these rights and freedoms, it has been alleged that the one most imperiled by antagonism, which emanates from pluralism, is the fundamental right to freedom of expression. Therefore, before examining the *de jure* impact of pluralism on the fundamental right to freedom of expression at the international, European and national level, it is importunate to grasp why precisely this particular right is imperiled by the contemporary civilizational clashes. In order to grasp this, in the second part of this research, the endeavor was to elaborate on the significance of this fundamental right within the pluralistic public realm, as well as the impact of this pluralism on this right. In so doing, the theory of Hannah Arendt is taken as our point of departure, the elucidation of which has thus made apparent why precisely the fundamental right to freedom of expression is central to the pluralist realm. For pluralism is not only an undeniable reality but even the prerequisite for such fundamental rights and freedoms[877], a denial of which would, however, result in alienation and worldlessness, with deprivation of rights and freedoms as its consequence, since freedom "[...] is actually the reason that men live together in political organization at all. Without it, political life as such would be meaningless. The *raison d'être* of politics is freedom, and its field of experience is action"[878] in general, and speech, as *the* authentic political action, in particular. In other words, speech, as the authentic political action, cannot take place in isolation, but is inevitably dependent on plurality and *vice versa*. As Arendt asserts, speech is the actualization of that same human condition of plurality, that is, appearance as a distinct and unique being among equals. Hence, the loss of human rights amounts to the deprivation of a place in the world that makes opinions significant and actions effective, for it is only in this realm that one can, by means of this authentic political action, appear and, thus, be free. This makes the inextricability and necessity of the freedom to this fundamental right evident and shows why, among all the fundamental rights and freedoms, it is precisely this right which is at stake in contemporary pluralistic societies.

Hence, pluralism does not only foster freedom of speech as suggested by the theory of Arendt, but due to the antagonism that emanates from it, it also confines speech (in the broadest sense of the term) and the freedom to it. This indicates that the exercise of this fundamental right, like all the other rights, is subject to limitations as our discussion has made evident. It is also this confining effect of pluralism that makes it exigent to grasp the theoretical limitation of speech and the freedom to it before we can scrutinize the *de jure* impact of this pluralism on the fundamental right to freedom of expression. For a theoretical assay of the possible limitation of this fundamental freedom, the philosophy of John Stuart Mill provided a cue. According to Mill's harm principle, speech ought to be constrained when it would entail mischievous acts that can inflict harm on others. However, he adds to this the notion of offense, and argues that although it is hard to determine the bounds of this notion, the freedom of expression in the public realm has to meet the civilized conditions of interaction, which he calls 'the morality of public discussion', the violation of which should result in the limitation of speech in the same way as action that harms others in society. This can become problematic when it is conceived against the background of utilitarianism, whereby the interest of the majority is taken as the standard, as we have also discussed in light of the reliance of this right on the body politic. Especially when we bear in mind that, besides the befuddlement of the distinction between speech and action, in contemporary multicivilizational societies, the threshold of morality of public discussion is reversed from the interests of the 'majority' to those of the 'minority' whereby, contiguous to governmental curtailments, this latter group also poses limitation on the fundamental right to freedom of expression which is, due to globalization, unprecedented.

---

[877] Hannah Arendt, *The Human Condition* (2nd edn UCP, Chicago 1958) 175
[878] Hannah Arendt, *Between Past and Future* (Penguin Books, New York 2006) 145

Nevertheless, little thought is bestowed upon the *de jure* delineations, if any, that are imposed on this fundamental right with the acceleration of multicivilizationalism, which is also designated by the term 'multiculturalism'. Thence, after having examined why, among all the fundamental rights and freedoms, precisely the fundamental right to freedom of expression is most imperiled by pluralism, and what the permissible limitations are that can be imposed on this right, it is high time to make due allowance for the *de jure* delineation, which tends to be imposed on the fundamental right to freedom of expression by the dichotomous antagonism that is fostered, if not brought about, by the pluralism that characterizes this age of globalization. Especially when we bear in mind that, thus far, the main attention has gone to the extrajudicial constraints, i.e. *de facto* limitations, with the consequence that little thought is bestowed upon the *de jure* delineations that are imposed on this fundamental right by the acceleration of pluralism. Accordingly, with the preceding discussion in mind, in the remainder of this research, the attempt is made to explore the *de jure* limitation which is thus deemed to be fostered by the accelerated pluralism at the global, regional, and national level. To put it differently, in the following parts of our inquiry, we will try to elaborate on the central question as to what extent, if any, pluralism has had a *de jure* effect on the fundamental right to freedom of expression at the international, European, and national level. In so doing, at each level, the scope and substance of the law in force is thoroughly expounded, whereupon, the delineating effect of the acceleration of pluralism is scrutinized.

At the international level, our survey has led to the conclusion that while expressions may be offensive, which could well be robust and critical in examining religious doctrines and practice, even in a harsh manner, they may, nonetheless, not amount to the advocacy of hatred that would constitute incitement to discrimination, hostility or violence. What is more, this fundamental right, besides the limitations imposed by the law, is also confined by its clash with other fundamental rights, the most important of which has been the fundamental right to freedom of religion and belief. Classically, this latter is aimed at protecting the human person and not religion and belief as such. Still, since 1999, the concept of 'defamation of religion' has grown in status within the UN framework, by means of which an attempt has been made to enact laws for extending the scope of protection beyond the bearer of this right in order to protect also the objects and symbols of veneration. This extension can be said to come down to the broadening of the ambit of the external dimension of religion, for not only the expression of conviction is covered, but also the means through which conviction is manifested. To put it simply, we have been witnessing a shift in protection from persons to ideologies in the broadest sense of the term, encompassing also the means and objects of veneration. The menace posed by this in a globalized era, wherein world affairs are characterized by civilizational clashes, is that such laws are vulnerable to arbitrary usage and can also lead to further limitations on the freedom of expression. Yet in recent years, we have seen a reversal of this development, whereby, once again, the emphasis is put on the fundamental right to freedom of expression in its classical sense. In this way, also the aim to protect religion as such has gone back to the original intention of the law, whereby only the human person has to be protected. However, the dividing line between the freedom of expression and hate speech is thin and perilous, which must be attentively guarded against abuses, especially in contemporary world affairs. Yet, it remains to be seen how the aforementioned reversal tendency can be maintained within a constantly changing landscape of world affairs with newly emerging powers and the accompanying alteration in international setups. What is more, as noted in the course of our research, the civilizational clashes do not only occur at the international arena but also, and perhaps even more so, at the European and national level.

As regards the European level, the scope of this research has been narrowed to the Council of Europe, and, more specifically, to the Human Rights Court that functions within the framework of this organization. This is because our research has been concerned with the mere legal effects, that is, *de jure* limitations of the civilizational clashes on the fundamental right to freedom of expression. And it is only this organization that is characterized by a court that functions on the basis of fundamental human rights and freedoms, whereas, as has been thoroughly discussed, other organizations are either not (yet) established on the basis of these rights and freedoms or they do touch upon them only sporadically and marginally. Furthermore, our inquiry has revealed that the fundamental right to freedom of expression has not remained unaffected by the civilizational tensions. This has been made evident through a survey of the case-law of the Human Rights Court and the legal developments therein. In the first place, freedom of expression has been broadly defined in scope, which can go so far as to offend, shock and disturb, all of which have to be tolerated in the name of tolerance and broadmindedness in a pluralistic democratic society unless violence is advocated.

However, we can observe a tangible shift when it comes down to the morals, rights or reputation of others who have made their presence felt in Western pluralistic societies, as we can find in the vast jurisprudence of the European Human Rights Court. This means that the scope of protection has been widened so as to also cover insulting, offending and provocative expressions. In other words, our discussion has shown that the acceleration of pluralism tends to have a detrimental effect on the balance that, for the sake of pressing social needs, has to be struck among elements that are considered necessary in a democratic society. It is also in this context that the notion of 'hate speech' has been brought within the ambit of prohibited speech. Thus, whereas previously offending, shocking and disturbing utterances had to be tolerated, currently we have been witnessing a shift in view, whereby the Court argues in favor of tolerance and respect within a pluralistic democratic society, for the sake of which it considers it necessary to sanction or even prevent all forms of expression that spread, incite, promote or justify hatred based on intolerance, including religious intolerance. In a word, although previously pluralism and tolerance, as prerequisites of democracy, demanded a certain openness to expressions that could be offending, shocking and disturbing, with the introduction of the notion of hate speech, however, the demand of (religious) tolerance within the democratic pluralistic society now requires the curtailment of such offending, shocking and disturbing utterances. In addition, as has been argued in this survey, a narrow margin of appreciation has generally been made available to the states, but when it comes down to the sphere of morals or religion, this margin tends to be wider in scope.

Such effects of the plurality of civilizations within Western societies on the fundamental right to freedom of expression have been recognized by the Court, for it has argued that in democratic societies in which several religions coexist within one and the same population, it might be necessary to place restrictions on this fundamental freedom in order to reconcile the interests of the various groups and ensure that everyone's beliefs are respected. In so doing, the emphasis is put on the 'duties and responsibilities', an example of which is – in the context of religious opinions and beliefs – the obligation to avoid expressions that are gratuitously offensive and profane as regards issues of veneration (that is, improper attacks on and provocative portrayals of objects of religious veneration), for such utterances imply a malicious violation of the spirit of tolerance. And yet, it has been argued that, since the *I.A. v Turkey* case, an inversion in the Court's attitude can be observed when it adopts a more protective demeanor towards freedom of expression. However, a change in attitude is noticeable only when the dissenting opinions are taken into consideration, but it is premature to draw decisive conclusions from mere opinions. Furthermore, the variable demeanor of the Court towards non religious and religious speeches has also become evident in this research. For while the Court limits non-religious expressions by lowering the threshold, it, nonetheless, allows religious utterances that are by definition incompatible with human rights and democracy. Thus, a difference in protection regarding religious and non-religious utterances can also be discerned.

The last stratum wherein the interactions between cultures is most direct and has led to perilous tensions and collisions is the national level, where for the most part multiculturalism underpins the reality of most national societies. In this study, we have also attempted to examine the *de jure* impact of pluralism of civilizations on the fundamental right to freedom of expression at this level. In so doing, after dealing with the applicable law at the national level, the jurisprudence of the national judiciary is inquired into, with the criminal law approach as our point of departure, since, as we have argued, this is the main instrument that, due to its coercive nature, has sweeping impact on the fundamental rights and freedoms in general and on the fundamental right to freedom of expression in particular. On this note, the Dutch judiciary has argued that only attacks against a group of persons – and thus not their views and conduct such as religious doctrines and practices – is punishable for the reason that in a democratic society there has to be room for debate. In this context, it is determined that expressions as such can be offensive in nature, which can, however, be softened if not eradicated by the *context* wherein they are uttered. But *how* to define such a context, is, according to some commentators, problematic in that religious expressions seem to gain more protection than non-religious ones, since subjective religious convictions underpin the context of religious utterances, whereas the same cannot be said of non-religious expressions. This development seems to be similar to the evolvement at the European level, whereby the threshold of freedom of expression tends to be lowered for religious expressions when compared to non-religious ones. Nonetheless, the observation has been made that this same subjectivity formula is applied not only to the person who expresses himself in a religious context, but also to the one who expresses himself on the basis of *political* convictions that have subjective relevance for him. Furthermore, according to the laws in force, and based on judgments rendered that are also in line with the European jurisprudence, defamation has to concern a 'group of persons' and not the doctrines and objects of veneration. However, at first sight the national judiciary seems to have accepted 'indirect defamation', which entails the lowering of the threshold that might, given the multicivilizational developments, result in the protection of symbols and doctrines of veneration as well. This, nonetheless, is a hypothetical assumption which time alone can clarify. On the other hand, the Dutch judiciary with its vast jurisprudence as well as the legislative branch with the abolition of the blasphemy law have shrunk back from such a development for the time being. Thence, based on the aforementioned discussion, it has been concluded that, at the national level, multiculturalism has, at least *de jure*, had no confining effect on the right to freedom of expression which has, thus far, been safeguarded by the Dutch judiciary. However, this in no way suggests that, as discussed in the course of this research, the right to freedom of expression is not *de facto* imperiled. Thus, it remains to be seen what the precise impact of multicivilizationalism (which we have also denoted as multiculturalism) will be on the fundamental right to freedom of expression, particularly with the digitalization of our world.

Bibliography

Books

Agamben G, *State of Exception* (UCP, Chicago 2005)

Ahmad A, *In Theory: Classes, Nations, Literatures* (Verso, London 2008)

Albrow M and King E (eds), *Globalization, Knowledge and Society* (SAGE Publications, London 1990)

Alfredsson G and Eide A (eds), *The Universal Declaration of Human Rights: A Common Standard of Achievement* (Martinus Nijhoff Publishers, The Hague 1999)

Arai-Takahashi Y, *The Margin of Appreciation Doctrine and the Principle of Proportionality in the Jurisprudence of the ECHR* (Intersentia, Oxford 2001)

Arendt H, *The Human Condition* (2nd edn UCP, Chicago 1958)

-- *On Revolution* (Penguin Books, New York 1965)

-- *The Origins of Totalitarianism* (Harcourt, Orlando 1968)

-- *Between Past and Future* (Penguin Books, New York 2006)

Ashcroft B and Ahluwalia P, *Edward Said* (Routledge, London 2001)

Barsamian D, *Culture and Resistance: Conversations with Edward W. Said* (Pluto Press, London 2003)

Benhabib S, *Modernity & Political Thought: The Reluctant Modernism of Hannah Arendt* (Rowman & Littlefield Publishers, Lanham 2000)

Blankley T, *The West's Last Chance: Will We Win the Clash of Civilizations?* (Regnery Publishing, Washington 2005)

Bonnett A, *The Idea of the West: Culture, Politics and History* (Palgrave Macmillan: New York 2004)

Bossuyt MJ, *Guide to the 'travaux préparatoires' of the International Covenant on Civil and Political Rights* (Martinus Nijhoff Publishers, Dordrecht 1987)

Brems E, *Human Rights: Universality and Diversity* (Martinus Nijhoff Publishers, Den Haag 2001)

Brouwer de ALM, *Supranational Criminal Prosecution of Sexual Violence: The ICC and the Practice of the ICTY and the ICTR* (Intersentia, Belgium 2005)

Buruma I and Margalit A, *Occidentalism: A Short History of Anti-Westernism* (Atlantic Books, London 2005)

Callewaert J, *The accession of the European Union to the European Convention on Human Rights* (Council of Europe Publishing, Strasbourg 2014)

Christians CG and Merrill JC (eds), *Ethical Communication: Moral Stances in Human Dialogue* (UMP, Missouri 2009)

Clifford J, *The Predicament of Culture: Twentieth-Century Ethnography, Literature, and Art* (HUP, Cambridge 1988)

Cliteur P, *The Secular Outlook: In Defense of Moral and Political Secularism* (Wiley-Blackwell, West Sussex 2010)
-- *Het Monotheïstisch Dilemma* (Uitgeverij De Arbeiderspers, Amsterdam 2010)
Collini S (ed), *J. S. Mill: On Liberty and Other Writings* (CUP, Cambridge 2010)
Conte A and Burchill R, *Defining Civil and Political Rights: The Jurisprudence of the United Nations Human Rights Committee* (2nd edn Ashgate Publishing Limited, Surrey 2009)
Craig P and de Búrca G, *EU Law. Text, Cases, and Materials* (4th edn, Oxford, OUP 2008)

Dacey A, *The Future of Blasphemy: Speaking of the sacred in an age of human rights* (Continuum, London 2012)
Dekker P and Uslaner EM, *Social Capital and Participation in Everyday Life* (Routledge, Oxon 2001)
Droege P (ed), *Urban Energy Transition: From Fossil Fuels to Renewable Power* (Elsevier, Oxford 2008)
Drury SB, *Alexandre Kojève: The Roots of Postmodern Politics* (Palgrave Macmillan, New York 1994)

El-Enany R, *Arab Representations of the Occident: East-West Encounters in Arabic Fiction. Culture and Civilization in the Middle East* (Routledge, Oxon 2006)
Ellian A, Molier G and Zwart T (eds), *Mag ik dit zeggen? Beschouwingen over de vrijheid van meningsuiting* (Boom Juridische Uitgevers, Den Haag 2011)
Elliott C and Quinn F, *English Legal System* (9th edn Pearson Education Limited, Essex 2008)
Eriksson M, *Defining Rape: Emerging Obligations for States under International Law?* (Martinus Nijhoff Publishers, Leiden 2011)
Ron Eyerman, *The Assassination of Theo van Gogh: From Social Drama to Cultural Trauma* (DUP, Duke 2008)

Faber J, *Wat bezielde Volkert van der G.* (Nijgh & Van Ditmar Uitgeverij, Amsterdam 2008)
Fortuyn P, *Tegen de islamisering van onze cultuur: Nederlandse identiteit als fundament* (A.W. Bruna Uitgevers, Utrecht 1997)
Fukuyama F, *The End of History and the Last Man* (Free Press, New York 2006)

Giddens A, *A Contemporary Critique of Historical Materialism: Power, Property and the State* (vol 1 UCP, Berkeley 1981)
-- *The Constitution of Society: Outline of the Theory of Structuration* (UCP, Berkeley 1984)
-- *The Consequences of Modernity* (Polity Press, Cambridge 1990)
Gismondi MD, *Ethics, Liberalism and Realism in International Relations* (Routledge, Oxon 2008)
Gogh van T, *Allah weet het beter* (Xtra Producties, Amsterdam 2003)

Goldman DP, *It's Not the End of the World, It's Just the End of You: The Great Extinction of the Nations* (RVP Publishers, New York 2011)
Goodhart M, *Democracy as Human Rights: Freedom and Equality in the Age of Globalization* (Routledge, New York 2005)
Groen L and Stronks M, *Entangled Rights of Freedom. Freedom of speech, freedom of religion and the non-discrimination principle in the Dutch Wilders case* (Forum Institute for Multicultural Affairs, Eleven international publishing, The Hague 2010)
Gutmann A (ed), *Multiculturalism* (PUP, Princeton 1994)

Hanmer J and others (eds), *Home Truths About Domestic Violence: Feminist influences on policy and practice – A reader* (Routledge, London 2000)
Hare I and Weinstein J (eds), *Extreme Speech and Democracy* (OUP, Oxford 2009)
Harrison LE and Huntington SP (eds), *Culture Matters: How Values Shape Human Progress* (Basic Books, New York 2000)
Harrison R (ed), *Bentham: A Fragment on Government* (CUP, Cambridge 1988)
Harvey D, *The Condition of Postmodernity* (Blackwell Publishing, Oxford 1989)
Hastrup K (ed), *Human Rights on Common Grounds: The Quest for Universality* (Kluwer Law International, The Hague 2001)
Hertzke AD (ed), *The Future of Religious Freedom: Global Challenges* (OUP, Oxford 2013)
Hoe nu verder? 42 visies op de toekomst van Nederland na de moord op Theo van Gogh (Spectrum, Utrecht 2005)
Hopper P, *Understanding Cultural Globalization* (Polity Press, Cambridge 2007)
Horstman R-P and Norman J (eds), *Nietzsche: Beyond Good and Evil* (CUP, Cambridge 2002)
Hullu de J, *Materieel Strafrecht: Over algemene leerstukken van strafrechtelijke aansprakelijkheid naar Nederlands recht* (3rd edn Kluwer, Deventer 2006)
Hunter ST, *The Future of Islam and the West: Clash of Civilizations or Peaceful Coexistence?* (The Center for Strategic and International Studies, Westport 1998)
Huntington SP, *The Clash of Civilizations and the Remaking of World Order* (Simon & Schuster, London 2002)
-- *Who Are We? The Challenge to America's National Identity* (Simon & Schuster, New York 2004)

Ibn Warraq, *Defending the West: A Critique of Edward Said's Orientalism* (Prometheus Books, New York 2007)
-- *Why the West Is Best: A Muslim Apostate's Defense of Liberal Democracy* (Encounter Books, New York 2011)
Ignatieff M, *Human Rights: As Politics and Idolatry* (PUP, Princeton 2001)
Irwin R, *Dangerous Knowledge: Orientalism & Its Discontents* (Overlook Press, Woodstock 2006)

Jackson Preece J, *Minority Rights* (Polity, Cambridge 2005)

Jansen H and Snel B (eds), *Eindstrijd: De finale Clash tussen het Liberale Westen en een Traditionele Islam* (Uitgeverij Van Praag, Amsterdam 2009)
Janssens ALJ and Nieuwenhuis AJ, *uitingsdelicten* (2nd edn Kluwer, Deventer 2008)
Johnston RJ and others (eds), *The Dictionary of Human Geography* (4th edn Blackwell Publishing, Malden 2000)
Jowitt K, *New World Disorder: The Leninist Extinction* (UCP, Berkeley 1992)
Juergensmeyer M, *Global Rebellion: Religious Challenges to the Secular State, from Christian Militias to al Qaeda* (UCP, Berkeley 2008)

Katzenstein PJ (ed), *Civilizations in World Politics: Plural and pluralist perspectives* (Routledge, Oxon 2009)
Kennedy V, *Edward Said: A Critical Introduction* (Polity Press, Cambridge 2000)
Kesby A, *The Right to Have Rights: Citizenship, Humanity and International Law* (OUP, Oxford 2012)
Khomeyni AR, *Islamic Government: Governance of Jurisprudence* (UPPH, Hawaii 2005)
Kiiver P (ed), *Sources of Constitutional Law: Constitutions and Fundamental Legal Provisions from the United States, France, Germany, the Netherlands, the United Kingdom, the ECHR and the EU* (2nd edn European Law Publishing, Groningen 2010)
Koenig M and Guchteneire de P (eds), *Democracy and Human Rights in Multicultural Societies* (Ashgate Publishing, Hampshire 2007)
Kristeva J, *Hannah Arendt: Life Is a Narrative* (UTP, Toronto 2001)

Lemon MC, *Philosophy of History: A Guide for Students* (Routledge, Oxon 2003)
Lerner N, *The U.N. Convention on the Elimination of All Forms of Racial Discrimination* (Noordhoff International Publishers, Alphen aan de Rijn 1980)
-- *Group Rights and Discrimination in International Law* (International Studies in Human Rights,
2nd edn Martinus Nijhoff Publishers, The Hague 2003)
Lewis B, *What Went Wrong? The Clash Between Islam and Modernity in the Middle East* (Harper Perennial, New York 2003)
-- *The Crisis of Islam: Holy War and Unholy Terror* (Phoenix, London 2004)

Madison J, Hamilton A and Jay J, *The Federalist Papers* (Penguin Books, London 1987)
Marsh D and Stoker G (eds), *Theory and Methods in Political Science* (2nd edn Palgrave Macmillan, Hampshire 2002)
McCarthy C, *The Cambridge Introduction to Edward Said* (CUP, Cambridge 2010)
McIvor M, *Establishing a Heart Failure Program: The Essential Guide* (3rd edn Blackwell Publishing, Malden 2007)
Mendis P, *Glocalization: The Human Side of Globalization as if the Washington Consensus Mattered* (Lulu Press, Morrisville 2007)

Mill JS, *Utilitarianism* (Longmans, London 1879)
-- *A System of Logic, Ratiocinative and Inductive, Being a Connected View of the Principles of Evidence, and the Methods of Scientific Investigation* (8th edn Harper & Brothers Publishers, New York 1882)
Molan M, *Cases & Materials on Criminal Law* (3rd edn Cavendish Publishing, Oregon 2005)
Molier G, Ellian A and Suurland D (eds), *Terrorism: Ideology, Law and Policy* (Republic of Letters Publishing, Dordrecht 2011)
Morsink J, *The Universal Declaration of Human Rights: Origins, Drafting & Intent* (UPP, Pennsylvania 1999)
-- *Inherent Human Rights: Philosophical Roots of the Universal Declaration* (UPP, Philadelphia 2009)

Neff SC, *War and the Law of Nations: A General History* (CUP, Cambridge 2005)
Neusner J (ed), *Religious Foundations of Western Civilization: Judaism, Christianity, and Islam* (Abingdon Press, Nashville 2006)

O'Rourke KC, *John Stuart Mill and Freedom of Expression: The genesis of a theory* (Routledge, London 2001)
OSCE, *National minority standards. A compilation of OSCE and Council of Europe texts* (Council of Europe Publishing, Strasbourg 2007)
OSCE/ODIHR, *Hate Crime Laws: A Practical Guide* (OSCE Office for Democratic Institutions and Human Rights, Warsaw 2009)
-- *Preventing and responding to hate crimes: A resource guide for NGOs in the OSCE region* (OSCE Office for Democratic Institutions and Human Rights, Warsaw 2009)
Osei Kwadwo Prempeh E, Mensah J, and Adjibolosoo S B-S K (eds), *Globalization and the Human Factor: Critical Insights* (Ashgate Publishing, Hampshire 2004)

Parekh B, *Rethinking Multiculturalism: Cultural Diversity and Political Theory* (Palgrave Macmillan, Hampshire 2006)
Parekh S, *Hannah Arendt and the Challenge of Modernity: A Phenomenology of Human Rights* (Routledge, New York 2008)
Phares W, *The War of Ideas: Jihadism against Democracy* (Palgrave Macmillan, New York 2008)
Pipes D, *The Rushdie Affair: The Novel, the Ayatollah, and the West* (Transaction Publishers, New Brunswick 2003)
Plattner MF, *Democracy without Borders? Global Challenges to Liberal Democracy* (Rowman & Littlefield Publishers, Maryland 2008)

Sabet AGE, *Islam and the Politics: Theory, Governance and International Relations* (Pluto Press, London 2008)
Said EW, *Culture & Imperialism* (Vintage, London 1994)

-- *The Politics of Dispossession: The Struggle for Palestinian Self-Determination 1969-1994* (Chatto and Windus, London 1994)
-- *Orientalism* (Penguin Books, London 2003)
Sands P and Klein P, *Bowett's Law of International Institutions* (5th edn Sweet & Maxwell, London 2001)
Slapper G and Kelly D, *Sourcebook on the English Legal System* (Cavendish Sourcebook Series, 2nd edn Cavendish Publishing Limited, London 2011)
Smidt C (ed), *Religion as Social Capital: Producing the Common Good* (Baylor University Press, Waco 2003)
Stefanou C and Xanthaki H (eds), *Drafting Legislation: A Modern Approach* (Ashgate Publishing Limited, Hampshire 2008)
Strauss L and Cropsey J (eds), *History of Political Philosophy* (3rd edn UCP, Chicago 1987)
Swift S, *Hannah Arendt* (Routledge, London 2009)

Tibi B, *Islam in Global Politics: Conflicts and Cross-Civilizational Bridging* (Routledge, Oxon 2012)

Vermaat E, *Nazi's, Communisten En Islamisten: Opmerkelijke Allianties Tussen Extremisten* (Uitgeverij Aspekt, Soesterberg 2008)
Villa D (ed), *The Cambridge Companion to Hannah Arendt* (CUP, Cambridge 2000)

Winks RW (ed), *Oxford History of the British Empire: Historiography* (OUP, Oxford 1999)
Wood AW (ed), *Hegel: Elements of the Philosophy of Right* (CUP, Cambridge 1991)

Yourow HC, *The Margin of Appreciation Doctrine in the Dynamics of European Human Rights Jurisprudence* (Martinus Nijhoff Publishers, Dordrecht 1996)

Journals & Newspapers

Abaza M and Stauth G, 'Occidental Reason, Orientalism, Islamic Fundamentalism: A Critique' (1988) 3 Int Sociol
Awesta AG, 'Alle ruimte om gelovigen te kwetsen' *Nederlands Dagblad* (Barneveld 9 December 2013)
-- 'De afschaffing van het verbod op godslastering staat niet op zichzelf, maar heeft verdergaande consequenties' *Reformatorische Dagblad* (Apeldoorn 7 december 2013)

Barsamian D, 'They call all resistance "terrorism"' [2001], Issue 19, *International Socialist Review*

Bingham J, 'Islamic law is adopted by British legal chiefs' *The Telegraph* (London 22 March 2014)
-- 'Sharia law in UK: Calls for Parliamentary inquiry' *The Telegraph* (London 23 March 2014)
Bozeman AB, 'Civilizations Under Stress: Reflections on Cultural Borrowing and Survival' [1975] VQR 51

Cliteur P, 'Godslastering en zelfcensuur na de moord op Theo van Gogh' (2004) NJB 45
-- 'Pim Fortuyn en de multiculturele samenleving' (2004) Civis Mundi 80-84
-- 'State and religion against the backdrop of religious radicalism' (2012) 10 Int Jnl of Constitutional Law 127, 139
Connolly K, 'Angela Merkel declares death of German multiculturalism' *Guardian* (London 17 October 2010)

Dacey A, 'United Nations Affirms the Human Right to Blaspheme', *Religion Dispatches Magazine* (11 August 2011)
Doughty S, 'Britain has 85 sharia courts: The astonishing spread of the Islamic justice behind closed doors' *Mail Online* (London 29 June 2009)

Ellian A, 'Van Janmaat tot El Moumni: De Discriminatie tussen gewone en heilige meningen' [2003] *Justitiële verkenningen*

Fukuyama F, 'A question of identity' *The Australian* (Sydney 3 February 2007)

Huntington SP, 'The Clash of Civilizations?' (1993) 72 (3) Foreign Aff

Iontcheva J, 'Power Clashes in a Multicultural World' [1998] Theory & Event

Janelle DG, 'Central place development in a time-space framework' (1968) 20 The Professional Geographer
Jowitt K, 'After Leninism: The New World Disorder' (1991) 2 (1) JoD
Jusová I, 'Hirsi Ali and Van Gogh's *Submission:* Reinforcing the Islam v. women binary' (2008) 31 Women Stud Int Forum

Kuenssberg L, 'State multiculturalism has failed, says David Cameron' *BBC* (London 5 February 2011)

Lewis B, 'The Question of Orientalism' *The New York Review of Books* (New York 24 June 1982)

Philpott D, 'The Challenge of September 11 to Secularism in International Relations' [2002] World Politics: A Quarterly Journal of International Relations

Said EW, 'The Clash of Ignorance' *The Nation* (New York 4 October 2001)

Sen A, 'Democracy as a Universal Value' (1999) 10 (3) JoD

Tamanaha BZ, 'Understanding Legal Pluralism: Past to Present, Local to Global' [2007] Syd LR

Voogt de S, 'Openbaar Ministerie vervolgt Wilders voor discriminatie' *nrc.nl* (Amsterdam 18 December 2014)

Yalmiz I, 'The Challenge of Post-Modern Legality and Muslim Legal Pluralism in England' [2002] Journal of Ethics and Migration Studies

Table of Cases

International Cases

Persecutor v Akayesu (Case No. ICTR-95-4)
Persecutor v Furundzija (Case No. IT-95-17/1-T and IT-95-17/1-A

Bodrožić v Serbia and Montenegro, Communication No. 1180/2003
Coleman v Australia, Communication No. 1157/2003
Faurisson v France, Communication No. 550/93
Fernando v Sri Lanka, Communication No. 1189/2003
Gauthier v Canada, Communication No. 633/1995
Ilmari Länsman et al. v Finland, Communication No. 511/1992
Lovelace v Canada, Communication No. 24/1977
Mavlonov and Sa'di v Uzbekistan, Communication No. 1334/2004
Mika Miha v Equatorial Guinea, Communication No. 414/1990
Ross v Canada Communication No. 736/1997
Shchetko v Belarus, Communication No. 1009/2001
Shin v Republic of Korea, Communication No. 926/2000
Toonen v Australia, Communication No. 488/1992
Velichkin v Belarus, Communication No. 1022/2001

European Cases

Aksu v Turkey (App nos 4149/04, 41029/04) ECHR 15 March 2012
Autronic AG v Switzerland (App no 12726/87) (1990) Series A no 178
Axel Springer AG v Germany (App no 39954/08) ECHR 7 February 2012
Aydin Tatlav v Turkey (App no 50692/99) ECHR 2 May 2006

Balsyte-Lideikiene v Lithuania (App no 72596/01) ECHR 4 November 2008
Barthold v Germany (App no 8734/79) (1985) Series A no 90
Bergens Tidende and Others v Norway (App no 26132/95) ECHR 2000-IV

Bladet Tromsø and Stensaas (App no 21980/93) ECHR 1999-III
Burden v the United Kingdom (App no 13378/05) ECHR 29 April 2008
Burghartz v Switzerland (App no 16213/90) Series A no 280-B
Busuioc v Moldova (App no 61513/00) ECHR 21 December 2004

C.R. v the United Kingdom (App no 20190/92) (1995) Series A no 335-C
Castells v Spain (App no 11798/85) (1992) Series A no 236
Ceylan v Turkey (App no 23556/94) ECHR 1999-IV
Chaare Shalom Ve Tsedek v France (App no 27417/95) ECHR 2000-VII
Chauvy and Others v France (App no 64915/01) ECHR 29 June 2004
Colombani and Others v France (App no 51279/99) ECHR 2002-V

D.H. and Others v the Czech Republic (App no 57325/00) ECHR 2007-IV
Dahlab v Switzerland (App no 42393/98) ECHR 2001-V
Dalban v Romania (App no 28114/95) ECHR 1999-VI
De Haes and Gijsels v Belgium (App no 19983/92) ECHR 1997-I

Erbakan v Turkey (App no 59405/00) ECHR 6 July 2006
Erdogdu v Turkey (App no 25723/94) ECHR 2000-VI
ETA Deutschland v Germany (App no 43481/09) ECHR 18 March 2013

Feret v Belgium (App no 15615/07) ECHR 16 July 2009
Fressoz and Roire v France (App no 29183/95) ECHR 1999 I

Garaudy v France (App no 65831/01) ECHR 2003-IX
Giniewski v France (App no 64016/00) ECHR 2006-I
Gündüz v Turkey (App no 35071/97) ECHR 2003-XI

Handyside v the United Kingdom (App no 5493/72) (1976) Series A no 24
Hizb Ut-Tahrir and Others v Germany (App no 31098/08) ECHR 12 June 2012
Hoffer and Annen (App nos 397/07, 2322/07) ECHR 13 January 2011

I.A. v Turkey (App no 42571/98) ECHR 2005-VIII
Incal v Turkey (App no 22678/93) ECHR 1998-IV

Jersild v Denmark (App no 15890/89) (1994) Series A no 298

Kjeldsen, Busk Madsen and Pedersen v Denmark (App nos 5095/71, 5920/72, 5926/72) (1976) Series A no 23
Klein v Slovakia (App no 72208/01) ECHR 31 October 2006
Krone Verlag GmbH and Co. KG v Austria (App no 34315/96) ECHR 26 February 2002

Lawless v Ireland (No.3) (App no 332/57) (1961) Series A no 3
Le Pen v France (App no 18788/09) ECHR 12 May 2010

Lehideux and Isorni v France (App no 24662/94) ECHR 1998-VII
Leyla Sahin v Turkey (App no 44774/98) ECHR 2005-XI
Lindon, Otchakovsky-Laurens and July v France (App nos 21279/02, 36448/02) ECHR 22 October 2007
Lingens v Austria (App no 9815/82) (1986) Series A no 103

Malisiewicz-Gasior v Poland (App no 43797/98) ECHR 6 April 2006
Mamere v France (App no 12697/03) ECHR 2006-XIII
Metropolitan Church of Bessarabia and Others v Moldova (App no 45701/99) ECHR 2001-XII
Milanović v Serbia (App no 44614/07) ECHR 14 December 2010
Mouvement raëlien Suisse v Switzerland (App no 16354/06) ECHR 13 July 2012
Müller and Others v Switzerland (App no 10737/84) (1988) Series A no 133
Murphy v Ireland (App no 44179/98) ECHR 2003-IX

Norwood v the United Kingdom (App no 23131/03) ECHR 16 November 2004
Nur Radyo Ve Televizyon Yayinciligi A.S. v Turkey (App no 6587/03) ECHR 27 November 2007

Observer and Guardian v the United Kingdom (App no 13585/88) (1991) Series A no 216
Open Door and Dublin Well Woman v Ireland (App no 14235/88) (1992) Series A no 246
Otegi Mondragon v Spain (App no 2034/07) ECHR 15 March 2011
Otto-Preminger-Institut v Austria (App no 13470/87) (1994) Series A no 295-A
Özgür Gündem v Turkey (App no 23144/93) ECHR 2000-III

Pedersen and Baadsgaard v Denmark (App no 49017/99) ECHR 2004-XI
Petrovic v Austria (App no 20458/92) ECHR 1998-II

Refah Partisi and Others v Turkey (App nos 41340/98, 41342/98, 41343/98, 41344/98) ECHR 31 July 2001
Refah Partisi and Others v Turkey (App nos 41340/98, 41342/98, 41343/98, 41344/98) ECHR 13 February 2003
Rekvényi v Hungary (App no 25390/94) ECHR 1999-III

Schuler-Zgraggen v Switzerland (App no 14518/89) (1993) Series A no 263
Schwabe v Austria (App no 13704/88) Series A no 242-B
Sejdić and Finci v Bosnia and Herzegovina (App nos 27996/06, 34836/06) ECHR 22 December 2009
Smith and Grady v the United Kingdom (App nos 33985/96, 33986/96) ECHR 1999-VI
Socialist Party and Others v Turkey (App no 21237/93) ECHR 1998-III
Soering v the United Kingdom (App no 14038/88) (1989) Series A no 161
Soulas and Others v France (App no 15948/03) ECHR 10 July 2008

Stankov and the United Macedonian Organisation Ilinden v Bulgaria (App nos 29221/95 and 29225/95) ECHR 2001-IX
Steel and Morris v the United Kingdom (App no 68416/01) ECHR 2005-II
Sürek v Turkey (no. 1) (App no 26682/95) ECHR 1999-IV
SW v United Kingdom (App no 20166/92) (1995) Series A no 335-B

The Sunday Times v The United Kingdom (App no 6538/74) (1979) Series A no 30
The United Communist Party of Turkey and Others v Turkey (App no 19392/92) ECHR 1998-I
Timishev v Russia (App nos 55762/00, 55974/00) ECHR 13 December 2005

Van Raalte v Netherlands (App no 20060/92) ECHR 1997-I
Vejdeland and Others v Sweden (App no 1813/07) ECHR 9 February 2012
Verein gegen Tierfabriken Schweiz (VgT) v Switzerland (no. 2) (App no 32772/02) ECHR 30 June 2009
VgT Verein gegen Tierfabriken v Switzerland, (App no 24699/94) ECHR 2001-VI
Vides Aizsardzības Klubs v Latvia (App no 57829/00) ECHR 27 May 2004
Vogt v Germany (App no 17851/91) (1995) Series A no 323

Wingrove v The United Kingdom (App no 17419/90) ECHR 1996-V

Yazar and Others v Turkey (App nos 22723/93, 22724/93 and 22725/93) ECHR 2002-II
Young, James and Webster v The United Kingdom (App nos 7601/76, 7806/77) (1981) Series A no 55

Case C-617/10 *Åklagaren v Hans Åkerberg Fransson*, 26 February 2013, ECLI:EU:C:2013:105
Case C-309/96 *Daniele Annibaldi v Sindaco del Comune di Guidonia and Presidente Regione Lazio* [1997] ECR I-7493
Case C-540/03 *European Parliament v Council* [2006] ECR I-5769
Case 6/64 *Flaminio Costa v ENEL* [1964] ECR 585, 593
Case 11/70 *Internationale Handesgesellschaft* [1970] ECR 1125
Case 4/73 *Nold v Commission* [1974] ECR 491
Cases C-465/00, 138 & 139/01 *Rechnungshof v Österreichischer Rundfunk* [2003] ECR I-12489
Case 29/69 *Stauder v City of Ulm* [1969] ECR 419
Case 5/88 *Wachauf v Bundesamt Für Ernährung und Forstwirtschaft* [1989] ECR 2609

National Cases

Germany

Internationale Handelsgesellschaft mbH v Einfuhr- und Vorratsstelle für Getreide und Futtermittel [1974] 2 CMLR 540

The Netherlands

HR 27 February 1951, *NJ* 472
HR 27 February 1951, *NJ* 473
HR 24 January 1967, *NJ* 270
HR 30 May 1967, *NJ* 1968
HR 22 September 1987, *NJ* 1988, 300
HR 22 March 1988, *NJ* 1988, 785
HR 22 February 1994, *NJ* 1994, 379
HR 28 March 1995, *NJ* 1995, 454
HR 21 April 1998, *NJ* 1998, 781
HR 18 May 1999, *NJ* 1999, 634
HR 16 November 1999, *NJ* 2000, 125
HR 9 January 2001, *NJ* 2001, 203
HR 9 January 2001, *NJ* 2001, 204
HR 9 November 2001, *NJ* 2002, 76
HR 2 April 2002, *NJ* 2002, 421
HR 14 January 2003, *NJ* 2003, 261
HR 15 April 2003, *NJ* 2003, 334
HR 27 January 2004, *NJ* 2004, 121
HR 16 November 2004, *LJN* AR3040
HR 9 January 2007, *LJN* AZ 2497
HR 25 September 2007, *LJN* BA7257
HR 10 March 2009, *NJ* 2010, 19
HR 23 November 2010, *NJ* 2011, 115
HR 16 December 2014, ECLI: NL:HR:2014:3583

Hof 's-Gravenhage 18 November 2002, *NJ* 2003, 24
Hof Amsterdam18 July 2003, *NJ* 2003, 580

Rb. Amsterdam 13 June 1995, *NJ* 1995, 664
Rb. Amsterdam 15 April 2003, *LJN* AF7291
Rb. Amsterdam 26 July 2005, *JIN* 2005, 360
Rb. 's-Gravenhage 7 April 2008, *LJN* BC8732
Rb. Amsterdam 23 June 2011, *NJ* 2012, 370

The United Kingdom

R v R [1992] AC 599 (HL)

Table of Legislative Instruments

International and European Legislation

An Agenda for Democratization
Camden Principles on Freedom of Expression and Equality
Charter of the United Nations
Convention on the Prevention and Punishment of the Crime of Genocide
Declaration on Criteria for Free and Fair Elections
Declaration on the Elimination of All forms of Intolerance and of Discrimination based on Religion or Belief
Declaration on the Human Rights of Individuals Who Are Not Nationals of the Country in Which They Live (1985)
Declaration on the Right and Responsibility of Individuals, Groups and Organs of Society to Promote and Protect Universally Recognized Human Rights and Fundamental Freedoms
European Convention for the Protection of Human Rights and Fundamental Freedoms
International Convention on Civil and Political Rights
International Convention on the Elimination of All Forms of Racial Discrimination
International Covenant on Economic, Social and Cultural Rights
Rome Statute of the International Criminal Court
Siracusa Principles on the Limitation and Derogation of Provisions in the International Covenant on Civil and Political Rights
Supplementary Convention on the Abolition of Slavery, the Slave Trade, and Institutions and Practices Similar to Slavery (1956)
UNESCO Convention on the Protection and Promotion of the Diversity of Cultural Expressions (2005)
UNESCO Universal Declaration on Cultural Diversity (2001)
Universal Declaration of Human Rights
Universal Declaration on Democracy
Vienna Declaration and Programme of Action
Warsaw Declaration: Toward a Community of Democracies (2000)

ICCPR General Comment No. 3
ICCPR General Comment No. 4
ICCPR General Comment No. 10
ICCPR General Comment No. 11

ICCPR General Comment No. 18
ICCPR General Comment No. 19
ICCPR General Comment No. 22
ICCPR General Comment No. 23
ICCPR General Comment No. 25
ICCPR General Comment No. 29
ICCPR General Comment No. 31
ICCPR General Comment No. 34
ICCPR General Comment No. 34
CERD General Recommendation No. 15
CERD General Recommendation No. 30

National Legislation

Dutch Constitution
Dutch Penal Code
Dutch Code of Criminal Procedure

Sexual Offences Act 1956
Criminal Justice and Public Order Act of 1994

Other Instruments

Parliamentary Papers II 1969/70, 9724, nr. 6
Parliamentary Papers II 1975-1976, 13872
Parliamentary Papers II 1980-1981, 16905
Parliamentary Papers II 2007/08, 31570, nr. 3
Parliamentary Papers I 2009/13, 32203, nr. 11

UNGA Res 1780 (XVII) (7 December 1962)
UNGA Res 1781 (XVII) (7 December 1962)
UNGA Res 36/55 (25 November 1981) UN Doc A/RES/36/55
UNGA Res 55/97 (4 December 2000) UN Doc A/RES/55/97
UNGA Res 60/150 (20 January 2006) UN Doc A/RES/60/150
UNGA Res 61/164 (21 February 2007) UN Doc A/RES/61/164
UNGA Res 62/154 (6 March 2008) UN Doc A/RES/62/154
UNGA Res 63/171 (24 March 2009) UN Doc A/RES/63/171
UNGA Res 64/156 (8 March 2010) UN Doc A/RES/64/156
UNGA Res 65/224 (11 April 2011) UN Doc A/RES/65/224
UNGA Res 16/18 (12 April 2011) UN Doc A/HRC/RES/16/18

UNGA, Second session 'World Conference Against Racism, Racial Discrimination, Xenophobia and Related Intolerance, Preparatory Committee' (22 March 2001) UN Doc A/CONF.189/PC.2/24

UN Doc CCPR/C/13/D/24/1977 (1981)
UN Doc CCPR/C/50/D/488/1992 (1994)
UN Doc CCPR/C/52/D/511/1992 (1994)
UN Doc CCPR/C/87/D/1009/2001 (2006)
UN Doc CCPR/C/85/D/1180/2003 (2006)

UNCHR Res 20 (1986) UN Doc E/CN.4/RES/1986/20
UNCHR Res 60 (1995) UN Doc E/CN.4/RES/1995/60
UNCHR Res 57 (1999) UN Doc E/CN.4/RES/1999/57
UNCHR Res 23 (1999) UN Doc E/CN.4/RES/1999/167
UNCHR Res 47 (2000) UN Doc E/CN.4/RES/2000/47
UNCHR Res 84 (2000) UN Doc E/CN.4/RES/2000/84
UNCHR Res 4 (2001) UN Doc E/CN.4/RES/2001/4
UNCHR Res 9 (2002) UN Doc E/CN.4/RES/2002/9
UNCHR Res 46 (2002) UN Doc E/CN.4/RES/2002/46
UNCHR Res 4 (2003) UN Doc E/CN.4/RES/2003/4
UNCHR Res 36 (2003) UN Doc E/CN.4-RES/2003/36
UNCHR Res 6 (2004) UN Doc E/CN.4/RES/2004/6
UNCHR Res 3 (2005) UN Doc E/CN.4/RES/2005/3

UNCHR 'Racism, Racial Discrimination, Xenophobia and all Forms of Discrimination' (20 April 1999) UN Doc E/CN.4/1999/L.40
UNCHR 'Civil and Political Rights, Including the Question of Freedom of Expression: Report of the Special Rapporteur on the promotion and protection of the right to freedom of opinion and expression' (13 February 2001) UN Doc E/CN.4/2001/64
UNCHR, Fifty-ninth session 'Civil and Political Rights. Continuing dialogue on measures to promote and consolidate democracy. Report of the High Commissioner for Human Rights submitted in accordance with Commission resolution 2001/41' (27 January 2003) UN Doc E/CN.4/2003/59

UNHRC Dec 1/107, 'Incitement to racial and religious hatred and the promotion of tolerance' (30 June 2006) UN Doc A/HRC/DEC/1/107
UNHRC Res 4/9, 'Combating defamation of religions' (30 March 2007) UN Doc A/HRC/RES/4/9
UNHRC Res 7/19, 'Combating defamation of religions' (27 March 2008) UN Doc A/HRC/RES/7/19
UNHRC Res 10/22, 'Combating defamation of religions' (26 March 2009) UN Doc A/HRC/RES/10/22
UNHRC Res 12/16, 'Promotion and Protection of All Human Rights, Civil, Political, Economic, Social and Cultural Rights, Including the Right to Development' (2 October 2009) UN Doc A/HRC/RES/12/16

UNHRC, Fourteenth session 'Report of the Special Rapporteur on the promotion and protection of the rights to freedom of opinion and expression' (25 March 2010) UN Doc A/HRC/14/23/Add.2

UNHRC, 'Report of the Special Rapporteur on the Promotion and protection of the right to freedom of opinion and expression' (2012) UN Doc A/67/357

UNHRC, Nineteenth session 'Racism, racial discrimination, xenophobia and related form of intolerance, follow-up and implementation of the Durban Declaration and Programme of Action' (16 March 2012) UN Doc A/HRC/19/L.7

UNHRC, Twenty-second session 'Report of the Special Rapporteur on the promotion and protection of human rights and fundamental freedoms while countering terrorism. Framework Principles for securing the accountability of public officials for gross or systematic human rights violations committed in the context of State counter-terrorism initiatives' (1 March 2013) UN Doc A/HRC/22/52

UNHRC, Twenty-second session 'Racism, racial discrimination, xenophobia and related form of intolerance, follow-up and implementation of the Durban Declaration and Programme of Action' (18 March 2013) UN Doc A/HRC/22/L.40

Other Works

Committee of Ministers of the Council of Europe, 607th meeting of the Ministers' Deputies 'Of The Committee of Ministers to Member States on "Hate Speech" ' (30 October 1997) Rec No R (97)

-- Appendix to Committee of Ministers of the Council of Europe, 607th meeting of the Ministers' Deputies 'Of The Committee of Ministers to Member States on "Hate Speech"' (30 October 1997) Rec No R (97) 20

-- 607th meeting of the Ministers' Deputies 'Of The Committee of Ministers to Member States on The Media and The Promotion of a Culture of Tolerance' (30 October 1997) Rec No R (97)

-- 872nd meeting of the Ministers' Deputies 'Declaration on freedom of political debate in the media' (12 February 2004)

Concluding observations on the United Kingdom of Great Britain and Northern Ireland-the Crown Dependencies of Jersey, Guernsey and the Isle of Man (CCPR/C/79/Add.119)

Conference for Security and Co-operation in Europe (1992 Summit, Helsinki), 'CSCE Helsinki Document 1992, The Challenges of Change' (Helsinki Summit Declaration)

Council of Europe, European Court of Human Rights, 'Preparatory Work on Article 10 of the European Convention on Human Rights' (5 March 1975) Confidential CDH (75)

ECRI General Policy Rec No 7 'On National Legislation to Combat Racism and Racial Discrimination' (13 December 2002)

European Commission for Democracy through Law (Venice Commission), *Preliminary Report: On the national legislation in Europe concerning blasphemy, religious insults and inciting religious hatred* (adopted by the Commission at its 70th plenary session, Venice, 16-17 March 2007)

Inglis C, 'Multiculturalism: New Policy Responses to Diversity', UNESCO Management of Social Transformation, *Policy Paper* (1997) No.4

Lamy P, 'Humanising Globalization' (Speech at the World Trade Organization in Santiago, 30 January 2006)

Loenen M.L.P. (Titia), 'Mensenrechten en diversiteit in Europa: gelijke monniken, ongelijke kappen?' (Oratie (in verkorte vorm) uitgesproken door Prof.dr. M.L.P. (Titia) Loenen bij de aanvaarding van het ambt van hoogleraar op het gebied van Mensenrechten en Diversiteit aan de Universiteit Leiden op vrijdag 15 november 2013)

Lord Phillips, Lord Chief Justice, *Equality before the Law*, East London Muslim Centre (3rd July 2008) "The speech was organized by Pro Bono in the LMC and the London Muslim Centre"

Mautner M, 'Religion in Politics: Rawls and Habermas on Deliberation and Justification' (2013) Tel Aviv University Law Faculty Papers. Working Paper No. 167

-- 'A Dialogue between a Liberal and an Ultra-Orthodox on the Exclusion of Women from Torah Study' (2013). Tel Aviv University Law Faculty Papers. Working Paper No. 180

Office of the Deputy Prime Minister, 'State of the English Cities' (2006) Vol 1

Opinion 2/13 EU Accession to the ECHR [2014]

Organization for Security and Co-operation in Europe, 'Mandate of the OSCE Representation on Freedom of the Media' (5 November 1997) PC.DEC No.193, PC Journal No 137

Parliamentary Assembly of the Council of Europe Rec 1396 'Religion and democracy' (27 January 1999) CoE Report Doc 8270

Parliamentary Assembly of the Council of Europe Res 1510 'Freedom of expression and respect for religious beliefs' (24 June 2006) CoE Report Doc 10970

Parliamentary Assembly of the Council of Europe Rec 1805 'Blasphemy, religious insults and hate speech against persons on grounds of their religion' (29 June 2007) CoE Report Doc 11296

Parliamentary Assembly of the Council of Europe Res 1691 'Rape of women, including marital rape' (2 October 2009) CoE Report Doc 12013

Peters R (Mei 2005) "De Ideologische en Religieuze Ontwikkeling van Mohammed B.: Deskundigenrapport in de strafzaak tegen Mohammed B. in opdracht van het Openbaar Ministerie opgesteld voor de arrondissementrechtbank Amsterdam"

Poorter de JCA and Roosmalen van HJThM, *Rol en betekenis van de Grondwet: Constitutionele toetsing in relatie tot de Raad van State,* (Raad van State, Den Haag 2010)

Report and Recommendations of the President's Review Group on Intelligence and Communications Technologies, '*Liberty and Security in a Changing World*' (12 December 2013)

The joint declaration [1977] OJ C103/1 by the European Parliament, the Commission, and the Council

UN Development Programme, 'Globalization with a Human Face' (1999)

UN Inter-Parliamentary Union, "Human Rights: A Handbook for Parliamentarians", No.5, 2005

UNESCO Integrated Framework of Action on Education for Peace, Human Rights and Democracy (1995)

World Plan of Action on Education for Human Rights and Democracy (1993)

Websites

Benjamin Netanyahu (Speech at the UN on 27 September 2012) <http://www.algemeiner.com/2012/09/27/full-transcript-prime-minister-netanyahu-speech-to-united-nations-general-assembly-2012-video/> accessed 4 January 2013

Muslim Arbitration Tribunal <http://www.matribunal.com/> accessed 10 December 2012

Speech at the Conference "Twenty years of the Helsinki Final Act – Towards a New European Security Model" delivered on 17 July 1995 in Moscow <http://www.osce.org/secretariat/15666> accessed 6-10-2013

UN Economic and Social Council, Preliminary Report <http://www.unhchr.ch/Huridocda/Huridoca.nsf/0/75ccfd797b0712d08025670b005c9a7d?Opendocument> accessed 10 December 2012

<http://www.hoover.org/publications/policy-review/article/5664> accessed 8 March 2012

<http://www.un.org/en/events/humanrightsday/> accessed 15 June 2013

<http://www.un.org/Depts/dhl/udhr/> accessed 15 June 2013

<http://daccess-dds ny.un.org/doc/UNDOC/GEN/G03/171/69/PDF/G0317169.pdf?OpenElement> accessed 20 June 2013

<http://eur-lex.europa.eu/en/editorial/abc_c02_r1.htm#h7> accessed 3 October 2013

<http://legislationline.org/> accessed 5 November 2013